pin-ups 1972

Also by Peter Stanfield

*A Band with Built-In Hate: The Who
from Pop Art to Punk*

*Body and Soul: Jazz and Blues in
American Film, 1927–63*

The Cool and the Crazy: Pop Fifties Cinema

*Hollywood, Westerns and the 1930s:
The Lost Trail*

*Hoodlum Movies: Seriality and the Outlaw
Biker Film Cycle, 1966–1972*

*Horse Opera: The Strange History of the
Singing Cowboy*

*Maximum Movies – Pulp Fiction: Film Culture
and the Worlds of Samuel Fuller, Mickey Spillane
and Jim Thompson*

pin-ups
1972

THIRD GENERATION ROCK 'N' ROLL

Peter Stanfield

Reaktion Books

For Graham Henderson and Eddie King

Published by
REAKTION BOOKS LTD
Unit 32, Waterside
44–48 Wharf Road
London N1 7UX, UK

www.reaktionbooks.co.uk

First published 2022
Copyright © Peter Stanfield 2022

Printed and bound in Great Britain
by TJ Books Ltd, Padstow, Cornwall

A catalogue record for this book is available from the British Library

ISBN 978 1 78914 565 6

CONTENTS

INTRODUCTION: FIRST IS FIRST, SECOND IS BEST AND THE THIRD GENERATION IS NOWHERE

That's how fast pop is: the anarchists of one year are the boring old farts of the next.

Nik Cohn, *Pop from the Beginning* (1969)

This is a book about the rock acts that became the pin-ups of 1972, that year's anarchists. To tell their stories, *Pin-Ups 1972* pivots around a commonplace catchphrase in early 1970s pop criticism: 'third-generation rock 'n' roll'. The term was introduced to London's rock cognoscenti by Alice Cooper on a promotional visit to England in 1971; he said his band and The Stooges were third-generation rock's best representatives.[1] It was likely he intended it to be no more than a pithy aphorism to differentiate his and Iggy's band from the competition, to signal that they were the next in line, but the idea behind the phrase found a receptive audience among those who wrote for Britain's Underground press.[2] They ran with the concept, putting it into wider circulation, and turned it into a refrain that became a summary definition for rock's current predicament, namely: if The Beatles followed Elvis, and they were now sundered, who was their heir apparent? The need to find an answer was motivated by the fear that the scene was fast burning out, smothered by conformity to the demands of the marketplace. The heat once generated by rock's seditious intent was turning to cold ash. Who then might fan the dying embers and put some fire back into rock 'n' roll? For rock journalists, aesthetes and muckrakers alike, their role was to act as the accelerant for the conflagration they ardently hoped was to follow.

The first-generation were the original rockers: Elvis, Little Richard, Chuck Berry, Buddy Holly, Gene Vincent and Eddie Cochran. The second-generation were those who were directly and immediately inspired by these innovators: The Beatles, Bob Dylan, the Rolling Stones, The Kinks, The Who. But where it was easy to see the break between first and second iterations, the end of the second cycle and the start of the third was less obvious.

It was widely accepted that things had fallen apart when Elvis joined the army, Little Richard got religion, Chuck went to jail and Buddy and Eddie were killed. Following the wake, the vanguard of the resurrection shuffle was never in doubt. The contention in 1970–72 was over whether or not the succeeding generation had now reached its end point. All who cared about such things could agree that something had changed with the break-up of The Beatles, with Altamont, the Tate–LaBianca murders and the deaths of Janis Joplin, Jimi Hendrix, Brian Jones and Jim Morrison between 1969 and 1971. Whatever its end-of-days symbolism, the difficulty with this particular cut-off point was where it left those rockers, such as the Rolling Stones and The Who, who were still active and creatively valid, never mind figures such as Bowie and Bolan, who had roots deep into the second-generation, even as they themselves were seen as defining actors in the third.

As the 1960s rolled into the '70s and Dylan, Lennon and Jagger edged into their thirties, the truism that rock was about the now, the new and the immediate, that it was fundamentally teenage in orientation, needed to be reassessed. How was the discrepancy between the ideal and the reality, between youth and maturity to be managed? Some ignored the question, their taste confirmed by displays of virtuosity and grandiose concepts measured against the fickle values of the teen pop consumer. Others, greaser revivalists, smothered the question under a shroud of nostalgia for the prelapsarian 1950s. A third camp dealt with it by redefining the canon to better classify just what rock was so that its latest iteration could be named and fêted. *Pin-Ups 1972* is about this last group.

♀ ♀ ♀

Iconoclasm would play a key role in helping to define the generational shift. Nik Cohn's earlier and somewhat unique pursuit of the contrary in pop criticism was a model of sorts: few others at the time, or since, have proselytized with such passion and conviction for an outlier while showing an equal measure of disdain for the masters of the idiom, P. J. Proby and Bob Dylan respectively in his case. With the new cohort of rock writers – Ian MacDonald, Charles Shaar Murray, Duncan Fallowell, Roy Hollingworth and Nick Kent among them – the cultivation of a discriminating sensitivity, in which an amplification of cultish preferences underlay critical evaluations, became the norm. Dylan, The Beatles, the Stones and The Who stopped being the markers against whom all might be judged. They were, for the most part, beyond contention, with the gods so to speak. In their earthly place, the process of canonizing the Velvet Underground and The Stooges, who occupied the hinterland between the second and third generations, took hold.

Running in parallel with a critic's show of discerning taste was an archivist's pursuit of the arcane pleasures found in the juvenile delirium of punk bands from the first psychedelic era, the high-school drama of girl groups, and the delinquent rhythms of rockabilly. Such forms represented paradise lost, but as guides they might yet point to the Promised Land. In becoming a pretender's champion, the critic linked them to such predecessors and explained how they held true to rock 'n' roll's core values as embodied in Shadows of Knight, The Ronettes, Charlie Feathers. Through showing a connoisseur's appreciation for the finer points of rock's chequered history, critics set out their bona fides when it came to revealing the new challengers, as with Hollingworth and the New York Dolls, Richard Williams and Roxy Music, Fallowell and Krautrock, and MacDonald, Murray and Simon Frith, in a rather more congested field, with Bowie. In near splendid isolation, Kent chose to occupy the teenage wasteland with Iggy and the Stooges.

Rock's three generations are partitioned and examined in Nik Cohn and Guy Peellaert's illustrated volume from 1973, *Rock Dreams*, which begins with the idea of rock and roll as a 'secret society, an enclosed teen fantasy' and as an obsession.[3] The authors track the cycles of rock, how visions of it changed, became more complex and diversified, 'and the ways in which they remained always the same . . . Its ever-changing, never-changing rituals.'[4] In a key image, Elvis sits at the centre of a table. In front of him is a last supper of cokes and burgers, and surrounding him are his twelve disciples (of a decidedly British bias) – Vince Taylor, Tommy Steele, P. J. Proby, Billy Fury, Tommy Sands, Rick Nelson, Tom Jones, Eddie Cochran, Terry Dene, Ritchie Valens, Fabian and Cliff Richard. Like Jesus, Elvis is a figure big enough to contain multitudes. In other images, he is a street punk loitering outside a poolhall, a devout Christian and a married man. Those who followed his lead are mono-dimensional versions of one or other of these aspects. In a British pub surrounded by rockers with greasy quiffs and leather jackets, Gene Vincent threatens a police detective with a flick knife; homely Eddie Cochran hangs out at the ice cream parlour waiting for the right girl to drift by and save him from his summertime blues; and the Everly Brothers make out with their girlfriends, wives to be, at the drive-in.

The first generation of rockers are followed in Cohn's tale by Dylan and the British Invasion, an era that lasted until around 1968 when rock, he writes, got complicated. It could no longer be 'contained in a single direction, one overall fantasy, and it broke apart into different factions and schools . . . From now on, all was chaos; sometimes hopeless and sometimes splendid confusion.'[5] What was left was a mess, populated by serious musicians, poets and bogeymen. Some looked to the future, others to the past; some mixed things up with Country and Western, others with Jazz, or the pseudo-Classical and mock-Oriental. The effect was that rock had 'grown self-important, predictable, flat'.[6] The kinship between performer and audience had vanished. Solemnity, jadedness and exhaustion followed. Decadent rot had set in, and the moment of rock had passed:

Real energy survived only in pockets, where scattered groups or individuals refused to be sucked under by the general smog and, steering clear of movements, fads, classifications, quietly went their own way. The Rock dreams that remained were bred in isolation: private visions, personal obsessions.[7]

Marc Bolan and Rod Stewart are among those that slip out of the amorphous crowd to become guarded passions, but it will be David Bowie (linked with Lou Reed in Peellaert's illustration) who best helped define the fallout after the legacy of the second-generation had been squandered.

The location for the action was not Memphis, Liverpool, Laurel Canyon, Haight-Ashbury or Detroit, but London. Despite Alice Cooper's coining of the term, third-generation rock proved to be an English obsession, decidedly metropolitan in its scheming and very suburban in its dreaming. Those ambitions and fantasies were haunted by the ghosts of 1950s American rebels without a cause, the wild ones, who held in thrall the visionaries with a more romantically inclined disposition. To many, first-generation rock 'n' roll, as it was presently being reanimated on the streets and in the boutiques and clubs of London, was a talisman of what made music life-affirming, or at least a sufficiently disruptive influence to upset the drag of the everyday. Others, less inclined to suspend disbelief, saw it as sodden trash spilled out along Wardour Street.

Soho: Take It or Leave It, We're Leaving
Of all the world's red light districts Soho must be the most
depressing.
Our advice is stay away – it's healthier that way.
Curious – The Sex Education Magazine for Men and Women (1972)

The tagline for *Curious*'s Soho supplement was, as is in the
nature of these things, both a warning and a solicitation. If
provincial readers were unable to stay away, to resist the lure
of the West End, even at its most depressing, then the sex magazine provided them with a guide to its sights and prospects and
a complementary map to aid in their nocturnal perambulations.
Piccadilly Circus and Coventry Street mark the southern end,
Oxford Street the north, Charing Cross Road the east and Regent
Street the western extreme. Inside these trig points, there was a
circuit of 'creep-crawly routes' marked by blue arrows that go
around Soho Square, south down Greek Street, turning west
into Old Compton Street, then, depending on whether you are
heading north or south on Wardour Street, it affords the option
of side trips along Shaftsbury Avenue, Brewer and Broadwick
Streets.

In the pull-out's lead article, a 25-year-old author reflects
on his first visit to Soho as a fifteen-year-old virgin; his story
is obvious and boring. Other equally dull pieces follow on strip
clubs and strippers: dancer Maureen is trying to earn enough
money to get out of London, which is at least novel since the
traffic is usually in the other direction. Judy, from Guyana, works
as a prostitute. She walks the same streets as the rent boys who,
in the rain, hang out in the amusement arcades with the drug
peddlers. Off the streets there are also the sauna clubs, photographed by JP Smut (the pseudonym for Jay Myrdal and Pete

Smith). Not much else is on show in *Curious*'s '*last* look at Soho';
all is as tawdry and quotidian as can be managed. Even a creep-
crawly flaneur would surely hurry on his way to something a
little more delirious.

With its title and cover image inspired by *West Side Story*,
'West End Story', as *Curious*'s exposé of Soho was imagin-
atively named, promised something more than the dreary
circadian grind it actually provided. The cover model is styled
as an American 1950s tomboy with lascivious intent, her gang
affiliation sprayed on the toilet wall she's leaning against. She
is wearing Converse sneakers, rolled Levi's and a satin bomber
jacket, open, provocatively, to reveal her breasts. Inside the
magazine, she reappears as a centrespread, same pose, location
and backdrop, with its 'Jets' and 'K.K.K.' graffiti. What's
changed is that her top is buttoned and it's her Levi's that are
open. At the head of the spread 'baby, baby, where did our
love go?' is the ironic caption, quoting the Supremes' 1964
hit, while at its base is the cynical 'No. 1' in the 'Seen It All
Before Gallery'.

As hawked in *Curious*, nostalgia is exhausted; there's no
frisson of desire left, only a blank stare behind a pair of aviator
shades worn by a 1970s approximation of a 1950s teenager
exposing herself in a Soho lavatory. Same year, and just a little
detour off one of the creep-crawly routes down Brewer Street,
going right a little up Regent Street and then across the road
is Heddon Street. This is where Bowie posed for the images
– outside the furrier's, beneath the K. West sign, and inside
the red telephone box – that were used on the cover of *The
Rise and Fall of Ziggy Stardust and the Spiders from Mars*.
In his quilted two-piece, designed by Freddie Burretti, boxer's

The Curious 'West End Story': a last look at Soho.

boots and cropped hair, Bowie is an otherworldly apparition; a premonition of the transformation of the everyday into something more exciting; the mundane made marvellous.

Bowie had earlier shared the front cover of *Curious* (May 1971) with Burretti (aka Rudi Valentino). The couple appear at their most epicene, with Bowie wearing a man's dress designed by Mr. Fish.[8] They were promoting their band Arnold Corns:

> Bowie says that Rudi is the leader of the whole gay scene, but Rudi himself is a little more modest – 'I really want to be a big name and make it in America,' he says. 'I have a single out written by David called Moonage Daydream and that's only the beginning. An album *Looking for Rudi* will be out very soon . . .'
>
> 'I believe that the Rolling Stones are finished and Arnold Corns will be the next Stones,' said Bowie.[9]

Rudi didn't stay the course but, as Ziggy, Bowie fulfilled his ambition for a new order in the age of rock's third generation.

Pop's ability to generate excitement, desire and the promise of fulfilment, which the Soho sex industry so abjectly failed to deliver, was best carried, as Bowie knew, by the nation's young. In late 1971 into 1972 that fact was dramatized with savage effect in the film *A Clockwork Orange*. Director Stanley Kubrick and costume designer Milena Canonero borrowed freely from the youth culture fashions of the day. The black boots, white shirt, braces, box and jeans, supplemented with an aristocratic cane and banker's bowler, differ only in small matters from the contemporary figure formed out of the skinhead's transition into something altogether more complex. It was a journey undertaken by Richard Allen's antihero, Joe Hawkins, in the 1971 novel *Suedehead*:

> In his pin-stripe suit and clean white shirt with his conservative tie clipped in place by a Stratton gold pin, Joe felt quite the City gent. *Funny*, he mused, *how clothes change a guy's outlook.*
>
> He could remember those far-off days when he *was* ten foot tall dressed in his bovver boots, union shirt, tight trousers with the loud braces boldly showing. He could touch his hair and recall the pride of a skinhead cut. *Recall!* His hair was growing now. In another month or two it would be suede . . . in between being a skinhead and being what the Establishment liked to call 'normal' styling. *Suede* – smooth, elite, expensive.[10]

Like Joe, the protagonist of *A Clockwork Orange*, Alex, appropriates the badges of authority as adornments to his more functional attire, especially the bowler hat. This was in much the same manner of sartorial presentation that The Who had practised, with their transformation of flags into jackets. That was before Townshend retreated away from such trappings of pop display to wear a white boiler suit and Doc Martens – looking every bit, minus the hat, make-up and horror-show eyeballs, like a model for Kubrick's droogs.

Billy Boy and his gang, who rumble with Alex in a derelict music hall, are likewise styled on a contemporary youth cult, the very British DIY version of California's Hells Angels. They have the requisite Nazi regalia and coal bucket helmets, though the leathers are traded for a set of camouflage jackets. Each gang member, somewhat incongruously, wears a frilled dress shirt of the sort favoured by nightclub entertainers, but the effect of the costuming is the same as with Alex and his droogs: the ready and easy identification of the day's delinquents.

Kubrick's adaptation of Anthony Burgess's novel made the most of contemporary culture, from the new town high-rises to brutalist concrete architecture and 1960s modernist homes, used to suggest a near future setting that is wholly recognizable. By avoiding pre-war buildings, except for the interior of the music hall, and with only minor modifications to décor, the *mise-en-scène* achieves the same effect Jean-Luc Godard had managed in 1965 with *Alphaville*: tomorrow is already here.

Running counter to much of the futurity of *A Clockwork Orange* is its use of pop design that was past its sell-by-date. The influence of Allen Jones's s&m sculptures on the Korova milk bar may have been genuinely of the moment – his key pieces, *Table* and *Chair*, had been first exhibited in 1969 – but the entrance at the foot of the stairs to the subterranean bar is decorated with psychedelic posters randomly liberated from a head shop, including a prominently displayed Michael English and Nigel Waymouth poster promoting long-gone 1968 events at Middle Earth. Such images were already showing their age in 1971, and definitely would be anachronisms by the time the film was distributed.

That juxtaposition of pop's yesterday with a tomorrow that sits in the present is replayed when Alex has exchanged his bovver boy chic for a purple Regency-inspired double-breasted suede frock coat with fake snake-skin cuffs, collar and lapels under which he wears a yellow Ben Sherman shirt. All in all, the perfect attire for a stroll along the mirrored corridors of a record boutique, where he picks up two devotchkas.

The flashing board showing the Top Ten at the record counter is full of fictitious artists and their records, yet the racks are loaded with albums of the day, including a *2001 Space Odyssey* soundtrack that sits at the front of the 'Underground' section and alongside John Fahey's *The Transfiguration of Blind Joe Death*. Other long players seen as Alex takes in the sights during his circular stroll, which begins and ends where the devotchkas browse idly through the discs, are progressive rock stalwarts Stray, Keef Hartley, Pink Floyd and Rare Earth. What especially dates the moment is a picture-sleeved copy of T. Rex's 'Ride a White Swan' displayed behind the counter. Released in October 1970, like all great pop singles it had a relatively short shelf life, and was displaced by 'Hot Love' in February 1971. It is still there, however, just over a year later, on the film's initial release and ever thereafter.

The sequence was shot in the Chelsea Drugstore, which opened in 1968. The building had three floors, was clad in brushed steel, stood on the corner of Royal Avenue and the King's Road (it's now a McDonalds) and was immortalized in the Rolling Stones' 'You Can't Always Get What You Want'. A world away from Soho's sex attractions or Wardour Street amusements, it provided a sensation-filled environment for Alex's idle amble. In dandy threads, he is as much at home in this space as a nineteenth-century Baudelairean flaneur was in the Paris arcades. Six or seven years earlier London had swung; in 1972 it swaggered and swished in a pair of 'flip horrorshow boots for kicking' borrowed from *A Clockwork Orange*.

Alex is what Barney Hoskyns calls a 'gutter-aristocrat'; a contradictory construct that he uses to describe figures such as Bolan, Bowie, Lou Reed and Iggy Pop, whose peacock-like ostentatious displays took place in a kind of street theatre, glitter in the grime – the latest iteration of Baudelaire's maxim: 'Dandyism is the last flicker of heroism in decadent ages.'[11] They were performers who worked on and then blurred the line between pop and art, artifice and authenticity, surface and depth, fantasy and reality, the plebeian and the noble. 'Hoodlum poets', metropolitan figures who performed for an audience of suburbanites whose fantasies of the city's attractions they fulfilled, was another term Hoskyns used to describe them.[12]

Early in 1972, a *Rolling Stone* correspondent, Jerry Hopkins, visited London and sent back a report on the return of Britain's Teddy Boys. He started his tour at the Black Raven pub in Bishopsgate where 'Awopbopa-loobop, awopbamboom' on the jukebox was 'the sound of falling through a time warp':

> Outside, parked at the curb, are half a dozen Fifties American cars. Inside there are at least 150 Teds, attired in their weekend flashback best: velvet-trimmed Edwardian suits, jackets reaching mid-thigh, drainpipe pants so tight the Teds look as if they've been dipped in ink, frilly shirt fronts, bootlace ties, glow-in-the-dark salmon and chartreuse sox, suede shoes with thick crepe soles, creepers is what they're called ... All you can see is hair.
>
> Plumes and cascades and whirlpools of hair, all of it greased and obsidian-black, thumbing its nose at gravity as it stretches four inches from the brow, wobbling, glistening: the classic Elephant's Trunk; sweeping

back in shiny sheets past earringed ears to plunge into a perfect D.A. or splash over the velvet collars in hirsute waterfalls. Towers and arches and walls of hair. This isn't just extraordinary styling – it's architecture.[13]

No one called them 'hoodlum poets', but the Teddy Boys were the day's true gutter-aristocrats: 'fashion for effect, not function', Hopkins wrote, 'Soft as velvet, sharp as razor blades. It's possible to be a dandy, yet tough.'[14]

Cutting across town, past the Chelsea Drugstore towards the end of the King's Road, Hopkins called in at Let It Rock. The proprietor was Malcolm McLaren, and his shop catered to Britain's rockers:

Malcolm stands there in a wide-lapeled powder-blue sports jacket and luminescent peggers . . . Warren Smith . . . is wailing on the jukebox. Malcolm . . . goes into a story about the day a full charter busload of Teds arrived. 'They came boldering in 'ere, all dressed up in their gear, their drapes and everything, they spent three hours playing the records, buying glow-in-the-dark sox and pants and magazines. It was quite dynamic, really. All the way from Wakefield in Yorkshire, which is a bloody long way, it really is. It's about 150–200 miles nearly. They'd especially 'ired the coach for the day.'[15]

McLaren, dressed in a grey drape, was captured by David Parkinson in a series of photographs he took in Let It Rock that Paul Gorman has documented in his history of rock and pop fashion, *The Look*. With the Situationist theory of *dérive* stashed in his hip pocket, McLaren believed that you could change your life by inhabiting the streets.[16] 'Chelsea chose Malcolm McLaren', writes Gorman, 'just as he plumped for it.'[17]

Other American tourists and exiles followed Hopkins to Chelsea and Let It Rock, including the New York Dolls, Lou Reed and Iggy Pop. Iggy thought McLaren's artless display of winkle-pickers was the 'most punk thing I ever saw in my life'.[18] Comparing Let It Rock to the much hipper boutique Granny Takes a Trip, which was located 180 metres (200 yd) further down the King's Road, he described McLaren's store as a 'worthless box of shit' but in its casual refusal to conform to the faddish present it was 'like a time bomb against the status quo because it was saying that these violent shoes have the right idea and they are worth more than your fashion, which serves a false value'.[19] Or at least that was the spin Iggy put on it from the viewpoint of 2014.[20] Others back in the day saw it more simply as part of a widespread nostalgia for the 1950s.

In May 1972, Let It Rock and the Teddy Boy revival was covered in a double-page spread in the tabloid newspaper the *Daily Mirror*. The piece on the 'decade that just won't fade away' was not solely about the puritanical revivalism of rock 'n' rollers. Beneath the photograph of a gamine figure ran the tagline 'It's the 1972 Fifties fashion show. A mixture of the awkward tomboy and the ultra-feminine. The ultimate in the bad taste look which is now good taste.'[21] This was the light to the dark of *Curious*'s 'West End Story'. All clothes and accessories worn by the model were sourced from Biba.

Biba was then situated at 120 Kensington High Street where it had been since 1969, located just a little way down the road from Kensington Market at 49/53. It was at the market that Iggy Pop, living locally at Seymour Walk with the rest of The Stooges, bought the Wild Thing jacket that is pictured on the rear of the *Raw Power* sleeve. The image of the roaring leopard head, designed by John Dove and Molly White, printed onto black T-shirts, was worn by Bolan, Steve Marriott, The Sweet's Brian Connolly and Mott the Hoople's Overend Watts. In *Diary of a Rock 'n' Roll Star*, Ian Hunter wrote about Mott's preparations for the autumn 1972 tour of the USA, 'Now we've got to look groovy so our manager, Tony Defries, gave us £100 each to buy clothes. That's O.K. but the clothes are all shit – Carnaby Street, Ken Market, King's Road – ridiculous prices for rubbish that doesn't last five minutes – that's show biz.'[22]

Until Bowie put their career onto a different track, Mott were fairly indistinguishable from any of the era's progressive bands in denim, afghan coats, shapeless hats and lank hair. The backdrop for a promotional shoot might be woodland for that return to the country aesthetic or a brick wall with 'Urban Guerrilla' graffiti for that street-fighting revolutionary Ladbroke Grove look. 'All the Young Dudes' put them in Kensington satin and tat that was not made to last, was inauthentic, but was designed to make an onlooker gasp with shock or delight, preferably both. In that sense, 'Dudes' was a return to a fundamental pop trope of immediacy and built-in obsolescence: pop as symbolized by the rip in P. J. Proby's trousers and the flash style and confrontational attitude of The Who.

Just a stop up the circle line from Kensington High Street is Notting Hill and the adjacent areas of Westbourne Grove, Ladbroke Grove, Holland Park and Bayswater. It was here that the Underground had centred itself. The community of Freaks were sustained by the ready availability of cheap housing or

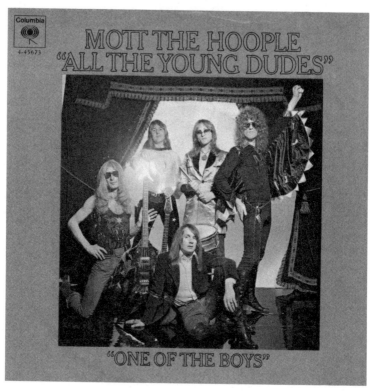

Mott the Hoople: All the Young Dudes in their satin and tat.

squats, a network of services such as the Release offices, which provided legal advice and representation, and London's Free School. It was also the base for the Underground press, *Frendz* and *Oz*, and spiritual home of IT (*International Times*), the area providing a locus (centred on the performance and rehearsal space in All Saints Church Hall) for the leading Freak ensembles, The Deviants (later Pink Fairies), Hawkwind, Edgar Broughton Band, Stray and Mighty Baby among them. The scene is captured in the 1970 documentary *Getting It Straight in Notting Hill Gate*, which features footage of Quintessence playing and rehearsing in the hall and an interview with Caroline Coon in the Release offices. However, the style and myth is better grasped that same year by Christopher Gibbs's interior designs for Nicolas Roeg and Donald Cammell's film *Performance*, starring Mick Jagger and James Fox. Gibbs, the 'King of Chelsea', defined the era's bohemian style affectations with his mix of rich exotic Middle Eastern fabrics overlaying Victorian furnishings and carefully chosen, and placed, antique objects. The lovingly worn-and-torn-with-age-and-wear look of a Gibbs interior, the perfect distressed environment for the Grove's gutter aristocrats, was at the opposite end to the Pop art spaces of *A Clockwork Orange* on the spectrum that defined the day's aesthetic of hip.

By the early 1970s, the Underground was struggling to maintain an image of unity and shared purpose. For outside observers and participants alike, it was as if that coterie had begun to eat itself. Journalist, agent provocateur, frontman of an art-brut rock 'n' roll band and scene-maker par excellence, Mick Farren had fictionalized this dystopian scenario in a short story, 'Once It's Started', published in the final issue (Winter 1973) of *Oz*.[23] Cannibalism is where the promise of the counterculture ends more certainly than in either Charles Manson's Helter-Skelter or stage front in Altamont. The setting is Dirty Edna's bar, where a group of Freaks and drug fiends are holed up. Like a stage set for one of Joan Littlewood's Theatre Workshops, the scene is lit by a pulsing red neon sign and a guttering candle. Alice stares at the flame, a cowboy spins Merle Haggard records on the stereo, while Monk and Easy, strung out on speed, are 36 hours into their rap about Kennedy conspiracy theories and whether

Hitler was a junkie. All this is going on as our narrator ponders whether he should share his pill stash. Before he can make a decision, Haggard is replaced by Johnny Cash and Ice and Belinda join the cursed. Now, all the six of them have to do is to get it together. Yeah, just get it together.

Farren's view of the Underground echoed his then current interpretation that the promises made by the first rock 'n' roll revolt had been despoiled by the present generation. He opens his short story 'Bedsitter Loving' with the unnamed narrator getting ready to go out one Saturday night.[24] He is putting on a clean shirt in front of a mirror, 'legs straddled, feet apart, shirt collar turned up, head dipped like Elvis singing "Lonesome Cowboy"', when he's hit by a Proustian moment. The flashback is to the teenage ritual of dressing for the weekend before heading out to meet the gang in the café, where the jukebox plays Eddie Cochran and the Hollywood Argyles. A world of possibilities seemed to be theirs for the taking, but as the narrator returns to his present situation those 'punk adventures' are now far behind him and his old cohort of rebels are clerking for the town council.

'Bedsitter Loving' was published in the men's magazine *Club International*, which had previously carried other bits of fiction, as well as some essays, by Farren. Not the least of these was an unalloyed piece of nostalgia for the 1950s, 'Back to That Teenage Heaven'.[25] In his 2001 autobiography, *Give the Anarchist a Cigarette*, Farren spent little time reflecting on his fiction and none at all on these short stories. After the Underground press had gone the way of The Beatles he earnt rent money writing for soft porn magazines. Though he appreciated the cheque given for his labours, Farren had little positive to say about the experience: the world of pornography was tacky at best, and, at worst, wretched. Believing he deserved better, he took up employment in 1974 with the NME and put his real energy into writing novels.

Farren was not alone among the Underground alumni in finding employment in Soho's skin factories. Caroline Coon was at the posing end of the camera; she had modelled, circa 1967, for the West End's pornographer-at-large Harrison Marks. The Deviants/Pink Fairies' manager-of-sorts, Jamie Mandelkau, wrote reportage and fiction for *Club International* and *Men Only*. Mick's spouse, Joy Farren, similarly contributed pieces to these Paul Raymond magazines. Photographers who were working in the music field, such as Mick Rock, Byron Newman, Jay Myrdal and Pete Smith, also provided pin-up material for Soho's publishers. Design group Hipgnosis played a significant role in early issues of *Club International*, as did illustrators George Underwood (friend and collaborator of Bowie and Bolan) and his partner Terry Pastor.

Another of *IT*'s leading lights, Jonathon Green, had briefly produced copy for nudie magazines. Giving the people what they want, provided for the sum of £20 per thousand words, however, had not helped to transcend his contempt for a porn journal's 'art, or is it artifice'?[26] Like those journalistic pieces on the thwarted delights and dim sights of Soho in *Curious*, Green found it was the sure weight of the humdrum that numbed the senses. Looking to get a pop kick in a glamour magazine is a fool's errand but, with the allure and intrigue generated by cross-dressing, gender-blurring, swishy pop stars of third-generation rock as a topic, the soft porn magazines of the early 1970s were often happy to sell the contemporary scene, found between the per per.

images of girls in various stages of dishabille in Christopher Gibbs-like interiors, as the new transgressive thrill.

The dirty-sweet line between selling pop in a porn magazine and selling sex in a pop journal had an equivalent in how rock's representations of contemporary social blight crashed into the blast of a new pop excitement as found, say, in *Riding on the Crest of a Slump*, the 1972 Ellis album, and The Sweet's bubblegum music. Denim, leather and long greasy hair contrast with the bright colours of Tommy Roberts's T-shirts, satin trousers and feathered haircuts. The style difference is hard-edged social realism used as a prop for young men to confirm their authenticity (and then sell that truth on to other earnest young men) up against the dishonest plastic flash of a pop group (marketed to an audience of teenage girls). Such a construct was perceptible to all in the manner that third-generation rockers played out their moment in the light by traversing the continuum between the two extremes. As The Jook, in their Skinner jeans and rugby shirts, could tell you, the divide was never so great as to be unbridgeable. Bands might have to modify their attitude and style, adjust the cut of their trousers and perfect their song craft, but that had worked out fine for Slade even if The Jook's version of aggro-pop failed to make an impression with record buyers.

This blurred line between pop and rock is embodied in the otherworldly starman figure in dingy Heddon Street and in the slack between the street chic of Manhattan's Velvet Underground and the foppish dandyism of Beckenham's David Bowie; in the tension between the wraithlike aura of Tyrannosaurus Rex and the cosmic suburban boogie of T. Rex; in the back to the future movement, with its radical yet conservative design aesthetic, of Let It Rock and in Roxy Music; in the grubby authenticity of a Ladbroke Grove headshop and the frivolity and glamour of Biba; and it is there in the seductive tug of teenage lust purveyed by the New York Dolls on those fans not yet, but soon to be, old at thirty. The point of convergence between the poles produced a play of attraction and repulsion that defined third-generation rock 'n' roll, which was cursed, or blessed, to return again and again, in a myriad of ways, to its origin point in the 1950s. The ambition behind *Pin-Ups 1972* is to make visible once more the set of plays along the line that ran between the pop-rock extremes.

♀ ♀ ♀

Mick Farren worked harder than anyone to remain true to the promises and rituals scripted by first- and second-generation rockers. As the scene splintered and diversified, and in some cases floundered and ossified, Farren proselytized and advocated, organized and fought for an ideal of rock 'n' roll that could match the zeal of young people who were agitating for change, renouncing their parents' culture and, as a result of the commercial success of the second-generation rockers, were now squaring up to the market forces that would absorb their energy, monetize their dreams, co-opt their hopes and aspirations, and then sell it all back to them through their proxies – the rock stars of the day.[27]

Ex-art student, doorman at the UFO club in Tottenham Court Road – the centre of the then emerging hippy culture – writer and editor at *IT*, and vocalist with The Social Deviants, Farren was the perfect figurehead for the part of the Underground brought up in the hothouse school of rock 'n' roll rather than in university halls and debating chambers. In his rants and raves in the Underground press he rarely, if ever, quoted Marx, but Eddie Cochran he knew by heart. Asked if he had any answers to the questions he was posing as singer with The Deviants, Farren said,

> That's a different thing. Maybe I'll write a book with all the answers. What we are doing is setting emotions to emotions – not intellect to intellect. Dylan started doing this with a formalised statement of policy. People may know and realise the things we sing about, but we all have different answers, otherwise it's a return to Marxist theory. What we are doing is putting situations into perspective. I think music goes down the drain if it comes up with answers.[28]

Farren was a spokesman for the Freak scene, and a pace-setter for rock 'n' roll as an outlaw creed that, regardless of whatever musical form it took, must speak for and to the community that sustained and nourished it. John Sinclair, aided and abetted by the MC5, was a model of sorts, though Farren was effortlessly cooler than the older Detroiter. Working out of Ladbroke Grove and the West End, he looked as good as Jim Morrison in his leathers, as sharp as Dylan behind his aviator shades and he had a head of hair that gave him the appearance of being Hendrix's electric brother-in-arms. Farren exuded the style and attitude of a true rocker. Even if he couldn't sing for shit, he looked every inch the part and was perfect casting for Marc Bolan's gutter-gaunt gangster in lizard leather boots in T. Rex's 'Ballrooms of Mars'.

Bolan was also a singular part of the Underground community, but with Tyrannosaurus Rex he worked on the other side of the street to the corner from which Farren, on his soap box, heckled and cajoled passers-by. Bolan espoused a gentler attitude, a patchouli-scented folkie airiness rather than a steam blast of amplified amphetamine-sweat noise. However, that was only if you took him at face value, as Nik Cohn attested. Cohn had known Bolan since at least the autumn of 1966, when he was taken under the wing of manager Simon Napier-Bell, and most certainly knew him by the time he had joined John's Children in the spring of the following year. Bolan had been one of Cohn's three studies of the evolving cycles of Mod culture for an *Observer Magazine* article published in the summer of 1967. The feature used a picture of Bolan, then known as Mark Feld, from a 1962 edition of *Town* magazine, which had documented working-class youth's obsession with looking smart and staying ahead of the crowd. For Cohn, Bolan recalled how the early Mod scene was 'mentally a very homosexual thing' but he had not much noticed that aspect at the time:

I was too hung up on myself to be interested in anyone else . . . I didn't think at all. The only thought I ever had was, Oh, I just bought one suit this week and I should have bought three. That was all. I was completely knocked out by my own image, by the idea of Mark Feld. Even though I was so young, I was regarded as very cool, very fast, and I was quite a figure. I still meet people who talk about Mark Feld like a great hero and they couldn't care less about Marc Bolan. It's as if we're two completely separate people.[29]

Following the release of Tyrannosaurus Rex's debut single, Cohn wrote a short profile on Bolan for *Queen* magazine. He described him when first they met as appearing 'gentle' and 'soft-spoken' but that was just a front, basically; he was as 'tough as old rope. Definitely, he wasn't angelic.'[30]

When Bolan pulled Tyrannosaurus Rex out of the Underground and into the charts as T. Rex he had already gone through so many character changes and phases that he gave the impression to those he left behind of being a flighty cheat – a dandy in a turncoat. Little wonder then that during the years of T. Rextasy he was repeatedly challenged on his sincerity and authenticity. For himself, and for all his newfound teenage fans, he feigned indifference and played the role of pop star as someone still completely knocked out by his own image.

When Farren and Bolan sermonized on the youth revolt encompassed in 1950s rock 'n' roll, which they both did frequently and volubly, it was invariably channelled through the prism of a romanticized idea of Eisenhower's America. Britain under Harold Macmillan rarely got a look-in except as that place of dreary repression from which they planned their escape. The first generation of British rock 'n' rollers – Cliff Richard, Johnny Kidd, Billy Fury, Vince Taylor and all the rest – were ignored for Eddie Cochran, Gene Vincent, Elvis, Little Richard and Chuck Berry. The 'Summertime Blues' was their anthem, sung while perfecting a stance in front of the microphone based on James Dean's slouch. In their mind's eye, they drove around town in Cadillacs, smoked Lucky Strikes and wore Levi's over cowboy boots. New legends were not created in Stamford Hill or the Surrey suburbs where Bolan and Farren, respectively, grew up, but in some altogether more exciting space. Bolan and Farren were both coke drinkers from way back. What they had learnt from worshiping at the church of rock 'n' roll was that youth culture had to signify the new if it was to mean anything, and that meant a total break with their parents' generation.

The idolization of Cochran and Vincent by the two Underground figures was shared with any number of the nation's youth. Rock 'n' roll revivalism was in full flow in 1972, symbolized by the gathering of the tribes at Wembley that summer where Little Richard, Chuck Berry and Jerry Lee Lewis shared top billing. Lower on the bill were Detroit's MC5, who were on their second tour of the UK; their first had taken place a year earlier when they played at a free festival organized by Farren and his gang. In 1972, they were joined by other American visitors, including San Francisco's The Flamin' Groovies, New York's Lou Reed and fellow Detroiters, Iggy and the Stooges (the New York Dolls would pay a fleeting visit in the autumn). Reed and Iggy, in particular, brought with them a cultish mystique that matched that of Cochran and Vincent, which Bowie, with his willing accomplices in the music press, promoted and exploited in equal measure.

The speed and apparent certainty with which Bowie moved from being a one-hit wonder – 'Space Oddity' – with a critically approved album (*Hunky Dory*), only just released and barely promoted in January 1972, into a full-on media assault as Ziggy Stardust that reached a first, heady peak in June when the album hit the shops, still has the power, fifty years later, to startle and amaze. Reading over the weekly music press for the first six months of 1972 it's possible to see Bowie enter from stage left, pushing his way past the backstage hands, supporting cast and chorus girls, to take up his place in the spotlight; just as Bolan, still transfixed by his own image, exits on the right. 'Bowie has been a long time coming,' wrote Ray Coleman in *Melody Maker*, 'but a more certain Bolan-chaser I never saw . . . Bowie has arrived – a worthy pin-up with such style.'[31] The first Ziggy tour started at the most inauspicious of venues, the Toby Jug pub, and ended in a considerably more ostentatious venue, the Royal Festival Hall, where Bowie was joined on stage by Lou Reed. A week or so later, in July, Bowie had also pulled Iggy Pop and Mott the Hoople into his media circus. The fiction, at the start of the year, of a singer who had cast himself as the rock 'n' roll star Ziggy Stardust had become fact six months later.

While Bowie refitted yesterday's men into figures fit to play a part in the 1970s drama he was busily writing, ad-libbing even, they gave him in return the frisson of rock's hoodlum-poet pose. The character of Ziggy demanded he insinuate, if not exude, an aura of danger; dark sex with a violent twist. Nothing in Bowie's career thus far had prepared him to take on such a role, so he did this by association. First with Mick Ronson, transformed into a sidekick who posed with his guitar as if he were an alley punk with a switchblade, and then by a form of osmosis, absorbing the gang mentality of a band like Mott, especially the relationship they had with their fans. 'The Phantom of Rock', Lou Reed, helped to take him deeper into the shadows and taught him how to feign a (New York) street accent, while the physicality of Iggy Pop, his aggressive recklessness, put yet another dimension of threat into the demi-monde Bowie was assembling. Before 1972 was done with he had even co-opted the New York Dolls into his dramatis personae.

These somewhat disparate characters were pulled together, and given a very contemporary, London-based edge, by Bowie's references and quotes from Kubrick's *A Clockwork Orange*. The film had premiered in the West End in December 1971 to great critical acclaim and shrill moralizing. When it opened in provincial cinemas, the best part of a year later, becoming more widely accessible to the nation's juvenile delinquent wrecks, the outrage it caused was amplified exponentially. Bowie cannily exploited the film's plaudits *and* tabloid-inspired censure and made the media hype that is built on the altercations between admiration and disapproval his subject and his means to achieve stardom.

Begun as a fantasy of a star and his fans – a mix of science fiction and street-corner punk poses – Ziggy Stardust had become a veritable truth by the middle of 1972. This slide from the imaginary to reality was made no less astonishing by the simultaneous arrival of Roxy Music, a band, unlike the Spiders from Mars, that was not a figment of their leader's imagination. With no prior existence in the pop market, Roxy Music even better personified the now of today.

The contradiction Roxy Music had chosen to ride was to temper their futuristic leanings with a retro aesthetic that matched the glossy chrome sheen and subject-matter of an Allen Jones sculpture or Peter Phillips canvas: a 1950s Pop art phantasmagoria for the new space age. Unfortunately for Roxy, critics tended not to share their set of cultural reference points and instead directed their readers to compare them to Sha Na Na, who also wore gold lamé trousers and had greaser haircuts. Though the American revival band had better dance moves, Roxy Music had style and class, albeit somewhat aspirational.

On the other hand, the New York Dolls were without class, and that suited them just fine as they tore apart whatever patchwork critics had stitched together in an attempt to hold on to some semblance of order in the era of third-generation rock. The Dolls were discovered, almost fully formed and with a matching gang of followers, by a clutch of critics in the early summer of 1972. For those who fell under their spell it was as if they had found again the thrill of their first love: the Dolls allowed their twenty-something-year-old fans to play at being teenagers again. At the Mercer Arts Center the Dolls parlayed a brand of rock 'n' roll that was as pure *and* as tainted as that of any first-generation rocker, Jerry Lee Lewis and Little Richard among them. They were like Jodie Foster's teenage prostitute in *Taxi Driver*, childlike and innocent yet aged and corrupted by experience that should have been beyond their earthly years.

The New York Dolls played the scene as decadent wrecks, impersonating teenage longing and insouciance, and in so doing they encapsulated the idea of third-generation rock better than any of their contemporaries. Who knew (or cared) that singer David Johansen was not 19, but in fact 22, when the Dolls gave the best teenage head of any contender on the corner? The Dolls played a brand of rock 'n' roll that was seeped in the past, especially that formed in the likeness of the Rolling Stones and The Pretty Things. Trying to explain where his band, Silverhead, and the Dolls sat with regard to their influences, Michael Des Barres said, the vibe might be the Stones, but that was because it was the 'dirtiest vibe' and that's what the bands were about, getting 'as dirty as possible'.[32] Like the Dolls, he loved R&B, 'but my roots are in the Stones, not in Elmore James as it was for Jagger. You could say I'm twice removed from the origins of

R&B', which is to say that his band and the Dolls were third-generation through and through.

Though the Dolls shared with others the Rolling Stones and The Pretty Things as avatars of the primal in the new theatre of third-generation rock 'n' roll, uniquely among their peers, they dressed their Anglo predecessors in the raiment of 1960s girl groups, producing a *Rock Dreams*-like twist to their presentation of self. The Stones had toured with The Ronettes, they were their contemporaries, but the Dolls came later and conflated the image of the bad boys and girls of pop, making them into a fetish to better play out a role in their wild, mad masquerade. The Dolls were like characters from a Fellini film (it was said of them) who, following a midnight screening of a double-bill of *Studs on Main Street* and *Bike Boy Goes Ape*, had spilled out from a 42nd Street grindhouse onto the sidewalk in their high heels and dime store glad rags. Having momentarily gathered themselves together, they were now all set to deliver *The Teenage News* . . . 'Extra! Extra!! Buy yourself a copy.'

1

ROCK 'N' ROLL UNDERGROUND: MICK FARREN LOOKING TOUGH — KICKING DOGS

As empty of disorder as rock 'n' roll was in 1975, [Malcolm] McLaren understood that it remained the only form of culture the young cared about, and at thirty in 1975, he clung to a sixties definition of young – youth was an attitude, not an age. For the young everything flowed from rock 'n' roll (fashion, slang, sexual styles, drug habits, poses), or was organized by it, or was validated by it. The young, who as legal phantoms had nothing and as people wanted everything, felt the contradiction between what life promised and what it delivered most keenly: youth revolt was a key to social revolt, and thus the first target of social revolt could be rock 'n' roll.

Greil Marcus, *Lipstick Traces* (1989)

Heard on the early records by the Rolling Stones, The Pretty Things and The Yardbirds is the sound of adolescents parsing a new language, the blues. These young men had every expectation that their exercises in a foreign tongue would give them ready access to the mysteries of adulthood. This was not the workaday world occupied by their parents, with their squandered suburban lives, but one filled with potency and magic. Learning the blues would be a transformative experience, a journey of discovery that was best undertaken in the company of likeminded malcontents. In their gangs, a social contract only slightly corrected from the one they had at school, they presented an indifferent and stroppy face to the world even as they reassured each other that their endeavours were honest and their motives true. To get to where they were heading, destination Skedaddle, they renounced all bequests and made a solemn vow to one another that they would kill their fathers.

Other than a shared patricidal resolve, Mick Farren held in common with the Stones, the Pretties and the 'Birds a fondness for more generally confronting authority. It was a stance that led him to call his band The Social Deviants, later shortened to The Deviants. The variant was less specific but still suggestive of a refusal of accepted standards – sexual values and good taste among them. As they attempted to find themselves in the immediate aftermath of The Beatles' and the Stones' success, The Deviants' name made a direct link with other second-generation rockers whose collective identities similarly advertised a truculent pose – Them, The Who, The Others, The Measles, The Flies, The Ugly's, The Troggs, The Downliners Sect, The Sorrows, The Attack and The Kinks.

In his autobiography, Farren writes about his teen fantasy life in which he envisaged his first band as an 'outlaw ensemble' that drew on the Cochran, Holly and Vincent song books, 'and I'd be clinging to a mike stand in a bike jacket and one black glove'.[1] Rock 'n' roll, he firmly believed, 'harboured a solid, if unshaped core of insurrection, long before it could even form or spell the word'.[2] Farren embodied the period's idea of the non-conformist, self-identifying with the founding figures of rock 'n' roll he celebrated above all else. 'Elvis', he wrote, 'was white, greasy, and had the sullen good looks of a successful hubcap thief.'³ Vincent and Jerry Lee Lewis were 'fuelled on pills and bourbon', and 'pumped out hard, uncompromising rock music that made it very clear that their romantic interests were mainly directed towards getting some'.⁴

Ptooff! was the title given to The Deviants independently produced and distributed 1968 debut album. It came wrapped in a six-panel poster sleeve, a lysergic Pop-art triumph of in-your-face graphics and effusive sleeve notes courtesy of DJ John Peel and *International Times* editor Barry Miles. In his note, the latter called the record a 'prime, over-ripe example of a gratu-itously obscene, rockin', stompin', post-psyche-delic, neo-rock 'n' roll, UNDERGOUND freak record'. Sometime after the fact, Farren defined The Deviants as 'British amphetamine psychosis music'.⁵ It was a near perfect description. Miles thought their music contained 'secret mystic rites', like those found in old 78s on the Cobra or Sun labels. Were that it was so; the band channel much of the attitude Farren valued in rock 'n' roll but are wholly lacking in finesse. They pound like a mallet rather than slash like a blade and for all their effort they produce very little heat and flash. The album is lumpen, a set of gestures. The template is Bo Diddley, via The Pretty Things and, indisput-ably, 'Gloria' by Them. The Deviants are acolytes at rock 'n' roll's shrine, their stance a genuflection towards the keepers of the mystic rites, but it was not the thing itself. They practised a form of outsider art, savage and untroubled by profession-alism, unadulterated and raw.⁶ After The Downliners Sect, critic Richard Williams, echoing numerous others, said Farren's combo were the worst band he ever saw.⁷

Whatever the merits of his music, to supporter and foe alike, Farren left an impression. In the final accounting, his stamp

The Deviants in *Beat International* (January 1969).

on things was less a musical legacy than the promotion of a particular style and attitude formed out of the iconography of the 1950s rebel that he adapted for the Underground rock scene of the late 1960s and early '70s. Dave 'Boss' Goodman described to Deviants' biographer, Rich Deakin, the impact of first seeing the band:

> From the bottom up, he's got his Acme cowboy boots on, he's got his leather trousers on, he's got his yellow Ben Sherman shirt open to the waist and an enormous great studded belt, and hair that had gone completely fucking Hendrix like . . . and then some. And he just looked . . . you know? . . . this huge broken nose, and he can't sing a note in tune, and it was the most fearsome thing the pair of us had ever seen in our lives.[8]

With Caroline Coon as its cover model, the bastion of British society magazines, *Queen*, reported on the Underground scene in its February 1969 edition. Coon worked for Release, advising those who found themselves ensnared in bureaucratic and legal red tape: 'The English system stinks and the underground is very aware of the smell,' she said.[9] The six-page spread, written by Jenny *'Groupie'* Fabian, with photographs by Clive Arrowsmith, included profiles of *Oz* and *Time Out* designer John Goodchild, DJ and scenester Jeff Dexter, dancers Mimi and Mouse and outlaw couple Joy and Mick Farren. Whatever the politics of the individuals, the emphasis is firmly on fashion and looks. Joy's handwoven nightgown is from Forbidden Fruit, Portobello Road, and Mick made the leathers himself while his jacket came from a Brighton speed shop. His hair is natural (a point Farren often made, as if to deflect any accusation of inauthenticity).

Despite being married, neither Joy nor Mick believed in the institution. A 25-year-old Mick is described as the leader of

Promoting the grease burger diet with Joy and Mick Farren in *Queen*,
cover star Caroline Coon (February 1969).

The Deviants – 'an extreme underground group who specialize in revolting':

> We're a nasty group, and now we've started to make
> a bit of money we're getting nastier. The underground
> is fragmented, disorganised and uncomfortable, but
> extremely necessary because it's a move for a change.
> The system hangs me up and makes me intensely angry
> at times. We express this in our music.[10]

Farren volubly rejected the macrobiotic lifestyle eschewed by Dexter and others: 'It's all right eating rice if you're going to sit on your backside and meditate all day,' but he was having none of that, 'I eat greaseburgers,' he said.[11] In the full-page portrait by Arrowsmith, Farren's fuzzed-up hair, black leathers and the generally snarky demeanour of his pose attest to the idea that he is not in the least fearful of any kickback on his views about hippie lifestyle choices from his fellow contributors (or *Queen*'s readers); rather he invites their opprobrium. He is out to make his mark.

Flash forward four and a half years to September 1973 and Farren is on the cover of the *Daily Telegraph Magazine* – his notoriety now such that he can function as poster boy for the Underground. Neither a celebration nor exposé of the scene, Charles Nicholl's article instead asks what had gone wrong for the Underground press? It now found itself in decline and its young idealists 'veterans of progress':

> The label 'Underground' always concealed a vague and
> unhelpful generalisation. Now, perhaps there is nothing

behind it at all – the debris of an ideal, diminishing
echoes of a war-cry that no one quite understood.[12]

Frendz, *Ink* and *Oz* had folded and only *IT* was still publishing. Increasing overheads, waning sales, a dearth of advertising
revenue, poor distribution and expensive court cases had taken
their toll, but lack of purpose, he suggested, had also added
to the cost.

The Underground is made up mostly of middle-class,
college-educated under-thirties, Nicholl argued, who self-
identify as anti-establishment. They are, he maintained, less
concerned with revolution and being doctrinaire than with
managing their chosen lifestyle, which is an activity that is
'communal, egalitarian, drug-oriented' but beyond that 'its
protagonists are reluctant to define it in conceptual terms. It
is something tribal, to be lived rather than explained.'[13] If the
Underground was not easily defined, Nicholl was still able to
point to the first issue of *IT* in 1966 as its origin, and the community of long hairs in Notting Hill Gate that had formed
around the nucleus of John 'Hoppy' Hopkins, Michael X, Mick
Farren and Alexander Trocchi as its guides. Writing for *IT* gave
this disparate set of individuals a focus and a shared identity
and in turn they helped promote 'an intuitive sense of community' for its readers.[14]

Within two years of its founding, sales of *IT* went from
5,000 to 45,000 fortnightly. By 1971 the Underground press
was bursting with activity and ambition, a UK edition of *Rolling
Stone* had been launched in 1969 which, after its U.S. publisher,
Jann Wenner, withdrew support, became first *Friends of Rolling
Stone*, then *Friends* and finally *Frendz*. *Oz* had been in

circulation since February 1967 and had been successful enough for a spin-off, *Ink*, which was first published in 1971 in an attempt to find the middle ground between the Underground and the *New Statesman*. But success was the father of the Underground press's failure. Even as sales soared for *Oz* and *IT*, following the Director of Public Prosecutions' obscenity charges against their editors, advertising revenue diminished, with companies unwilling to align themselves with publications being dragged through the courts. Printers and distributors were also reluctant to support a paper struggling with litigation. Nicholl reported that *IT* was hit by a £3,000 fine for publishing gay contact ads (ruled liable to corrupt minors) and then went a further £500 into debit when it defended the obscenity charges employed against the *Nasty Tales* comic book that Farren edited with cartoonist J. Edward Barker.[15]

The key problem was that independence was always illusory, and the Underground press existed on a contradiction – it depended on the establishment: whether advertisers such as the big record companies, or distributors, or printers that had the necessary technology and capacity needed to produce enough copies to make the whole operation sustainable. Not all was doom and gloom in Nicholl's report, however. He also noted the increasing number of alternative community papers that served a local readership, the rise of special interest journals such as *Spare Rib* and *Gay News* and the 'startling success' of the listings magazine *Time Out*: 'The Underground press, perhaps, is not dead only scattered and tired,' he concluded.[16]

When he recorded just where the protagonists had scattered to, Nicholl did not mention the burgeoning market for the weekly music press, *Melody Maker* (MM), the newly arrived *Sounds* and most especially the rejuvenated *New Musical Express* (NME). He had described Mick Farren as sporting 'Afro-hair, sun-glasses and a vague aura of exhaustion' and now dedicating his time to science fiction, which in 1973 was true enough. Farren, however, was also paying his bills by selling short stories to, as well as writing anonymous copy for, Soho's soft porn publishers. The following year Farren would further expand his interests by taking up full-time employment at the NME, alongside other Underground alumni such as Nick Kent from *Frendz* and Charles Shaar Murray from *Oz*. As the latter said, 'The idea was to hijack the NME and have an underground rock weekly being produced by a major corporation for a mass audience.'[17] In Murray's telling, the contradiction the Underground had existed on is subverted as long as writers didn't succumb to the lure of mammon.

That there was a readership for journals dedicated to taking rock music seriously had been demonstrated by *Rolling Stone* and it was a perception clearly held by the editors at *Frendz* who, in 1972, with Nick Kent as a key contributor, gave ever-more space to the evolving music scene.[18] Kent, like Farren, was enthralled by the scene built around Detroit's *Creem* magazine, founded in 1969. Defining *Creem*'s ethos, two of its contributors wrote in 1971 that it had been conceived as 'a cross between a rock magazine, an underground newspaper and a rock and roll band'.[19] The journal, they added, 'is operated on a communal basis; it remains the only successful rock publication to be edited in this fashion. The conspirators live and breathe in the same atmosphere, housed under one roof where they deal not only with a unified purpose but with the complexities of each other as individuals as well.'[20] What surely appealed to writers in the UK with a commitment to the music scene was the idea that 'Creem sprang directly from Detroit's burgeoning rock community, and in its infancy it maintained exclusive lines of communication and nourishment to that community.'[21]

First published in 1969, Zigzag waved the flag for a dedicated British journal, but its earnestness was unleavened by the likes of Creem's irreverence and humour. Zigzag would be joined by Cream in 1971 and Let It Rock in 1972. Further evidence that there was a potentially receptive readership for a UK rock journal came in the form of Strange Days, a short-lived biweekly music paper that was published over the autumn and winter of 1970/71 and edited by Mark Williams, who had previously been music editor at IT. Strange Days promoted itself as an alternative to the establishment pop papers, especially Sounds, which was initially funded by Rupert Murdoch, and the still conservative MM and NME. Though it mimicked the fold-over cover of Rolling Stone, Strange Days offered little else in the way of comparison with the groundbreaking San Francisco publication. Nevertheless, it had ambition and hubris to spare, proclaiming itself 'The British Rock Paper'. Produced on a shoestring budget, it ran adverts for a motorcycle dispatch company the editors had formed to offset the cost of printing the paper.

Editorial content highlighted motorcycle culture alongside articles on whatever band was currently in the frame with new product to push, but it also dealt with themes such as god-rock, kids-rock, Black rock and white soul, and reggae as the true underground music of the day. The first issue had Elvis Presley in his gold lamé suit on the cover and the main feature was a long item on the Isle of Wight Festival. Given its promotion of first-generation rock 'n' rollers, m'cycles, the MC5 and festival culture in its debut, it was not surprising that Mick Farren was granted space in the paper's second edition. The piece on the Underground star runs beneath the heading 'We Want the World and We Want It Now!' Jim Morrison's rallying cry is ironically juxtaposed with a photograph of Farren marching down a London backstreet with a small group of followers all provocatively, yet splendidly, attired in Nazi military uniforms of jodhpurs, boots, swastika armbands and holstered Luger pistols. Only Farren's sunglasses, muttonchop sideburns and frizzed-out hair, pushed down by his cap, suggested something was amiss with this drama.

Sarah Malone's interview with Farren focused on his and his confederates' attempts to cause maximum disruption to the Isle of Wight Festival. He was still angry at what he saw as the personal profiteering through the exploitation of the Underground. He laid into Jim Morrison for paying only lip-service to the scene as he flew in on a private helicopter and stayed at luxury hotels and got 'paid probably something in the region of £500 a minute for putting out that ethic'.[22] Specifically, Farren was at war with 'anybody who lives considerably better than their brothers, while still attempting to maintain the ethic of brotherhood'. For a while, he had been espousing common cause with Detroit's John Sinclair and the MC5 to the point where he had helped form the British chapter of the White Panthers. This was intended to be a movement that aligned the white youth of the counterculture with militant Black youth. As Farren raged against the appropriation of the Underground's radical agenda by commercial interests, it seemed the contradictions in that gesture of solidarity with the Black Panthers were as invisible to him as they had been to Sinclair. The gesture itself was what mattered, however; the fight was on and Farren had Uncle Tom hippies in his sights.

Extreme gestures, he had come to understand, did not make anyone any money. Play the game, be polite and accept the status quo and you'll get along fine: 'when you're a good boy, you can make more than when you're a bad boy.' Nevertheless, being the 'bad boy' was where it was at for Farren. Perhaps that was why he and his pals decided to raid a Shaftesbury Avenue theatrical costumers and parade around as Nazis, the ultimate bad boys. This was one pose that could not be easily exploited and sold back to the kids; he was not yet willing to concede that youth rebellion would always be co-opted by commercial interests. The MC5, Farren argued, at least in that time before Sinclair was incarcerated on drug trafficking charges, challenged the simple binary between pop and rock with The Monkees on one side and Led Zeppelin on the other. 'Though MC5 are not as technically proficient as Led Zeppelin, they're putting down a lot heavier trip . . . They were giving you rock that was actually telling you about their situation. You know . . . "Motor City Burning".'[23] But as Malone concluded, the MC5 eventually sold out and even John Sinclair's 'faith in the Rock-based revolution that he launched together with the Five must be sadly diminished now that both parties have surrendered to the system or been swallowed by it'.[24]

In his history of the Underground press, Nigel Fountain compares the literary, American Beat influence on Barry Miles with Mick Farren's 'somewhat more street-based style', which was 'born of the rock culture':

Out of rock came a stance of the rock concert rebel, where the crisis and the contradictions of the times could be played out as theatre. The problem was that adherents to the vision had nowhere to go, as time passed, but onwards to the next gig. But in 1967, as the high tide of commercial hippiedom flowed onwards, who cared?[25]

Farren's response to the problem of the cul-de-sac Fountain argued he was lost within was to write *Watch Out Kids* – a cartoon polemic or a polemical cartoon. Published in 1972, with illustrations by his *IT* pal Edward Barker, the book claimed to be 'The first hippy-yippie-freak political and pointers-to-survival-and-good-times statement to come out from under in this country.'[26] Farren promised to reveal how 'Elvis gave birth to the Angry Brigade' and to explain 'where the rock generation's been and where it is going'.[27] In case anyone accused Farren and Barker of personally profiteering on the back of the Underground, the cover blurb concluded with the self-deprecating justification for writing the book: 'They promised us money.'[28]

Like the aesthetic of much of the Underground press, the book blurred the divide between image and text. Graphic layout often said as much if not more than pictures and words on their own. The book is easily consumed in a single sitting. To set the scene for today's situation, Farren's charge began with an innocuous history of teenagers and their music. Images of *The Wild One* (released in 1967 after fourteen years of censorship by the British Board of Film Censors) jostle with James Dean in one of his iconic poses, and then comes Elvis. Farren's view of the origin of youth in revolt is almost exclusively American, as Jonathon Green observed in his review of the book for *IT*, and has little to say about Britain in the 1950s beyond representing a scene of youth loitering outside Soho's 2i's – the home of British rock 'n' roll.[29]

The thesis is that the 1950s is where it – teenage culture and the rock revolution, which was founded on the simple opposition of us (teenagers) versus them (adults) – all started. Suppression and regulation, rules and obedience, parents and school rose up against the new beat. After Elvis came Gene Vincent, Farren explained, a working-class hood. Then there was Eddie Cochran, who wrote with a rebel heart for the rebel even if compared to Vincent he appeared unthreatening. Next up, Little Richard, the best rocker of the lot, who brought race to the table. The reaction to these rebel teen-savants was immediate and inevitable. The adult world shut them down, Farren wrote, contained and emasculated them by drowning them out under a tidal wave of teenage products.

Whether dealing with early rock 'n' rollers or the current situation the Underground found itself within, Farren depicted youthful rebellion as being in a constant struggle to assert itself, to claim autonomy. But, inevitably, 'the system will outnumber and out-manoeuvre us.'[30] The artist will compromise and the community they came from and spoke for will scatter and split. However,

> If that singleness of purpose can be recaptured and developed it might enable us to survive and hold tiny pieces of territory in which we could live according to our own ideals, and by living in this way we may remind the population that an alternative to the system actually exists.[31]

While images, music and words can be legislated against, controlled by censors and the police, what cannot be suppressed is the way you walk, hold yourself and speak. Style and attitude matter and have force for someone like Farren. Dylan embodied this way of being; his lucid lyrics escaped the bounds of early rock, Farren thought, speaking in a code that his audience implicitly understood even as they argued over a symbol's meaning. Dylan as a gnostic prophet spoke only to the young. Elder generations who had not grown up on rock 'n' roll could never fully comprehend what he was singing about. They were excluded from the sect. Yet, as Farren readily admitted, it is difficult to use style to change anything, its elusiveness working for and against itself.

The competing working-class teen styles of Mods and Rockers seemed only to confirm the political dead end of such juvenile revolts against the adult world. The more educated, slightly older teenagers – sixth-formers, art school attenders and undergraduates – suggested to Farren the possibility of a more creative (and subversive use) of style to better contest the joust he was proposing with repressive forces – opponents who he might effectively define himself against – that he saw ranged around him and his peers.

The term Farren commonly used in this period to describe himself and those he felt most keenly aligned with was 'Freak'. As a term for group identification, as popularized by Frank Zappa and his Mothers of Invention, 'Freak' was American in its origin and thus, post-Beatnik and rock 'n' roll, inscribed with revolutionary intent. The name had resonance because it invoked the idea of the outsider, a freak of nature or society. The sideshow attraction of abnormality – Siamese twins, the bearded lady and the chicken man – the concept of the object of fascination, ridicule and fear was appropriated and hurled back at the straight world as a provocation and as a challenge to recognize the self within the other:

> Like the Jews, blacks and gypsies before them, the freaks began to experience the prejudice, repression and hostility that is levelled at minorities by a paranoid and corrupt civilisation. Their case, however, was made even more ugly and bizarre by the fact that it was society directing its oppressive powers against its own children.[32]

Farren took it as a given that he was writing for white, educated, male heterosexual youths.

He considered the youth movement to be 'revolution in its purest form'.[33] Previous revolutions had involved changing the organizational structure of an already established culture, Farren argued. The result led, symptomatically, to bad art:

> The rapid spread of youth culture on the other hand ... is the result of the kids themselves evolving a new way of living despite all the massive opposition thrown against them. Hundreds and thousands of white kids prepared to become social outcasts rather than join their parents' death culture.[34]

Nigel Fountain had made his criticism of Farren's politics in 1988. Charles Shaar Murray had been equally critical sixteen years earlier in his review of *Watch Out Kids*. Murray thought the book was overpriced, which 'doesn't really strike one as an acceptable revolutionary act', and not much more than a long essay for IT that 'reads like twenty thousand lapel badges laid end to end'.[35]

Farren may have been a romantic and politically naive, but he was not unaware of the weakness in his stance and arguments. At least until the early 1970s he saw his belief and trust in the Underground as evidence of his incorruptibility and his armour against co-option.[36] The Freak scene of 1967, especially as it was realized in San Francisco, was, for Farren, one of 'the greatest revolutions in style and attitude' despite the eventual failure of the bonds that tied the community together. If that revolution did not last, the idea of it at least prevailed. In March 1972 the White Panther Party UK report was published in IT: 'We bring our music to our communities with revolutionary, high-energy bands like the Pink Fairies. Our lifestyle becomes our politics, our politics our lifestyle.'[37] Indisputably, Farren lived that maxim.

Outside of his activities with The Deviants and his writings for IT, Farren's most noteworthy attempt to pull the people together was with the free festival Phun City that was held over three days in July 1970. That the event even got off the drawing board was a feat in itself, but run it did despite legal injunctions and the withdrawal of funding:

> none of our original plans had come together, we were no longer in control and the kids, the audience (although the word was now meaningless), had taken over the event. They were getting down, making it happen, and having the time of their lives.[38]

If the physical and mental cost of organizing things meant running a festival was not something Farren again contemplated, it did not mean he had lost faith in the idea.[39] His obligation to what he considered to be his community was why he took the monetarization of festivals, especially as applied to the Isle of Wight Festival, so very seriously.

Farren's first novel, *The Texts of Festival* (1973), looked further and harder at what was at stake for the Freak scene. Set in a post-apocalyptic landscape, Farren slotted his dystopian view into a generic Western framework of a frontier fort under siege from marauding natives: Phun City as Fort Apache. The fortified town of Festival is run by a despot whose power is enabled by the keepers of the texts, celebrants who hold on to bits of rock lore and lyrics by the likes of Dylan, Jagger and Morrison. The town is built around an old stage with an antique PA system and light display. The idea of a people's festival – a celebration of community – was, by the time of the story's setting, fixed into a repressive ritual. Its final reckoning was now long overdue.

Out in the countryside the outlaws led by Iggy, an unhinged figure high on crystal, have formed an alliance with a tribe of hill people intent on ransacking Festival. The image of a band of outlaws led by a figure named after Iggy Pop is an amusing conceit, but Farren no more saw him as an answer to the repression of authoritarian power than he did the figure of the gambler, Frankie Lee, based on Wild Bill Hickock, who helps lead the resistance. However romantically inclined he is towards society's outliers, Farren had already reached the same question that Nigel Fountain was to make: after the revelry what next?

In *Watch Out Kids*, he was unequivocal about rock stars
as the problem not the solution: when the musician becomes
a star he becomes decadent. The music produced by pop stars
is introspective and divorced from the situation the kid on the
street finds himself in. Farren has little time for rock ego bands
such as Led Zeppelin or Ten Years After, The Who too. For a
while he thought of The Who as the 'people's band', but with
Tommy they had become 'non-committal'.[40] For some kids, the
answer, he wrote, was to 'delve back into the fifties', to return
to the roots of 'revolution that began when teenagers rejected
Eisenhower and embraced James Dean'.[41] But that shift away
from a rock star's appeal could be retrogressive if all it did was
to 'feed the sad rock 'n' roll revival'. Who then to look to for
a lead if it wasn't to the stars of the past or present? What
might third-generation rock 'n' roll look like?

In a letter to *Friends* (September 1970), Farren contested
one writer's use of the term 'people's band'. He claimed, 'The
fact that people go to and see the pop stars at Bath [Festival]
does not mean those bands get to qualify. They may be bands
for the people but they are not bands that belong to the people.
Quite the reverse, they in fact belong to the same capitalist
interests that exploit and rob the people daily.'[42] A genuine
'people's band' had to return what it had received from its
audience, and its aim can 'only be the total accomplishment
of revolution'.[43] Such a band must show the same dedication
to the cause as the Panthers and Weathermen. To his mind,
only the MC5, when they were under the guidance of John
Sinclair, and David Peel and the Lower East Side, qualify as
'people's bands', but the Pink Fairies might. If they 'don't fuck
up they could make a positive contribution to the overthrow

of the pigs that rule us'.[44] The debate continued to play out into the following year.

In its review of Goodbye Summer, the autumn 1971 charity rock extravaganza starring The Who, The Faces and Mott the Hoople, *Frendz* asked the question 'what would you rather do – see the Who for 25 bob at the Oval, or the Pink Fairies and Edgar Broughton for free at Glastonbury Fair?'[45] In one context or another, these bands were all being touted as 'people's bands'. As 1970 unfolded, holding the centre together became increasingly problematic. 'The Underground Music Is Dead Long Live Pop' ran a headline inside *IT*. Did it matter whether or not Jethro Tull were designated as an Underground band? And, post-Altamont, was there even an Underground community any more that might be supported by an Underground band, asked Arthur A. Pitt, as the Dead, Airplane, MC5 and The Stooges did in America?

> In Britain a group has a job supporting itself, even a big group, and the only time a band demonstrates any altruism is when it does a free concert in Hyde Park or maybe someplace else, which the music press will notice, editorially confirm the Underground image of that band, which will in turn sell a few more records to Underground record buyers. Get the Picture? It's a hype.[46]

Mick Farren responded by refuting the suggestion that the Underground was dead, not least because those outside cannot distinguish between the Underground musician and the progressive musician, between the Hells Angel and a Zen macrobiotic. The Underground is defined by those who oppose it, by external forces, he argued.[47] The point was to end the 'internal factional bullshit . . . We have to learn to relate together, have fun together literally before it is too late.'[48]

One third-generation group that was in the business of communicating the kind of information Farren wanted to disseminate was the Edgar Broughton Band who, in 1970, had twice been made the cover stars of *Zigzag* magazine. By their second appearance there was a presumption of familiarity, and this left their critic, Ian (no surname given), free to focus on the question of how bracketing and categorizing such a band would inevitably lead to things becoming predictable and therefore easily dismissed. It was not musical pigeonholing that concerned him, but the political labels a band carried. The Broughtons, however, escaped such ready-made patterns, Ian argued:

> The band hasn't got any consistent and precisely defined plans, except to have an effect, to take those people who come into contact with them through an experience so that when they come out the other side they will feel or think a little different. They want to involve people, if only for a while, involve them in anything, especially confusion, because to struggle out of confusion you have to go by way of thought, and thought is therapeutic.[49]

The band's unpredictability, its ambiguity around certain political positions on the left (if not on the right), and their refusal to be readily classified are what he valued. Fear of being too po-faced has Ian qualify things by celebrating the band's sense of humour, but what is not countenanced, not even mentioned, is the idea the band might simply be out to entertain anyone. The presumption is that the band's main purpose is to bring their audience with them to face the reality of apartheid, Greek Colonels and other power-hungry politicians, or whatever the manifestation of inequality and oppression is that has been identified: 'Out Demons Out' band and audience cry in unison.

A news story about 'Out Demons Out' spray-painted around Aylesbury's County Hall and Market Square is quoted in the *Zigzag* story: 'What point of significance was behind this example of graffiti we wonder,' asked the reporter from the *Bucks Herald*. Unable to decipher the script and regardless of meaning, it was, he concluded, an act of vandalism done at a cost to the ratepayers.[50]

> The mere phrase 'Out Demons Out' has been causing a lot of puzzlement and worry to some people in official posts – in places as far apart as Birmingham and Belgium. The slogan has appeared on walls, road signs, doors and windows. Local council officials, questioned by the press, elaborate various theories about exorcism and black magic; obviously they haven't heard of the Broughton Band yet.[51]

To initiates, the meaning of the chant was obvious but to those it was aimed at the purpose remained obscure.

This is rock 'n' roll as a secret language, which Mick Farren described, in a little pamphlet that accompanied the release of the third Deviants album, as a way of communicating that 'the rulers cannot understand' and so they fear the rock musician, 'but since he is a marketable commodity (product?) they allow him to continue'. Farren's point about commodification was underscored by an advert for CBS records publicizing their artist roster as 'the sound of the seventies'. The tag line was 'don't compromise, because the music doesn't.' The advertisement appeared in the January 1970 edition of *IT* and was clearly riffing on the company's earlier, deeply contentious, declaration that the man can't bust our music. It was no more than another appropriation of the counterculture's political sincerity, which was then sold back as product. Such commercialization of the Underground diminished its authenticity and thus its authority to make the claim that it was speaking for the people. In the realm of record company marketing, the debate about whose side are you on was refigured as what product of ours have you bought this week?

Inside the closed world of the Underground rock scene the question was temporarily being reframed as who, the Broughtons or the Pink Fairies, were the most credible and trusted purveyors of messages stealthy or bold? The debate kicked into high gear following a shambles of a gig at Keele University in Staffordshire. The Broughtons were pissed off with the organizers who, they felt, were abusing their good will and comradeship by putting on a free gig and ripping off the band. The night turned into something of a riot and the band were given fines and costs of almost £1,000. In the aftermath, it seemed to some that the band were the hapless stooges of their management, who had been exploiting their reputation as a people's band. Peter Jenner at Blackhill Enterprises, who represented the Broughtons, didn't dispute that he was in a business that was out to make money. It was no secret that Blackhill was an entertainment agency, he said, but this did not mean they were without an ethos that allowed them to support good causes.[52]

IT responded that the Broughtons, as a committed 'revolutionary band', had sold out and their 'sense of values had changed'.[53] Jenner responded that the band's revolutionary credentials were intact and compared them to the Stones, who drive around in 'their fuckin' Jaguars or whatever'.[54] The Broughtons played more free gigs than any other, but they were 'burned too often by these bloody revolutionaries. They've appeared at too many benefits that have been a wank in all senses.'[55] Yet it is Edgar who had to take the criticisms and is held to account for 'fuck-up revolutionary tossers . . . You've got to have an efficient business before you can fight the system,' said Jenner.[56] IT ignored his argument and instead shifted tack and asked why Blackhill would not book the Pink Fairies onto the same bill as the Broughtons? Jenner pushed back: 'I'll tell you why I didn't want the Fairies. The Pink Fairies make me sick. I think they are a very bad group. Musically they suck. I've heard the same thing said about Edgar, but Edgar is fucking Stravinsky compared with the Fairies.'[57] The issue continued unabated in the letter pages of IT: 'Watch out! Broughton is a fake . . . the Pink Fairies are a damn sight more RED than ED.'[58] Whatever their relative musical merits, neither the Edgar Broughton Band nor the Pink Fairies articulated a political position or agenda that was ever anything more than a vague solidarity with the Underground movement: 'out demons out' chanted the Broughtons; 'keep it together' cried the Fairies.

Ignoring generational conflict and Freak politics, a band from Shepherd's Bush, the Third World War, showed just how indirect the other two bands were in their communiqués. Terry

'Chopper Guitar' Stamp and bassist Jim Avery preached violence against the bosses and aligned themselves unequivocally with the factory floor. Our music, Avery told *The Guardian*'s Geoffrey Cannon, 'should be played over factory PAS' for 'men and women who are too accustomed to being ignored'.[59] To help his reader grasp where this unsigned group was coming from, Cannon linked them to Mick Farren's old band The Social Deviants and his idea that rock music must be a catalyst in forcing 'the social and political revolution he thinks is vital in Britain'.[60] But neither The Deviants, the Pink Fairies nor Hawkwind, he wrote, 'produce music as forceful and clear in this context as the music of the Third World War'.[61] Moreover, when compared to Stamp's band, Cannon considered the leading lights of the Underground, such as Procol Harum and Jethro Tull, to encourage no more than 'self-obsessed lethargy'.[62]

'More Working Class Heroes?' asked *Friends* magazine about Third World War. 'Well, no . . . These are not cosmetic furies at all. This is not the Great Underground revolution (let's drop acid in the water supply, chaps). This is a long way from Pepperland, and a long way from the Good Earth, and a long way from the West Coast. This is class resentment, class rage, class anguish . . .'[63] The band appeared at a time when the promise of the 1960s meritocracy, symbolized by the social climbing of East Ender Michael Caine, Twiggy and David Bailey, had turned sour. Out of that failure came 'The Third World War . . . a London group, virulent with London resentment . . . This is real England . . . an England which still smoulders with class-rage.'[64] What happens if you get successful and end up on *Top of the Pops*, won't you just be like all the other bands that have gone before? asked Haden-Guest, *Friends*' reporter. 'I don't think it will happen,' said Stamp.[65] It didn't. But that sort of success was never their ambition anyway; rather their intention had been to stir things up, to influence the next generation, to communicate with 'young musicians who haven't got anywhere, and who are not even musicians, and who are going to say "You are just saying what we want to say."'[66] Perhaps this was just a throwaway line, without foresight, but it was loudly echoed in the dialogue punk bands, such as The Clash, had with their fans.

Watching Third World War play at North London Polytechnic, Mick Farren held out the hope that they would become

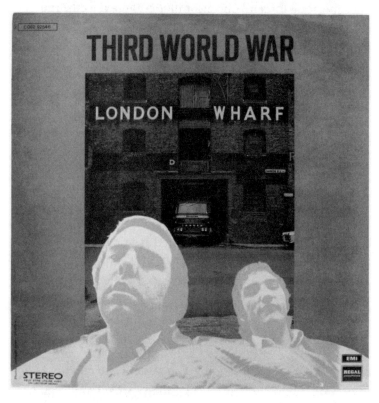

Class conflict with Third World War: French sleeve art for the debut album.

a force that will 'change the rock scene in a major way'. He thought they could be Britain's answer to the MC5: 'Not slim, camp, "Brother Wayne Kramer from Dee-troit City", but Terry Stamp (sniff) oo used to go up Tottenham Royal, like.' Along with the Pink Fairies and Hawkwind, he thought 'they could do a lot to move rock away from self-consciousness and artiness and bring it back to the street corner and parking lot.'[67] The following month Farren reviewed the band's debut album, which confirmed his impression of their live act as synonymous with being a British MC5. Hard-hitting lyrics in the mould of early Who, stomping minimal musical back-up in keeping with the Small Faces and The Creation and all done with the 'feel of 20th century English traditional left'. It was, he concluded, a fine album, which as 'crud rock' ranks with the MC5's *Back in the USA* and as 'fave rave crude rock', the lead track 'Ascension Day' being among the best street-fighting songs he has heard. All of which feeds into his predilection for early Pretty Things above Neil Young.[68]

The two Third World War albums, along with Terry Stamp's solo effort, *Fatsticks*, are crucial sonic documents of a moment in time; essential statements on a Britain divided along class lines. Stamp and Avery deliver vivid vignettes of life on the streets and in the pubs of West London, cranked out with all the drive and roar of a straight six-cylinder Jaguar with a hole in its muffler. While they give the bosses and the authorities no quarter, they are equally merciless in showing up self-pitying geezers – Shepherd's Bush cowboys – who spout prejudice and hate and amuse themselves with queer bashing, getting drunk, betting on the horses, spending their winnings on prostitutes and indulging in football violence before, inevitably, ending up in Wormwood Scrubs. Preaching violence is the debut album's rallying cry – one made on both sides of the line. The violence is done to us and by us, to self and to others; it's a truly scarifying vision. But in class struggle there is meaning and in their music there is an affirmation. The struggle takes place on the nation's stages, on 'Stardom Road', as much as on its shop floors, playing just a little bit of urban rock 'n' roll for those behind the wheel of a ten-ton Bedford, those listening to the canteen news, or for Commie sympathizers and agitators and, even, for the yobos, cosh boys, skinheads and bikers; Shepherd's Bush cowboys one and all. These are the raw recruits being called up to join the Hammersmith Guerrillas, who are just now waiting on the signal.

Further relief from the earnestness of CSNY and other denim-clad and bearded musos came in the early summer of 1971 with the release of Alice Cooper's *Love It to Death*. While the singer was doing promotion out of the Ladbrook Hotel in London, he was interviewed by Steve Mann for *Frendz*. Dismissing the Pink Fairies – the 'Toothless Fairies' he called them – Alice explained that 'England needs a jolt of energy – that's why Detroit Rock, Third Generation Rock is gonna do so well here.'[69] The Ann Arbor scene, he said, is 'a heavy revolutionary trip. Everybody wears black leather jackets and stomps around looking tough – kicking dogs.'[70]

Mann wrote that the music of Alice Cooper had been forged on 'a lifetime of American TV; *77 Sunset Strip*, *The Thin Man*, old Busby Berkeley extravaganzas, all mixed with the moon shots and the Vietnam war'.[71] With their second album of 1971, *Killer* (released in the UK in December), the band gained significant kudos with Britain's rock literati. Their Detroit bona fides (at least from the viewpoint of London), their delivery of straight-up 'hard dirty rock', augmented by theatrical props, chicken slaughter and gender dissembling in name, costume and make-up, made them an interesting proposition for those in the Underground press who were looking for a new sort of kick. *Frendz* reported, with enthusiasm, on each subsequent career move, making them cover stars in July 1972.

In January 1972, Mick Farren responded positively to the directness of Alice Cooper's high-energy rock 'n' roll, which at least, on his terms, appeared sincere, but their camp provocations suggested a countervailing insincerity and so he called them the 'supreme' example of 'pooff-rock'.[72] Offensive, then as now, and used without any modifying sense of self-awareness (if that were even possible), such homophobia diminishes Farren, as it does others in his peer group, who were equally prone to using spiteful language. In this aspect of the Underground outlaws' public life they are as one with the lumpen, witless Shepherd's Bush cowboys.

In an account of rock fashion and the politics of flash, published in April 1974, Nick Kent looked back over the past two years or so and, in his casual chauvinistic quips, revealed just how deep rooted homophobia was within the scene. Was it Rod Stewart or Marc Bolan, asked Kent, who introduced the satin jacket, that 'squalid, cheap piece of clothing' which contrasted so cheerily with the 'Denim Rules OK' style of Jerry Garcia or Rory Gallagher?[73] Musically distinct, Rod and Marc were nevertheless linked in their 'mod-turns-poove get ups'.[74] Having moved from skinheads to glam rockers, Slade made the 'garish' acceptable, indeed made it 'cool for working-class kids to flash up and not get called fags'.[75] As 1971 rolled into 1972, homophobic terms became a commonplace in rock literature.

'Pooff', 'poof', 'pouf' or 'poove' rock, however it was spelt, was a defining strand of third-generation rock 'n' roll, used both to dismiss and celebrate an active rejection of the badge of authenticity. But whatever it was, 'pooff rock' was not played by a 'people's band' and it was not the sound of revolution; at least not as that idea was defined by Farren. However many lines of continuity would be drawn back to Elvis, Little Richard and Mick Jagger, what was certain was that it represented something novel if not new.

In an interview with Nick Kent, Alice identified Jim Morrison as the first of the third-generation performers, and Kent added his favourites the Velvet Underground and The Stooges to the pantheon, both bands 'perhaps too wild to catch on'.[76] As if recalling the *Zigzag* interview with the Edgar Broughton Band, where their inquisitor showed an utter lack of interest in entertainment (or art for that matter), Kent thought that Lou Reed and Iggy Pop, recently relocated to London, alongside David Bowie and Marc Bolan, confirmed that the 'freaking faggots' had stepped out of the closet and left the Underground behind.[77] A new order was afoot and, even though its roots were in the Underground, it was not Farren who had the lead.

Marc Bolan turned the tables on the Underground's commitment to community, sincerity and authenticity – rock 'n' roll as politics, politics as rock 'n' roll – and embraced wholeheartedly the *art* of entertainment. Bolan would find his pop moment a fickle lover. However for two good years, he put the heat back into a romance grown as cold as a morning after. T. Rex brought to a dishevelled affair a frisson of exhilaration, a gasp of pleasure, and put sex back into the rock equation to make it dirty-sweet once more.

2

DIRTY–SWEET:
MARC BOLAN – POP STAR

Underground: The label given to the late Sixties 'hippie' movement, with its network of clubs, magazines, shops, etc. For a while, Marc was a hero of the Underground – especially when John Peel was pushing him hard in the days of Tyrannosaurus Rex. But as T. Rex became popular, the 'underground' turned sour – with such headlines in their press as BOLAN SELLS OUT'.

T. Rextra: Your Jackie A–Z of T. Rex (1972)

In his July 1972 'Letter from Britain' column for *Creem*, Simon Frith told his American readers he was having the most fun since the release of Creedence's *Green River* album. Even in the face of the Irish Troubles, unemployment and the 'endless hum of B-52s' he'd still been able to spend more time dancing than thinking, and that was down to the Stones' 'Tumbling Dice', Bowie's 'Starman', the Grin album, Mott the Hoople live and the buzz of things being stirred up by the 'inescapable' T. Rex.[1]

Even though he was too old to be part of their audience, Frith enjoyed the pop moment of T. Rextasy. 'Am I sexy?', shouted Marc to his fans, 'and I thought no', wrote Frith, 'and all around the yes was screamed back'.[2] At the gig, he watched a long-haired DJ who played 'Imagine' incessantly get heckled and ignored in equal measure by the audience. 'Who, on a Monday night in Bradford, wanted to imagine no possessions when they had come to see Marc Bolan in his silver-green sequined suit? The DJ stood for every progressive thing T. Rex had destroyed and the audience smashed him.'[3]

Much of the rest of Frith's column deals with the schism between the demand that rock mean something, to have something to say about the present situation, and the thrill of the pop moment and its potential to help its audience escape from the everyday. He didn't feel T. Rex spanned that divide, but Budgie, Edgar Broughton, David Bowie and Roxy Music might plug into the 'new surge of teenage energy' Bolan had generated, 'a rejection of the dead end of progressivism, a refuelling of fun'.[4] Over the rest of the year, and into the next, Frith would return to what would increasingly become the central issue in debates on third-generation rock, between sincerity, commitment and honesty on one side and dissembling, promiscuity and fraudulence on the other. Eventually, he would side with the pop faction.

The fact was, however, that Bolan, in the transition from Tyrannosaurus Rex to T. Rex, had already laid out how the line from the Underground – Middle Earth – to the High Street – BBC's *Top of the Pops* – was to be negotiated even if the final value of reaching that destination remained still to be weighed and costed. Budgie and Broughton missed all the signs T. Rex had set in place so others might follow, and did little more than carry on to the next gig. Bowie and Roxy showed they were not only able to track the trail left by Bolan, but they could also get ahead of him and lay out a convincing ambush. Before 1972 was done with they had taken his audience with them.

Responding in 1968 to the 'rhythmic vitality' of Tyrannosaurus Rex's first single, 'Debora', Nik Cohn reflected back over Bolan's career to date. He considered him to be a 'walking teenage history of the 1960s' – from Mark Feld, 'self-styled Supermod of Stamford Hill', to 'minor teen celebrity' who, by any standards, 'had style and he had cool'.[5] He changed his name and became a singer, had a few mis-cues and then with 'Hippy Gumbo' he made a 'good record'. It wasn't a hit, wrote Cohn, but it 'was imaginative just the same, quite advanced, and it had me hooked'.[6] A press release for the single reported that 'Marc Likes: £9,000 cars. Marc Dislikes: £8,000 cars. Taste in Music: Rock and roll and Chet Baker. "I've never heard Chet Baker, but he looks great. I have all his album covers," said Bolan.'[7] You can imagine Cohn having written that little spiel but, whoever the author, the lines were spoken like a true Mod.

Bolan then became a member of the angelic Pop art disrupters, John's Children. Cohn thought this new band 'hilarious and entirely impossible, and they cut some of the worst singles ever released' but they also 'fluked one true classic . . . "Desdemona". This was pure rock, way before any revival and it went like a bomb.'[8] And now, Bolan has 'turned into a full-time beautiful person', Cohn wrote, 'I saw him onstage a few weeks back and he came out in robes, sat crossed legged and generally came on like Stamford Hill's reply to the giggling guru. I hardly recognised him.'[9]

In October 1970, Bolan was yet again reinventing himself. Tyrannosaurus Rex had shortened their name to T. Rex and put out 'Ride a White Swan' on the recently established Fly label. The single outsold all their previously released records and rose as high as number two in the charts. Until this point the band had as good as stalled; the first album with the new sidekick, Mickey Finn, was a poor follow-up to the delirious *Unicorn*, with Steve Took's inventive percussive and vocal support sorely missed and barely compensated for by Bolan's return to electric guitar. But now, with renewed momentum gained from the 45, with a cover of Eddie Cochran's 'Summertime Blues' on its flip, Bolan was moving once more. In *Melody Maker*, Chris Welch noted the energy and new direction of travel in his review of the single: 'T. Rex cunningly recapture the drive and simplicity of late-fifties pop.'[10] Echoing the now common take on T. Rex as both looking back and going forward, *Cash Box* wrote of the follow-up 'Hot Love' that it came over as an 'advanced early-rock variant'.[11] T. Rex: progressive primitives. With one-two knockout hits under his belt, Bolan became a star for a generation for whom Beatlemania was but a rumour.

Released a week before Christmas, the new album, *T. Rex*, confirmed the pull of the past on Bolan's music – 'it's basically simple energy-packed rock,' wrote *Melody Maker*'s Roy Hollingworth.[12] In its review, *Record Mirror* noted that the 'acoustic, gentle approach has given way to a harsher, electric based music, and the influence of early rock and roll and r 'n' b is very much to the fore'.[13] If Bolan's approach was shifting, so too was his position within the rock echelon. In its Christmas 1970 edition, NME led with a Nick Logan interview that was something of an end-of-the-year, state-of-the-union, address. The headline was 'T. Rex – Last of the Great Underground Groups', which was propped up with 'We've broken the monopoly ... the revolution is over says MARC BOLAN.' From subterranean depths, T. Rex had risen into the pop mainstream.

Bolan's material situation, however, had not changed much. Logan reported that when he first met the singer, Bolan was living in a cramped Notting Hill bedsit. He had moved only once since then, to the no-more-luxurious two-bedroom pad a floor below that apartment. He was now on the point of moving to slightly larger accommodation in Little Venice but, until that happened, 'our Top Ten Star' was sitting in the half-light waiting for his wife, June, to come home with some candles. They had forgotten to pay their electricity bill.[14] Bolan had bought a new stereo system, even if he couldn't play it that evening, and the band had acquired a bass player, Steve Currie. His audience had changed too; they were now 'a lot younger', he said. 'They come along with the kind of excitement that in the past has been associated with Zeppelin.'[15] The kids' exhilaration is 'like the old rock days' with 'people rushing the stage'.[16] Bolan called his new sound 'cosmic rock'.

He had joined the Underground, he said, 'to get away from the pop syndrome and, for me the Underground at the beginning meant similar-minded people with similar thoughts'.[17] Now that movement had borne fruit, he said, with hit records not only for T. Rex but for Family and Fairport Convention. T. Rex were now pop, but that did not mean, he suggested, that they had left the Underground behind; rather he had pulled it along with him. The Underground scene had grown, he said, and was 'now purely teenage music. It is youth music.'[18] Logan pushed Bolan a little harder and asked if it would 'be true to say that as [the scene] has become more a majority than a minority interest, musical standards have become lower and the initial ideals have become blurred?'[19] Put another way, he was asking Bolan whether working in the commercial pop arena constituted a corruption of the ideal of being a 'people's band', with inclusivity being replaced by exclusivity? It was *the* question that Mick Farren never tired of asking.

In turn, Bolan argued there was nothing to worry about. He had improved as a musician and, hubristically but characteristically, suggested that the ideal was safe with T. Rex because they were the embodiment of the Underground. His success meant that the struggle was now at an end. The music industry's 'monopoly is broken', Bolan said; 'there is total confusion. In that respect the revolution is already over.'[20] Nevertheless, he warned, with change there had come corrupt managers who were out to fleece gullible audiences willing 'to accept a group called, let's say, Ramases Bullet'.[21] But, he thought, you can still tell the difference between those groups who masquerade as progressive and those who genuinely are. He allowed for some uncertainty or ambivalence, so that a group like Black Sabbath would qualify as a genuine part of the scene, because their 'stompy feet music' was a gas, even though they weren't to his mind original. They nevertheless fit the bill, Bolan said, plus 'they've got a guitar star and crosses round their necks, and let's hope Jesus looks after them.'[22]

If a group was not true to the ideal, which Logan summarized as honesty and integrity, Bolan said they would be found out, whether or not they had Christ on their side. The minute their bubble burst, said Bolan, they'd end up as dustmen (such employment suggestive, for him, of utter failure). For himself, he said he was neither part of Tin Pan Alley nor was anyone he respected. He worked outside of that kind of commercial control and, like Lennon and Townshend, he had now achieved a kind of autonomy. Summing up the 'change from freak to funster', Bolan told Keith Altham 'I don't think we will lose any of the students because of the newer younger audience that Mickey Finn and I have got. I can't believe that our audience have that kind of intolerance but if they resent youth then fuck 'em.'[23]

Looking back from the middle of Bolanmania, in 1972, founding member Steve Took described the original Tyrannosaurus Rex as a 'very violent pop thing', a description clearly at odds with the perception of the duo as gentle otherworldly hippies, but in keeping with the idea of the band as intensely oppositional to the mainstream.[24] Bolan had changed and had lost that edge of dissent. The proof, Took said, was found in who came to his shows: 'let's face it his audience aren't hippies now anyway. I tried to score [at a T. Rex gig in Boston, Lincolnshire] and couldn't.'[25] To make his point, when rock critic James Johnson asked Took what his music was now about, he said, in contrast to Bolan and, as if prompted by his mate Mick Farren, that the subject was 'Sex, drugs and violence . . . Things that people get into around this part of the world, things that happen to kids on the street.'[26] Took and Bolan were moving in opposite directions. The percussionist's presence at the Boston gig had been noticed by a *Melody Maker* reporter, but for T. Rex fans he passed by unacknowledged. For the day's Bolan fan, Took was anonymous. The history, for it was now that, and the ideals of the Underground were unknown to them: 'He was walking around, not speaking much. Nobody recognised him.'[27]

Took had travelled to the gig as part of an entourage of representatives of the Underground press. The concert was being filmed for television, for which it had been organized. Took and his accomplices had arrived with the idea of creating a situation of sorts, causing trouble for Bolan. He had attempted to join the band on stage, but failed.[28] If a symbol was needed of the Underground's irrelevance in the face of the pop juggernaut T. Rex were riding, then Took's botched prank was it. Fact was, Took himself was the joke, the target of ridicule. In *Frendz*, beneath a photograph of Took, strumming an acoustic guitar on stage at Kensington Town Hall, was the catch-line, 'Ladbroke Grove's answer to James Taylor', who may have 'given up acid, mandies, speed and other noxious chemicals, but he's still falling over a lot'.[29]

The accusations of having 'sold out' followed Bolan throughout 1971. On the front page of *Melody Maker* in March, the 'original British underground hero' hit back at his detractors. They accused Dylan of doing the same, he said, and the move from acoustic to electric music hadn't done Bob any harm. Critics shouldn't then deny him and other groups the 'right to grow naturally', to change, Bolan appealed.[30] That argument presumed a creative equivalence between Bolan and Dylan, which only Bolan it seemed recognized. But with 'Ride a White Swan' still selling, and 'Hot Love' having already sold 40,000 in the first week of its release, what did it matter if only a few saw much similarity between the two. T. Rex's first American tour beckoned; talking about the trip, Bolan said, 'Over there people look upon us as an avant-garde English pop group. So far the vibes have been very intellectual so they are going to be very surprised.'[31]

The debate around pop and rock, the cerebral and the visceral, commerce and art, authenticity and artifice, honesty and fabrication, which revolved around T. Rex, refused to let up and became a major trope of the letters pages in NME and *Melody Maker* well into 1972. Susan Male's letter is a fair example of the arguments:

> What a load of rubbish Simon Belsher wrote to Mailbag. I am an ardent T. Rex fan but I also have most of the early Tyrannosaurus Rex albums. Do you really believe that Bolan will ever go back to playing a 'One Inch Rock' or 'Debora', whatever people say. What's the matter, why does everyone begrudge Marc the success he has had? Do you not agree that there are more people who like his music now than before? Stop being so selfish, let younger people enjoy his music. You did, a few years ago.[32]

In explaining the present, Bolan would often look past his time with Tyrannosaurus Rex and establish his true rocker's credentials by referring to the period he spent with John's Children: 'I used to have a silver whip at the time. I'd chain up whole banks of amplifiers and drag them across the stage and whip the guitar.' Bolan told NME's Tony Norman, 'I couldn't play but I used that whip really well.'[33] 'That happened', wrote Norman, 'before the Tyrannosaurus Rex folksy days. When Bolan went back to rock they'd said he'd sold out.'[34] But the debate was not about whether Bolan could rock, or even had the right credentials to roll; it was about his audience. The shift was from college-age boys, such as MM's correspondent Simon Belsher, stout defender of Tyrannosaurus Rex, to schoolgirls such as Susan Male, his respondent, who were admirers of T. Rex. The gender and age lines had been drawn. The Beatles had appealed across the divide, Marc Bolan not so much.

Zigzag, a journal that more or less defined the authentic in rock culture in the early 1970s, published its second interview with Bolan in the early summer of 1971. Editor Pete Frame had decided to catch up with the man after reading just one too many 'sell out' letters in the music rags and after having heard a 'plasticised version' of T. Rex's 'Hot Love' piped into an Oxford Street restaurant. *Zigzag*'s readers remained loyal to T. Rex, he wrote, despite the band's success. 'I see no reason why the freaks should not be represented in the charts,' said Bolan, 'but what bugs me is when they turn around and resent you for it.' Now living in Little Venice, Bolan was listening on his headphones to 1956-era Elvis when Frame arrived.

The interview began with how the star had dealt with all the criticism that had been levelled against him, and again Bolan turned to Dylan as his role model to explain his change in direction, although it was also justified in terms of his own self-perception: 'Two years ago I was very much into being a poet and I'm not anymore because I *am* a poet . . . I don't think about it . . . I've now become Marc Bolan, in fact, which I never was before.'[35] The act of becoming a star was confirmation of his artistry. 'Marc Bolan' had been a fantasy of stardom and that fantasy was now the reality. That was the shift he had to navigate. What then had changed? Everything and nothing. Yesterday the hippies were his audience, today little girls ask him for autographs, but he is still accessible, the heads can still converse with him, he said – 'forget all the "superstar" bit. Anyone can talk to me . . . I'll listen.'[36]

He was now that complete contradiction: approachable and aloof, knowable and unknown – an ordinary man and a cosmic being.

Melody Maker published a special edition dedicated to T. Rex early in 1972. It was among the first of the many one-shot magazine titles that exploited his fan base; although this example was perversely high-end, with the three contributors – Chris Welch, Michael Watts and Roy Hollingworth – honing, rather than abandoning, their critical faculties. Always the paper's most convivial reporter, Welch wrote about his friendship with Bolan and the fortunes of the star's career to date. With *Electric Warrior* Bolan had reached something of an apex, 'the best that Marc had recorded' and it, and the 'succession of chart number ones', had a 'happy and zestful content that no way denied the early ideals of that Tyrannosaurus Rex of long ago'.[37] Watts, who was one of the paper's most exacting, analytical and stimulating critics, ignored the Underground years and focused on the moment, T. Rextasy. He argued that Bolan's female fans 'feel an acute sense of identification' with him; they can relate to him. But unlike earlier pop superstars he doesn't project sex but romance:

> For how can one take seriously the idea of sex trips in association with a young man who's 24 but looks more like 16, stands little more than five feet tall, and wears spangles round his eyes, like a young chick making-up for her first big dance? . . . Sex is there, but it's sex courtesy of the Magic Prince. She'll wake in the morning to a kiss from Marc.[38]

The Bolan fan is fourteen years old, she is not 24 with her Beatles and Stones albums. T. Rex put an emphasis on singles and played a 'gutty simple music that strips away all the gloss and self-consciousness that has accrued around rock music in the past five years'.[39] Bolan was taking pop back to the beginning. Almost but not quite back to the music's rockin' roots, thought Watts, because T. Rex are not revivalists they are third-generation rockers, 'who have retained the idea of using post-Cream riffs, as in "Jeepster" in particular'.[40] Furthermore, Bolan's lyrics, with titles that 'reek of a passion for Americana' are all post-John 'I Am the Walrus' Lennon. Bolan's achievement, Watts wrote, is that he has reaffirmed that 'rock operates best when it is in close proximity with an audience ... He's only 24, remember. John Lennon's 31. That mean anything to you?'[41]

In February 1972, Logan tried to grasp what was happening in his 'analysis' of the T. Rex, Slade and Faces 'miniphenomenon'.[42] The scenario: a three-year waiting period after The Beatles' break-up, a time of rock limbo, one the Underground had occupied but a time now seemingly forgotten, or just despised by the demographic the three bands tapped into, and who were definitely not being catered 'for by the excesses of the 20-minute album trackers or, more simply', they had 'been at school up to now':

> In the latter cases these are the kids getting their first influential (in the sense of having the bread to influence trends) taste of rock music: the young brothers and sisters of the Stones, Dylan and even Zeppelin fans: the kids who haven't been programmed and conditioned by the 'accepted' norms of snob rock behaviour ...

who want to do what their elders did when they first turned on to rock and roll.

They want to feel the emotion and the sheer gut and crotch power of rock at least on par with, if not ahead of, the cerebral qualities that have been pushed down the throats of the older generation.

They want, as Marc Bolan puts it, to boogie.[43]

These kids, said Slade's Noddy Holder, want to 'rave from the start', just as others had done before with the Stones and The Who.[44] The teenage fan, fourteen to eighteen years old, occupied the middle ground, Logan wrote, between 'straight pop' and 'progressive factions'. Foreshadowing Bowie's 'All the Young Dudes', Jonathan King said about the conundrum of third-generation rock, 'I don't see "Johnny Reggae" or the Weathermen as the answer,' alluding to his own pop creations, but, he thought, maybe 'T. Rex and Slade are'.[45]

And the kids were born to boogie. On 18 March 1972 Bolan consolidated his pre-eminence in the pop sphere with two shows at Wembley. The NME put images of the concert on its front page and called it 'Bolan's Triumph', an 'incredible concert that changed the face of British rock . . . Bolan's time had come.'[46] Across the centre pages of Tony Tyler's report ran the headline 'Twenty Thousand Screamers and the Day That Pop Came Back'.[47] It was as if Nik Cohn's character Johnny Angelo had been made flesh. Here was pop as an extreme – noise, noise, noise – a spectacle of flash and glamour, magnificent splendour, and an audience enraptured by it all. Once more, there was a star worthy of idolatry who was mesmeric and not a little bit messianic: 'The Prophet of the New Age appears onstage with a built in swagger that sends them potty.'[48] Confirmation of his stardom, if needed, is that Bolan, like one of his fans, wears a T-shirt with his own face printed on it. And, as if to finally confirm that the break with the Underground was now absolute, IT showed its disdain for T. Rextasy when they used a full-colour image of Bolan on stage at Wembley on the front of the May/June 1972 issue. It ran with the head-line, 'Bolan: Who Needs Him?', and advertised its contents as 'Positively Jive Ass Teen Special', but inside there was not a picture or mention of the man and his fans, just the aura of IT's antipathy to all he had come to represent.

In April 1972 Nick Logan was once again interviewing Bolan for the NME. The talk was about doing business – 'turn-ing the glory into hard cash' with Bolan's custom EMI label, T. Rex Wax Co. and merchandising – while Bolan fought off lawsuits, and tried to cope without a manager.[49] He said he was not getting any cut of the sales from T-shirts, posters and what-ever else they put his name and face on. He told Keith Altham, 'All the lunacy and merchandising things going on around me are seldom anything to do with me. I mean, Bolan pillows! Please, people, it's nothing to do with me.'[50]

He'd just lost his seventh manager, Tony Seconda, who George Melly had described as a 'hustling motor mechanic of pop' whose only talent was 'an instinct for style'.[51] For now, Bolan was being helped and abetted by his publicist BP Fallon and Seconda's ex-wife Chelita. Tony's role, said Bolan, had been to establish the band in the States. Now that was done they could both move on. T. Rex were in fact far from being successful in America, but if Bolan said it was so then who, at this point, would challenge him? In the week following the second part of the interview, the NME ran a shorter report from their American correspondent, Ritchie Yorke. He had spoken with Bolan at the end of February after T. Rex's Carnegie Hall show. With the generally positive response to the gig and last year's hit 'Bang a Gong (Get It On)' behind him, Bolan exuded

Bolan: 'I mean, Bolan pillows! Please, people, it's nothing to do with me.'

confidence over being able to replicate his British and European success stateside. His conviction was misplaced.[52]

On the back of the autumn 1971 and early 1972 Atlantic crossings, a new tour of the States had been arranged for the late summer. That effort, plus the release later in the year of Ringo Starr's film of T. Rex at Wembley, *Born to Boogie*, intercut with scenes of tomfoolery, was expected to help consolidate and develop the band's standing in the USA. In June, Logan travelled with Bolan's entourage to witness a Manchester gig, where crowd hysteria was still growing and Bolan worried whether touring would become unmanageable, his audience no longer containable. The follow-up to *Electric Warrior*, *The Slider*, was released at the end of July. His record sales over the last twelve months were said to have reached 16 million.[53] But it was not all good news.

Writing from New York, Roy Hollingworth summed up Bolan's American predicament, which was not as the star believed. Bolan was looked on as a 'figment of the English imagination. He doesn't really exist, does he?'[54] And if he did exist then his audience must be the same as David Cassidy's because he has nothing to do with the older rock scene – 'so say the Americans':

> To put it simply, Bolan does not have an audience over here. The heavy freaks think he's teenybop, and the teenybops think he's heavy, and unlike England, there is no audience that exists between those two categories ... So here we have this rock 'n' roll star being forced to shine in daylight.[55]

A year later, Richard Cromelin reviewed a Santa Monica gig and essentially echoed Hollingworth on why T. Rex had failed to make it in the States: 'If you're going to be a star, you'd best be able to satisfy the fantasies you engender or else tone down the hype so that the expectations don't outdistance the reality of the person on the stage.'[56] *Creem* made a lacklustre attempt to echo the UK letters pages, but the arguments for and against Bolan didn't resonate in their mail section for more than an issue or two: T. Rex simply had no meaningful traction stateside, with either critics or audiences.[57]

From the American critical reaction to T. Rex it is clear that Bolan misjudged his audience, giving them very much the same show as he played before his British fans. Instead of coming on hard, fast and flash like a 1966 Who onslaught, he dragged out the length of the hit singles. It was as if he thought he should play it like Cream or Led Zeppelin, overdosing on the guitar pyrotechnics and then diluting whatever energy he had produced by sitting down cross-legged as if he were still treading the boards with Steve Took in Tyrannosaurus Rex. Cromelin wrote:

> Marc and his band do manage to build an intensity during some of his long, boring guitar solos, but then – snap! – the song ends, they dawdle and tune and wait for the energy to fade away before starting the next one. Pacing is an elementary requirement of a good rock 'n' roll show, but T. Rex indicate no consciousness of its necessity or existence. On stage his movements are repetitive, empty and forced. He's trying too hard and the result is a total lack of spontaneity. He deflates the illusion instead of giving it additional substance.[58]

When the band returned to Santa Monica the following August, writing for the *Los Angeles Times*, Robert Hilburn reiterated Cromelin's critique and added that, as for Bolan himself, 'he seemed little more than a computerised kewpie doll.'[59] The ultimate put-down of Bolan's American efforts was provided by the British monthly *Beat Instrumental* under the headline 'Why Has Bolan Flopped in the States?':

> On T. Rex's third tour, [he] played abominable guitar . . . Every solo was sheer noisy garbage; even the feedback was limp, and every song sounded exactly alike, not that he played that many of them – each song lasted a good ten minutes, dragged out so that the last inch of subtlety was blown up like a cancer growth on a full-sized screen . . . T. Rex are through in America, all washed up both artistically and commercially.[60]

Even if he was lost in the light in New York and unable to meet the fantasies of LA's demi-monde, in the UK, with a hit sequence that had begun with 'Ride a White Swan' followed by three chart-topping singles and another two that just missed the number one slot, the future could still be construed to be in Bolan's favour. The truth, however, was that he was no longer running ahead of the pack. The marketing push behind his old pal David Bowie, which had been going full tilt since January, was now paying off, with the release in the first week of June of *Ziggy Stardust*. A paired image of Bolan and Bowie in the NME highlighted the former's sellout concerts and the latter's forthcoming tour dates and suggested equal billing beneath the headline 'Glam Rock: It's Glam and Stardust Time This

Week for Boppers and Campers Everywhere with Bolan's T. REX and the Luvverly DAVID BOWIE on the Road.'[61] From here on into the best part of 1973, the two would be considered competitors, every move they made compared and evaluated overtly or tacitly against one another.[62]

Since his first chart success, the NME, especially when aided and abetted by Nick Logan, had been a staunch supporter of T. Rextasy but when ex-*Oz* writer, Charles Shaar Murray, became part of the editorial team at the end of July that cosy relationship changed. Murray was firmly in Bowie's camp. Hints of a shift were already in place, however. Roy Carr was looking for the next superstar after Elvis, Dylan, Hendrix and Jagger:

> the likes of Bolan may well be causing scenes of hysteria, but again, I feel that Bolan is much too likable. Nobody fears him, his music is inoffensive, he's acceptable to both kids and parents alike. It's as if someone has stuck the Good Housekeeping Seal of Approval under one of his facial tinsel stars. Most young girls would rather throw Teddy-Bears than their knickers at Boley.[63]

Bowie, Beefheart and Zappa are mentioned as contenders (the last two a puzzling choice by any reckoning); all had talent, wrote Carr, but are not 'image-makers or revolutionaries of longevity'.[64] Alice Cooper had made the 'bravest attempt so far', but Carr thought his 'undetermined sexuality' confused people:

> Rock music and soul music have always come from well below the belt, and when practised by the definitive

masters, the music hungry, raw, violent, primitive, and, most important of all, sensual. It drives young girls into fits of uncontrollable hysteria and gives young men arrogance and confidence. The male should be able to identify with that personality that makes the female of the species succumb. For example: Presley was a smouldering stud, Cochran a smart kid, Vincent a pool-room punk, Jagger a threat, Hendrix an animal.

And Little Richard? Carr had been far too reductive in the depiction of his rock 'n' roll heroes, missing or ignoring the way they all transgressed sexual and gender norms, and none more so than Elvis, who had posed as comfortably with a teddy bear or a motorbike and looked just as cute and as camp with either prop as Bolan or Bowie might. While the two latest pop stars lacked the threat of the pool-room hoodlum that Carr revered, Bowie, at least, was working out how he could foster that appeal by association. His answer was his soon to be revealed alliances with Iggy Pop and Lou Reed: a gutter aristocrat and a hoodlum poet, each of whom purveyed an aura of dark menace.

If Carr found Bolan to be just too damn nice to be a star of choice, then Charles Shaar Murray found him to be wholly lacking in artistic merit. In July he wrote a comparative review of *The Slider* and Rod Stewart's *Never a Dull Moment*. Remarkably, for the NME, his piece spilled across two pages rather than the more usual two- or three-column inches. Murray wanted to know 'what kind of music was attracting teenagers' and 'escaping out from under the personality posters, one-shot cheapo magazines and in-depth analyses'.[65] Bolan, Stewart and

Bowie, wrote Murray, were the 'most charismatic figures in British rock'. Stewart, he thought, had produced yet another triumph. Where the Faces albums were raucous but derivative, Rod's solo work was diverse and sensitive. On the other hand, T. Rex's music had become crudely simplistic, endlessly repetitious and was now 'dangerously close to a total artistic collapse'.[66]

Whatever the qualities of Bolan's music, Murray was clearly overstating the case against. His was not a weighed and considered critical response but an act of provocation geared to ensure a reaction from the paper's readers, which he got. The anti-Bolan stance would mark his arrival as the paper's enfant terrible. He accused Bolan of repeating not only himself but others' ideas, such as the poaching of Jimmy McCracklin's 'The Walk' as 'Beltane Walk' on the *T. Rex* album. That had been achieved with wit, thought Murray. On *The Slider*, where 'The Walk' had been appropriated for the introduction to 'Rock On', it was now done without any of the teenage charm Bolan had previously mustered. And 'Baby Strange', he argued, is nothing but a dead ringer for 'Jeepster'. Without humour and originality, *The Slider* was lumbered with pedestrian string arrangements, he wrote, which smother Mark Volman and Howard Kaylan's 'I was a teenage werewolf' vocal backups, and Mickey Finn's percussion had been left to run rampant. Murray concluded:

It has been an achievement to borrow musically from as many sources as he has and still come up with something instantly recognisable, but now he's just ripping off his own clichés. His music is chasing itself in circles and obsessively eating its own tail.[67]

The week after Murray's review a third of NME's letter page was taken up with irate acolytes responding to the 'reptilian' critic.[68] It now became a war of attrition, with neither side ceding ground.

The kick in the teeth for Bolan was not just the bad notices but the fact that in the same issue NME gave Bowie's July Dorchester Hotel press conference wide coverage. The report ran across two weeks and three pages. Murray was their correspondent. The combination of the poor review and Murray's attentive and deferential interview with Bowie was suggestive of the moment where the spotlight shifted and Bowie took centre stage while Bolan began his fade into the shadows. During the interview Murray made two passing references to Bolan, one of which was about Bowie's imitation of the man's warble on 'Black Country Rock'. 'I Bolanized it,' said Bowie.[69] Two weeks later, when Mott the Hoople's 'All the Young Dudes' was released, Bowie had gone from parody to homage as he asked: who needed all that revolutionary stuff when the kids had T. Rex?

What Bowie did, and Bolan had failed at, was flatter his interviewer. Bowie charmed Murray by playing to his prejudices and vanity. The interview is presented as a dialogue, with the pose on Bowie's part being that he and the journalist are equals, or at least confidants. In interviews with Bolan, the T. Rex man rarely acknowledged the other, speaking only of himself, which left him open to accusations of narcissism and an ego run riot. At least initially, Bolan's outspokenness was a boon for the music press's editors. Danny Holloway's interview with him in the NME, which ran across three weeks in February 1972, was captioned with hyperbolic subheadings: 'Hendrix said I'd be big but I don't give a **** so long as I can boogie'; 'I was a superior kind of being'; 'When Clapton played bum notes'; 'Lennon copied me'; and 'I'm as good as Townshend. He knows it.'[70] As it read, this haughtiness all but demanded a takedown. His publicist, BP Fallon, admitted as much when he wrote a letter to NME complaining about the way the quotes had been taken out of context and how they reeked of 'nasty sensationalism'.[71] Beneath Fallon's letter, incensed fans of Townshend hit back: 'Who the hell does Bolan think he is . . .'[72] The British music press, especially the NME, were becoming past masters at creating controversy as a means to produce drama and interest (sales).

A little more than a year later, Murray put together an overview of Bolan's career to date; it read like the star's obituary. Skipping over Bolan's first solo recordings and his time with John's Children, Murray weighs up the Tyrannosaurus Rex catalogue. Initially, the band had 'enormous charm and considerable authenticity . . . What post-acid teenage mystic could resist them? I was one of the 750 people who bought "Debora" the first day it came out.'[73] But the appeal of their recordings was limited both in terms of instrumentation and songwriting. With their third album, the use of studio technology and a more varied delivery opened things up and, Murray thought, it was 'probably the finest that Bolan ever recorded. It remains one of my all-time thirty favourite albums to this day.'[74] Having ensured the reader understood that he was writing as a fan, or at least as a critical friend, Murray then began to take Bolan apart. With the fifth album, and the shortening of their name, Bolan's new electric direction was signposted by toting a Les Paul guitar and 'looking pretty in white make-up' on the cover.[75] The songs, wrote Murray, were now closer to rock than ever before and were a 'pleasant dessert after a brain-bruising session with the Floyd or Led Zeppelin'.[76]

'Ride a White Swan' was a 'pleasure to hear' and you could sing along with it too, he wrote; Bolan's cult followers were thrilled he had 'showed the world what he could do'.[77] Then, with the band's addition of bass and drums, 'Hot Love' ensured that their 'celebration was unabated'.[78] 'Get It On' kept things lively with its sly quoting of Chuck Berry. But then the 'first hints of doubt oozed into some of our minds when *Electric Warrior* fell into our hands'.[79] From here on in, Murray shifted from a pointed but gentle criticism to a patronizing lambast delivered from on high. In interviews, Bolan had 'become unbelievably arrogant' and the title and packaging 'caused considerable misgivings'.[80] The star's pouting and posture was too much, 'affectionate parody' had now degenerated into 'shabby trickery', and 'sensitivity' was replaced with 'clumsy overkill'.[81] And images of Marc were everywhere while he 'shoplifted' riffs and sang 'complacently impenetrable' lyrics.[82] *The Slider* and *Tanx* continued the plunge in quality (and interest) for Murray. His critical position on Bolan may have been an extreme, with the focus on image, but it was not uncommon.

Murray, however, had been as guilty as Bolan of repetition, reduction and of rewriting history. Just before his tenure at the NME he had written a nine-page magazine article on T. Rex. The forum was *Cream*, a monthly journal that ran between spring 1971 and autumn 1973. Its intended readers were A-Level students and undergraduates. Charles Shaar Murray fitted right in. The piece is built around his attendance at one of the Wembley shows where, surrounded by teenage girls, he described his situation as being akin to a 'sixth former sitting

at the second-year dinner table'.[83] Much less focused on (West
Coast) American rock acts than *Zigzag*, *Cream* mostly concerned
itself with the contemporary British scene (and with writers of
the calibre of Charlie Gillett, Bill Millar and Tony Russell it also
offered a lively historical perspective).

Unlike his later articles on Bolan for the NME, Murray
professed no particular knowledge, nor much interest in the
recorded works of Tyrannosaurus Rex; he didn't claim here
to have been among the 750 who bought 'Debora' on its day
of release, and *Unicorn* was not among his thirty all-time favourites; he had instead, he wrote, acquired the band's back
catalogue specifically for the purposes of putting the essay
together. Murray was not writing as a one-time fan trying to
figure out where, along the way, his hero had got lost, but as a
critic positioning himself above the fray to better see and comment on the phenomenon that was T. Rextasy. What was being
played out through Bolanmania, Murray thought, was the latest
turn in the cycle of pop. Once albums had been a reaction to
the formulaic restrictions of singles, he explained; now a surfeit
of 'tedious long-players' had caused a counter-reaction that was
being led by T. Rex: 'the best singles band we've got'. But just
because the cycle is in rotation does not mean that this particular
moment is the same or even an equal to previous turns:

On *Top of the Pops* or Radio One or my local pub
jukebox, T. Rex's records shine out like diamonds in the
mud. But in the more competitive environment of an
evening at home playing records, they suffer by comparison with the Who or the Dead, or the Stones or
the Byrds, or Steeleye Span, or whoever your own best

friends may be. But it's good bopping music, and there'll never be too much of that.[84]

In the context in which his essay was published, the comparison between T. Rex and The Who and the Dead is reasonable, but the ground on which Murray's argument is built is inherently uneven and Bolan's efforts will always rate less favourably than those who have already earned a place in the rock canon. Murray may have turned a deaf ear to the codes tapped out by 'Telegram Sam', and worked hard to curry favour with the progressive rock faction, but others, Bowie among them, sided with the teenage girls, or at least made it a point not to patronize and dismiss their pleasures.[85]

After Iggy Pop had attended one of T. Rex's Wembley gigs he told *Melody Maker*'s Michael Watts that he thought Bolan was 'kinda chipmunky', but some of his compatriots, the New York Dolls among them, did not see him as a competitor but as a model to be emulated.[86] They did not care about the loss of sensitivity or sincerity in the shift from Tyrannosaurus Rex to T. Rex or the overblown imagery; what they cared about was the music's impact on an audience who had a predilection to dance rather than to get lost in a progressive haze of introspection parlayed by Gnidrolog, Murray's favourites. In Manhattan, when the Dolls were trying out a new number, and it wasn't working, their default was to draw inspiration from T. Rex: 'So that's what we did' with 'Looking for a Kiss', wrote guitarist Sylvain Sylvain, 'and not only did it sound fantastic, that became the blueprint for a lot of our early songs. We T. Rexed the shit out of *everything*.'[87]

Citing Dylan, Hendrix, Lennon and Townshend as his equals was an act of hubris on Bolan's part that left him open

to rebuke and ridicule. But Hendrix was dead, Lennon and
Townshend no longer boogied, Dylan never did (though Bolan
thought he had), and none of them had much appeal to fourteen-
year-olds. Critics took an age to wake up to this fact. Nick Kent
had been gesturing towards this in most of his pieces written
since the summer of 1972, but it was not until a year later that
he pulled his thoughts together and penned 'Too Pooped to
Pop, Too Old to Rock', which finally took the age gap between
the stars of the 1960s and 1970s teenagers as a given and an
insurmountable divide. Once more, Nik Cohn's pronouncement
that the Stones would be better off dead before they reached
the age of thirty was trundled out.[88] For the kids, what did that
matter? They didn't even know who Jagger was and wouldn't
have cared anyway; they had T. Rex. For young journalists
such as Kent and Murray, both 21 in 1972, trashing Bolan for
his pretensions, while suggesting they had kept any vaulted airs
in check by championing Iggy Pop and David Bowie as
alternatives, worked for them as they sought to establish their
critical credentials. Both had figured out that to make your
mark you had to be passionately against something, and that
something in 1972 was T. Rex.[89]

Writing in the 22 January 1972 edition of *Melody Maker*,
with Bowie on the cover for the first time, Michael Watts not
only covered the yet-to-be star's coming out as 'rock's swishiest
outrage' but reported on T. Rex's first UK gig (the one attended
by Took) since the end of their last tour back in November. The
Starlight Rooms was an unseated hall with a capacity of 2,000,
but had managed to cram in around 6,000 kids. Some 50 per
cent of the bill's attraction was 'Bolan posturing glamorously
and teasing the front row of the audience'.[90] The other half

is the music, wrote Watts, which represented a return to rock and roll roots, 'to singles music, pithy, danceable and catchy, to where rock and roll is at, in fact'.[91] To another reporter, Bolan said, 'you need singles for flash and the albums for substance.'[92]

'The feel of the fifties is very important,' Bolan told NME's Danny Holloway, '[it is] where my head is at. Rick Nelson and Eddie Cochran ... I saw my place as writing things like "Quarter to Three" or "Runaround Sue", but with better words.'[93] On 'Ride a White Swan', he said, he 'was consciously trying to play like James Burton. And "Get It On" is very much "Little Queenie".'[94] The changing of the words made the tune once again contemporary; he was doing, in effect, he argued, the same as Dylan had done with 'Subterranean Homesick Blues', which is really 'Too Much Monkey Business' with new words. 'It was the words that made it for me. You could boogie about to it.'[95] Bolan told Nick Logan that 'Metal Guru' was like a 'Sun oldie, a nice groove track vaguely Spectorish with 12 acoustic guitars', and for the B-side, 'Lady', he'd taken the intro, he said, from The Beatles' 'Eight-Days a Week'.[96]

With *Melody Maker*'s Roy Hollingworth, Bolan had discussed the power of Howlin' Wolf – name-checked on the fadeout of 'Telegram Sam'– and the inspiration he had gained from him over the work of more contemporary artists, 'because I know if somebody was doing the Howling Wolf thing now they would be absolutely massive. I'm sure of that.'[97] This was less an act of prophecy and more a veiled reference to the fact he'd just filched, wholesale, the riff from the Wolf's 'You'll Be Mine' for 'Jeepster'. Bolan was like a kid who had plagiarized his homework, got away with it, and then smugly demanded recognition from his teacher for his clever ruse.

Elvis and his disciples: U.S. promotional poster for *Rock Dreams*.

A Clockwork Orange: in the Chelsea Drugstore.

The flipsides of the teenage
dream, as represented by
Fumble and Silverhead.

Mick Farren's 'Bedsitter Loving', *Club International* (July 1975).

WHATEVER HAPPENED TO THE UNDERGROUND PRESS?
Number 465 September 28 1973

The face of the Underground: Mick Farren, cover star of the *Daily Telegraph Magazine* (September 1973).

Opposite: Authenticity, insincerity and aggro pop: Ellis, The Sweet and The Jook.

The Real Marc Bolan: a *Record Mirror* special (1972).

Cosmic Jive: a Bolan fan at T. Rex's Wembley show.
Born to Boogie (Ringo Starr, 1972).

David Parkinson's photographic spread for
Men Only's feature on Fuck Girls and Thrill
Kids (August 1971).

Towards the end of 1972, he gave an interview to the NME's Tony Norman for their 'Under the Influence' page. Elvis at Sun, Dion, Dale Hawkins with James Burton, Eddie Cochran, Tony Orlando's 'Chills', the Orlons and Buddy Holly are all given his stamp of approval, as are his more immediate elders, Cream, Hendrix and The Who. Bolan wore his influences on his sleeve, or on his T-shirts.[98] Effectively, he folded together Chuck Berry and Marc Bolan. He never saw any division between himself and the first-generation rockers he revered. It was a synthesis that some found endearing, John Peel foremost among his followers, but others, such as Charles Shaar Murray, found presumptuous: a creative over-reaching.

Mick Jagger was equally uncharitable towards Bolan: 'I don't want to bitch, I really don't . . . the only thing is that I wish the music was different. I like what Marc does, but I only wish it was something I'd never heard before. Ya know – something entirely new. I wish it wasn't based so much on those simple riffs.'[99] This was a common moan echoed regularly by critics, none more so than NME's Danny Holloway. His review of 'Children of the Revolution' went under the heading 'This Is T. Wrecks'.[100] 'Marc found a formula', he wrote, 'and made some goodies, but it is all past tense now. "Metal Guru" was a big disappointment for me and this confirms the fact that Bolan doesn't realise he's run a good thing into the ground.'[101] He concluded that 'the soldiers of the Teenage Wasteland will send this straight to number one.'[102] Holloway was back again knocking 'Solid Gold Easy Action' in November. It was, he wrote, 'Another rocker . . . like the others it consists of clichés reworked to sound their own.'[103] On the suggestion that all the T. Rex records were interchangeable, his producer, Tony Visconti, responded: 'That's a load of crap . . . T. Rex have a style . . . if you don't like their style you can listen to someone else.'[104] Changing a hit formula was never going to be more than a minor modification here and there. This may have been abhorrent to Murray and like-minded critics of T. Rex, who offered discriminating pronouncements from the roof of the NME's office while clutching onto their Zappa long-players, but Bolan's fans wanted all the noise of the party, the explosion of the 45-rpm single, not the meritorious hubbub of the sixth-form common room with a Carole King album spinning quietly in the background. 'But, you know, we're only here for a time', said Bolan, 'and you might as well make it exciting for yourself and the audience. The actual truth of what it's all about is irrelevant.'[105]

What Jagger missed (and Murray scorned) was that T. Rex were without guile; they may have played with familiar song structures, familiar anyway to Jagger if not Bolan's audience, but they did it without the dead weight of nostalgia and a crippling sense of ennui. There was nothing decadent in T. Rex's resurrection shuffle; it was instead reduction and abstraction, back to the directness and immediacy of 1950s rock 'n' roll, Americana as teenage customs and rituals, which Bolan then rendered in abstruse lyrical curlicues. Repetition was part of the record's art; it was not a flaw or weakness within the recording itself or across a run of releases. Progression was anathema; the records needed to stay in the moment. Rock 'n' roll revival bands were inferior, Tony Russell argued, not just because nostalgia was a pointless exercise in and of itself, but because there 'was more to rock 'n' roll than noise and sweat' that either Britain's The Wild Angels or America's Sha Na Na might recreate – 'its spirit', he wrote, 'was a divine carelessness'.[106] The heedlessness in rock 'n' roll disappeared as soon as crusaders, professional rock 'n' rollers, entered the scene. T. Rex were never revivalists; in their own peculiar pursuit of a godlike recklessness they forsook a conservative respect for the past but still made common cause with those who had gone before.

Intuitively or not, Bolan had absorbed the moves made by the early rock 'n' rollers; he could mirror and echo Eddie Cochran, Little Richard, Gene Vincent, Chuck Berry and Elvis. Like them, when he played, Bolan took his audience out of a run-of-the-mill existence and out of the classroom. He extinguished the quotidian – teatime with the family – and dull ambition and, in their stead, plied glamour and flash, fearlessness and daring, and a corkscrew philosophy to baffle reason and rhyme. While rock critics felt comfortable exhorting the hits of Spector, Motown and Leiber and Stoller – The Ronettes, Supremes and The Shangri-Las, finding adult value in a past era's teen fantasies and factory-line productions (*NME*'s Ian MacDonald had called The Shangri-Las' *Golden Hits* 'the disc of the decade' and he meant the 1970s not the 1960s, and wasn't being glib) – T. Rex were damned as a poor reverberation of that golden age of pop (before *Sgt. Pepper's*) and for being a schoolgirl crush that had sold out the Underground and, thus, were twice cursed.[107]

Reviewing the 1972 collection *Bolan Boogie*, Dave Laing wrote that you either loved or hated the music of Tyrannosaurus Rex 'because it was so extreme'; there was no middle ground.[108] He called them 'flower-punk', a distorted echo, perhaps, of Took's description of the band as a 'very violent pop thing'. Bolan's contemporary version, Laing thought, was the best example, since The Troggs' demise, of 'British punk rock'; a musical form he thought was 'quintessentially adolescent in its emotional and musical simplicity, and in the obsessive energy with which that simplicity is expressed'.[109] To think of T. Rextasy in this context made more sense to him than comparing the band with the early Beatles:

> Intensely successful bands often arouse resentment or hostility because they seem to be holding in thrall millions of listeners. But in fact, after the first couple of hits they become the prisoners of their audience's expectations, and the life of most of them is strictly limited by how long it takes for fans to get bored with their sound.[110]

The problem for Bolan was how to break out of this conundrum, but, in the moment of his success, did the next step really matter?

In 1972, T. Rex released a sequence of singles unrivalled by any other third-generation rocker. That year's run began with 'Telegram Sam' in January, continued with 'Metal Guru' in May, 'Children of the Revolution' in September and 'Solid Gold Easy Action' in December. Released in March 1973, '20th Century Boy' would be the last of his regal cosmic boogies. That set of chart explosions had been preceded by 'White Swan' in October 1970 and 'Hot Love' in February 1971, 'Get It On' in July and 'Jeepster' in November. As the run of hits began, Bolan, the least self-reflective of his peers, told Chris Welch that he had 'flaming hands and bleeding fingers. I steer the guitar like a ship and sing with my eyes closed.'[111] Typically elliptical, his gnomic pronouncement suggested gut intuition as a guiding principle alongside his belief in making music with a god-like abandon: 'He creates fast,' it was reported in a *Record Mirror* special: 'He wrote "Ride A White Swan" in about 10 minutes. "Hot Love" took the best part of quarter of an hour. "Jeepster" was done there and then in the recording studio . . . and "Telegram Sam" was a real marathon job. It took almost half-an-hour.'[112] Dirty and sweet, the best pop also has to move fast – like in a New York minute.

3

EX-PATRIA: IGGY POP
AND LOU REED
EXILED IN LONDON

But tell me, Iggy, is everything they say about you true? 'Yeaaah,
pretty much ... Maybe it gets a little distorted.'

Michael Watts interviews Iggy Pop in London (1 April 1972)

In his September column for *Creem*, Simon Frith continued
to feel the good vibes being generated by third-generation
rock 'n' roll in 1972. His piece, however, began with a put-down
– of the Great Western Express Festival that took place over
the final weekend in May. It had bored him silly – but he followed it up with a rapture: 'I came out of David Bowie's show
so happy that I can't remember how I got home.'[1] British rock
festivals are like battles, he wrote, 'they're all dire, windswept
occasions, when pleasure has to be fought for.'[2] Frith thought
Mick Farren had asked the right question when he led the
charge at the Isle of Wight: 'what kind of liberation do you buy
for a weekend?'[3] A line had been drawn between rock as experience and rock as entertainment. With Bowie's emergence, Frith
knew on which side of the line he stood: why settle for the stink
of 'stale beer, piss and wet wool' when you can go and see a
Bowie show that smelt, in contrast, of 'Pink Camay'.[4] He loved

the spectacle of the show, the lights, the choreography, the costume changes, the 'relentless, hard, imploring music'.[5] Bowie had created a rock star, Frith wrote, a 'perfect image, remote, androgynous and thrilling . . . Glamour rides again'.[6] Bolan would be toppled from his pedestal, he predicted, and Bowie would take his place. And, to cap it all, he exclaimed, the new star had written and produced Mott the Hoople's next single.

Elsewhere in the same issue of *Creem*, news of the magazine's 'favorite all-American boy, James Osterberg aka Iggy Stooge aka Iggy Pop aka Pop', was that he had made England the base for his 'comeback thrust': 'His hair is longer now, we're told, and he's given to wearing old hats and leopard skin jackets.'[7] Frith too had noted Iggy's relocation and added that the MC5, and the Flamin' Groovies, had joined him in London. Lou Reed was also in town and, like Iggy, he was being pulled into Bowie's orbit.[8]

The image of The Stooges as the ultimate outsiders was established right at the start of their career. In a short news stub from an April 1969 edition of New York's *East Village Other* it was reported the band were in town to record their debut album with the Velvet Underground's John Cale. The Stooges played 'Renaissance Music', whatever that was, and were notorious for 'carrying their theatre right into the audience', but it was where they came from and how that was reflected in their music that mostly held the reporter's attention:

Nowhere are audiences more primitive and the music more visceral than in the Midwest. Kids are known to shoot up in junior high school and smoke dope in their high school classes in Detroit. It's a skonko city with the youth having three choices for the future: go to war, go to college or go to the factory. It's America and it's no wonder that much of today's revolutionary activity is coming from the centre of the continent, the crotch of the nation – Detroit.[9]

In a world of strictly defined limits, The Stooges embodied an alternative force fierce enough to flatten convention and fleet enough to ignore any sense of propriety. And it was all done in an agreeably scatological manner. Iggy, it was reported, was known to 'urinate on delighted girls' in his audience and was rumoured to have once 'wiped his anal [sic] with toilet paper and flung the dung dipped remnants to his howling throng of admirers'.[10] What The Stooges represented was the abject, individual, social, political and teenage, albeit a fantastical version of wretchedness.

Nearly a year later *East Village Other*'s Karin Berg returned to the subject of Detroit's lost boys, this time skipping over the apocrypha of spent bodily fluids and soiled wipes – decadence at its most reductive – and focusing instead on how the band cut through the crap: 'Hard rock stripped of its pretentious bullshit. Iggy Stooge has a *concept*. He's touted as an icon of evil, of depravity, but that's wrong. He's closer to a messenger of redemption, but in no current saintly fashion. No pacific John Lennon he.'[11] From renaissance to restoration, quite some journey for a band channelling a Bo Diddley beat beneath a maelstrom of over-amplified wah-wah guitar and the look of a 'hip street gang'. For all the attraction of the noise and hoodlum postures, Iggy is the difference; the physicality of his performance, his taunts and provocations, both impolite and imbecilic:

The anger of the Ig is directed against sterility, defences, wall; he's always chopping away, trying to make contact in this society, especially among much of the hipguard that people rock audiences, it is a superhuman task but Iggy takes the whole thing on.[12]

'Crashing through boredom, the shitty ennui of white America, polyethylene hip, glib sophisticated rot' was the base line, Berg thought, of The Stooges' appeal; it is an attraction that still resonates today.[13]

But on the eastern side of the Atlantic, the story of Iggy Pop was only just beginning to be told. In the 1970 Christmas issue of *NME*, beneath a photo of Iggy standing on the upraised arms of the crowd at the Cincinnati Pop Festival in June, Nick Logan gave a capsule review of the UK release of The Stooges' *Fun House* album, which in the States had been on sale since July. He called The Stooges a 'particularly American group – from the same bizarre traditions as Alice Cooper and the MC5'.[14] *Fun House*, he wrote, had 'reasonably played rock tunes, sung by a tortured non-voice over repetitive riffs . . . if you can make a virtue out of that then the album is for you.'[15] Stone the Crows singer Maggie Bell echoed these sentiments in her *Melody Maker* 'Blind Date' review of *Fun House*. Her band had played with The Stooges in the States: 'they were terrible,' she said, and repeated the stories of Iggy's demented performances.[16] The Stooges were admired for producing 'pimply rubbish rock' by one U.S. critic, Logan noted, while another compatriot had 'drooled' over their debut album, which he himself had found tedious.[17] Six months earlier Mick Farren had also failed to join the party, knocking The Stooges debut for not working up 'sufficient energy to make the album effective'.[18]

But some British critics saw value in The Stooges' delinquent posturing. Writing in an autumn 1970 edition of *Strange Days*, Chris Hodenfield filed a feature-length article on the MC5 and submitted a short piece on 'Other Detroit Sounds' that included notes on Mitch Ryder, Catfish and The Stooges. The last of the three, he wrote, are a 'band born out of depression, boredom, sadness, perversion, hunger and television'.[19] Iggy, he reported, had graduated from high school as class valedictorian, 'and everyone had high hopes for the lad. He, on the other hand, had an idea for a demented rock band.'[20] Recruiting novice musicians, they created a band that glorified 'messed up and outta my mind living'.[21] Hodenfield thought they were a 'natural smash'.[22]

At the other end of the political spectrum from *Strange Days*, the right-leaning political journal *The Spectator*, in its recently inaugurated 'Pop' column penned by 21-year-old Duncan Fallowell, also gave some attention to the 'demented' Stooges. Beginning with a round-up of America's so-called 'good groups' – The Band, Chicago, Zappa, Creedence Clearwater Revival, Canned Heat – Fallowell declared that they left him 'disappointed from the neck up and dead from the neck down'.[23] The trouble is, he wrote, 'they are so *normal*. There is nothing extra-terrestrial about them.'[24] These bands, along with the likes of Jefferson Airplane and the Grateful Dead, were all faultlessly professional and they play beautifully and dexterously, but, he declared, they are also sterile, anaemic, lack a cutting edge and are automatic. Exceptions to this rule are Blue Cheer, who 'generated a very personal kind of mad energy in which absolute criticism has no place', and the MC5, who 'took the clichés of rock and inflated them to monstrously exhausting proportions. They did other interesting things too like defecating on stage.'[25] Unfortunately, both bands have since tidied things up, he wrote, and are now 'feeble beyond words'.[26] There was also the Velvet Underground, who, 'because they are kicking against a tacky pop ancestry, are extremely bizarre', but the 'strangest of all' is a new band called The Stooges,[27] led by Iggy Stooge, 'manic perverted goon and apotheosis of the "all messed up an' outta ma mind" school'.[28] Fallowell was riffing on American dispatches on the Detroit scene and embellishing Hodenfield's report.[29] Iggy, Fallowell wrote, 'is inclined to claw at his body until it bleeds, tear out hair, punch his face into purple shreds, and generally abuse himself'.[30] Acts of self-abuse, he noted, that were celebrated in a song called 'Your Pretty Face Is Going to Hell'.[31] The music displays a 'degree of mind-concussing insensitivity' and is 'a catharsis indeed for the accumulating frustration of American youth'.[32] All this was created by musicians 'who had never played a note in their lives ... The result? Well, it need hardly be said. Quite unlike anything else, which is some achievement these days.'[33]

The narrow bandwidth of these transatlantic broadcasts about The Stooges was boosted somewhat when *Creem* scribe Dave Marsh wrote 'The Incredible Story of Iggy and the Stooges' for the monthly British journal *Zigzag*. Written around the time of the recording of *Fun House*, it was published towards the tail end of 1970. Illustrated with pictures from the Cincinnati show, Marsh gave the lowdown on the prehistory of the band, especially Iggy's time with the Paul Butterfield-influenced Prime Movers, his friendship with Ron Asheton and how that led to the formation of The Stooges, and the philosophical shift from the impossible quest to capture the spirit of 'True Black Blues' to the pursuit of 'True Rock and Roll'.[34] The piece thereafter evolved and became less the story of the band and more of a psycho-trip deep into The Stooges' world with Iggy as principal agent and tour guide.

A good slice of Marsh's article is devoted to a lengthy citation from a transcribed discussion between Jackie Curtis and Rita Redd. Their appreciation of Iggy's appeal had been published in *Gay Power* earlier in the year. Marsh selected the following as a particular highlight:

J. Why did you say that Iggy has the magic touch?

R. He's putting an old number in new light.

J. What do you mean?

R. He's taking what Elvis Presley did, giving you a taste of Mick Jagger . . .

J. None of Jim Morrison?

R. No, Jim Morrison is really gross. The only thing Jim Morrison is into is displaying his cock so he can prove he still has one WHEN IGGY IS ON STAGE THERE'S NEVER ANY DOUBT.[35]

When it came to reporting on The Stooges, myth was always preferable to any dull reality. In a post-Beatles age, when rock was thought to be undergoing a period of decadence (all that excrement left behind on stages by The Stooges and the MC5), Iggy appeared as its ultimate dissolute apostle.[36]

Before recognition of Iggy had moved beyond a small coterie of followers, before Bowie appeared in his Ziggy mode, that is

The abject: The Stooges – Iggy Pop and Ron Asheton.

'People are both male and female'

Alice Cooper explains why a group of five male musicians are called Alice Cooper.

"The typical male American thinks he is all male—100%, but what he has got to realise is that he has got a female side."

Alice reached this conclusion while studying with a hypnotist in Phoenix, who taught him to become three equal parts: male, for strength; female, for wisdom; and child, for faith. In their stage act, they strive for a total integration of these qualities. Their feminine image, their powerful music, and the 'toys' that they play with on stage.

"We act as a mirror—people see themselves through us, many times they react violently because they don't like what they see. If they were judging us at face value they would say, 'Well, that's what it is', but they put their values on it and their values are sometimes warped. They will react because they are insecure. They consider it shocking, vulgar . . . People who are really pure enjoy it. They enjoy it for what it is, entertainment. They enjoy it because it is really strong, positive. The more liberated you become, the more you realize that you are not just this or that, but everything . . . That's in the future."

Alice Cooper Love it to Death

STS 1065

Manufactured and marketed by CBS Records

through much of 1971, Alice Cooper had best personified third-generation rock's descent into decadence. *Love It to Death* was advertised in the UK counterculture magazines and music press with the heading 'People Are Both Male and Female', which ran above an explanation of where the band were coming from: 'We act as a mirror – people see themselves through us, many times they react violently because they don't like what they see.' The gender ambivalence of the group and singer's name, the transgressive costumes and make-up, the act's Grand Guignol gestures and theatrical props, the live animal show with snake wrangling and chicken hurling, and their trash TV aesthetic had ensured a steady flow of critical interest in Alice Cooper.

On a promotional junket, Alice Cooper, the singer, met with London's Underground press in the early summer of 1971. Asked by *Frendz* for his view on why the band flirted with transvestitism, he told Steve Mann that they were about confounding expectations. The name might suggest they were a folk-singer, but instead the audience gets hit by something 'really tough' that comes on all 'chrome and streamlined and loud – it's turned the name around'.[37] Mann asked him about The Stooges:

A lot of people compare us because we're both really blatant – sexual. He's much more physical, just like Theatre of Cruelty sort of thing, that type of shit, which is really neat and I appreciate it, but mine's more of a mimist [*sic*] type thing. It's still sensual – based on

Love It to Death: 'People Are Both Male and Female'; UK promotional advertisement.

sensuality, sex – but I think ours has a little more finesse.[38]

In *IT*, Jamie Mandelkau described Alice Cooper as 'Five young men with long flowing hair, no moustaches or beards, wearing feminine clothes'.[39] They are 'a specimen of Third Generation Rock and Roll, of TV and moonwalks, or what some people call Dada rock . . . carried to its ultimate logical absurdity'.[40] Alice told him the band were a product of 'Pop-art Amerika' and they were as 'camp as possible'. The kids, Alice said, were getting back into rock and roll, 'ripping out seats and wetting their pants . . . Younger girls. I find you can influence them more easily than the college-educated intellectual who sits back at our gigs and says, "Oh, you know – it's art! You know – ART." I hate intellectuals.'[41] The anti-intellectual stance, or dumb show, was matched by only one other group Alice 'can think of who attack their audience and get the beast enraged and moving' and that is The Stooges: 'Iggy just destroys the audience. He spits on 'em, picks a fight, once he got knocked out and the band just kept on playing until he came round and got into singing again.'[42]

Towards the end of 1971, Mick Farren wrote that Alice Cooper were 'rough-trade from Venus' who 'leave David Bowie a long way behind and Marc Bolan really can stay in bed'.[43] But Alice Cooper, even as they took delight in upsetting America's moral guardians, were busy building an alibi against any accusation they were genuinely transgressive. They now hid behind the idea that they were just a show, a bit of vaudeville ('we still wear make-up . . . but it's not feminine in the least, the way it comes off is totally masculine').[44] Bowie saw that play of deception as clearly as anyone: 'He's a tease really . . . I think he's probably a perfect identity of America, probably young America personified. I'm glad they've got 'im 'cause I don' wan' 'im!'[45] Bowie scorned the idea of 'baby-bashing or self-hanging'; his own theatre, he said, was from the school of Lindsay Kemp.[46]

With 'School's Out' about to climb to the top of the charts, Nick Kent interviewed Alice for *Frendz*, and The Stooges once more made an appearance:

> We had to move out of L.A. eventually, so we all checked out the States and found Detroit to be the best. That place has such incredible high energy scenes, it was unbelievable. The audiences there are amazing y'know, and the bands all live together. Bands like the MC5 and Iggy and the Stooges – Iggy was probably the finest performer ever. Have you heard *Fun House*? That must stand as one of the classic rock albums – the whole primal buzz, y'know? It's such a drag that the whole Detroit scene had to get so smacked out, because that was *the* rock 'n' roll city.[47]

The story of Iggy's gang had shifted to the past tense and references to them were now being elicited by the interviewing journalist rather than freely offered: Kent was less interested in the fact of pop star Alice than he was in the myth of Iggy.

One of the chief propagators of the myth was David Bowie, who used The Stooges to help provide an element of frisson for his Ziggy persona that he was busy introducing to journalists during the early months of 1972. With the just-released *Hunky Dory* garnering any number of critical plaudits, Bowie had cropped and dyed his hair and dropped the Lauren Bacall look, as it was often described, but which was more like a drag impersonation of Veronica Lake if truth be told. To complement the haircut he had new costumes made and tapes of his next project ready to play to critics who were invited to Haddon Hall in Beckenham, to meet the star in waiting. *Hunky Dory* was so last week.

Little space in the write-ups of these interviews held at his home in early 1972 is given over to discussing Bowie's music; instead the focus is on his image manipulation, his play with personas, especially sexual. Michael Watts's cover story for *Melody Maker* in January is seen as the piece that brought this all to the fore, but it is there too in the interview for the NME, conducted by Danny Holloway, and in a piece photographer Mick Rock wrote, which incorporated many of his now iconic images, for the recently launched men's magazine *Club International*. He's not 'totally gay', wrote Rock, he likes boys *and* he likes girls. Bowie tells him: 'I'm just a bisexual person. Whether that means I'm a boy who comes over very gay or what, I don't really know.'[48] In each of the interviews, Bowie plays up ambiguity around his sexuality and gives each journalist the impression they are receiving a candid, somewhat spontaneous, certainly unguarded, insight into his life. Yet the repetition across the key interviews suggests things were actually carefully planned and scripted. Little, you might safely wager, was left to chance. All is stage-managed, even the incidental props: 'On the carpet lies a copy of *Forum* magazine, a Yamaha steel string acoustic and a Fender Jaguar guitar as well as scores of albums including the first Pretty Things albums, The Yardbirds and The Stooges . . . "I'm just an image person.

I'm terribly conscious of images and I live in them",[49] Bowie told the NME.

With those Pretties, 'Birds and Stooges albums, Bowie was, in a calculated manner, displaying a refined and discriminating taste. It all gave a solid indicator of where his new creation was coming from: his music would be instilled by bands with an over-inscribed gang mentality that would balance the swish and flounce of his image play. He had first name-checked Iggy Pop in a May 1971 edition of *Melody Maker*, listing him alongside Paul Rodgers and Christopher Milk as among his favourite singers. The last of the three, under his real name, John Mendelsohn, had introduced Bowie to The Stooges during an American promotional tour in February.[50] Naming his alter-ego 'Ziggy' was as much a homage to The Stooges' singer as it was opportunistic and inspired on Bowie's part. Where The Stooges first touched and stirred the consciousness of British critics they did so as myth built out of half-truths and rumour, which was what Bowie was doing with his new conception.[51]

♀ ♀ ♀

Two years after Logan's review of *Fun House*, Hodenfield's introduction and Fallowell's blatant apocrypha, that myth arrived in London. On 30 March 1972 the first public announcement of his presence in the UK was made in a *Times* classified advertisement in the 'For Sale and Wanted' column beneath the listings for good wines, ceramic tiles and Persian rugs:

WHAT'S SKINNY and pink, throws itself into the audience, and rips chunks out of its own flesh? Iggy Stooge, that's what; Iggy is New York's most frightening rock hero, the master of Dada-Rock, Sade-Rock, and every-thing in between; right now, he's in London, and this week he talks to *Melody Maker* – out now.[52]

With guitarist James Williamson, Iggy Pop had moved to London in the early spring of 1972 on MainMan's ticket (Bowie's management). They were soon to be joined by the brothers Ron and Scott Asheton. The band played only one gig during their time in England, but the impact of that single performance resonated long after. Mick Rock's photographs of Iggy as a street-walking cheetah and pop god, featured on the sleeve of 1973's *Raw Power* album, have become iconic, transcending that July night in 'the inauspicious surroundings of King Sound, at London King's Cross'. It was here, according to Rosalind Russell in *Disc*, where he 'slimed offstage and wound his way among a somewhat nervous audience, still screaming into his mike, and berated the people for being so apathetic'.[53] Listing Iggy Pop as his best hope for 1973, as he looked back over 1972, Nick Kent said of the gig that it 'may well go down in history as some sort of event in rock 'n' roll'.[54] He was right;

'What's skinny and pink . . .?' The first public
notice of Iggy Stooge in London.

it was a singular, unrepeatable moment, the reviews and photographs of the night now holy relics.

In a four-page article headlined 'Pouf Rock' for the men's magazine *Knave*, Vaughn Masterson recalled that night in London and enlightened his readers, lovers of female pulchritude, on the fad for cross-dressing and the new swishing pop stars such as Alice, Marc, Gary, Bryan, Lou and David. The last of these, he wrote, dealt in 'gay adult pantomime that is all flash . . . a kind of greaser camp'. And then there's Iggy,

> whose appeal is strictly physical . . . his words and music have been reduced to a minimum. Frantic fuzz-tone rocking provides a background to Iggy screaming a key phrase over and over. In his song 'I'm Hungry', he just yells the title . . . hysteria growing in his voice as the song progresses. The originality of his act comes in the presentation. Stripped to the waist and wearing silver trousers and make-up, he has the body of a diminutive Adonis and the coordination of a gymnast, and from the start of the show he uses these attributes to mount a total physical assault on the audience. He pouts, he postures and screams, rushes round the stage in frenetic dance, and without warning collapses like a puppet with cut strings. Between songs he harangues the audience, provoking hecklers and then attempting to pick fights with them. The high point of the act comes when he leaps from the stage, pawing, cuddling and even climbing into the laps of members of the audience irrespective of age or sex.[55]

Iggy's crossing of boundaries, his acts of trespass, is as much about the dissembling of gender as it is about violating the performer/audience divide. All this takes on a heightened, almost delirious, sexual frisson when it is being played out in the pages of a magazine that is ostensibly directed at heterosexual males. That which is sublimated in girl's teenage pop journals is pushed to the fore in *Knave*, where sexual desire is less circumspect. But in either case, desire is dependent on imagining the self as the other. A performer's play with gender boundaries dramatizes the instance where fear and longing merge. No one performed this moment better than Bowie or perhaps better understood how it worked.

Spurred by the sight of The Sweet 'wearing heavy eye make-up and generally camping it up' on *Top of the Pops*, 26-year-old scribe John Brown, writing in *Cream*, noted you couldn't pick up a weekly or monthly music rag without coming across an article on Alice Cooper, David Bowie or Lou Reed. All three were 'curious forms of advertisements for themselves' and symptoms of a wider confusion around violence and promiscuity, gender and sex: 'And so, lipsticked, sequinned and armed with plastic machine-guns we thunder off towards the New Apocalypse.'[56] Alice was the cover star, and his picture was used under the article's headline, but it was a Pennie Smith shot of Iggy Pop, onstage in London, shaking his backside at the camera, that best illustrated Brown's idea of fear, loathing and the countervailing attraction of gender bending in 1972's pop scene.

Enamoured by the thrill and entranced by the danger of Iggy Pop, Nick Kent had introduced him to readers of *Cream* the month before, in October 1972, as the 'Punk Messiah of

Nick Kent's 'Punk Messiah of the Teenage Wasteland' in *Cream* (October 1972).

the Teenage Wasteland', 'brash, well-hung and mean as hell', illustrated by another of Smith's photographs from the gig.[57] Having clipped 'teenage wasteland' from The Who's 'Baba O'Riley', Kent had first repurposed it in his review of *The Rise and Fall of Ziggy Stardust and the Spiders from Mars* for *Oz* magazine in July 1972. As vital as Bowie's album was in his intent to be the 'messiah of the Teenage Wasteland', Kent claimed it was all a hype too far: the true leader of that domain was the 'amazing Iggy Stooge'.[58] A month later, Kent was still sitting in the shelter overlooking Margate's sands, conversing with the ghosts of Mod rioters and T. S. Eliot, but this time it was Hawkwind that held his attention: 'renowned for their journeys into the depths of Teenage Wasteland'.[59] He had found his mantra.

'Yes, friends,' wrote Kent in *Cream*, 'this is a story that Nik Cohn, David Bowie and even Willy Bee (Burroughs to all the squares) himself would find a trifle hard to conjure with.'[60] He went on to track the upward curve of The Stooges' rise from Ann Arbor garage bands, signing with Elektra, followed by the downward spiral after the release of *Fun House* in 1970 – an album of 'pure, undiluted teenage debauchery' – caused by Iggy's heroin dependency, and then his Lazarus-like rebirth in Maida Vale under the authority of Tony Defries, Bowie's manager.[61] Giving a more truncated report on Iggy's career and the London show for the NME, Kent thought the 'total effect' of the performance 'was more frightening than all the Alice Coopers and *Clockwork Oranges* put together'.[62] As things currently stood, he wrote, Iggy 'intends to work purely on teenage circuits, ignoring the mature student venues. To paraphrase one of Iggy's fave raves, Jim Morrison: the men may not know, but doubtless the little girls will understand.'[63]

Kent pushed his fantasy of teenage renegades overthrowing the old guard at every opportunity he was given throughout 1972, pulling together, as he did so, an image of 1950s American leather-jacketed street punks, Kubrick's droogies, and Iggy Pop. His review of an imaginary import album by 'Johnny Milkshake & The Hot Biscuits' on the Tampax label incorporated all these elements:

> OK so you're getting all this decadent ultra-violence third-generation rock thing . . . You smashed all your Alice Cooper albums in a fit of rage one night, the feds have confiscated your switchblade, you're fed up with queueing every time you go see 'Clockwork Orange' for inspiration and someone just stole your Iggy Stooge poster. Well, shit, I've got just the remedy for you . . .[64]

Kent befriended Iggy and guitarist James Williamson and led the charge of righteous believers who witnessed the band's gig in King's Cross. An album, he reported, was in the planning stage, perhaps helped along by Bowie. Iggy, Kent predicted, was going to be big, he was poised for superstardom, 'while the children, like Bowie and Roxy Music, who were weaned on the third-generation work of Reed and crazed Detroit bands like The Stooges are sweethearts of the hour. Iggy is the real deal, though, the true contender for the title of Punk Messiah of the Teenage Wasteland.'[65]

The most nuanced report of the King's Cross gig is from Michael Oldfield (not the musician) for *Melody Maker*. Unlike Kent he wasn't convinced by what he'd witnessed. He was aroused, certainly, but not smitten. What marked the performance for him was the lack of any theatrical props, or even the ballyhoo, of an Alice Cooper show, because 'Iggy's point is that it's not the artist who's depraved – it's the audience.'[66] Without fanfare, Iggy walks onto the raised stage, which is pitched below the audience, who sit in the raked seats still left from when the space was the upper circle of a cinema. The floor beneath the specially erected stage covers the void above the lower circle and stalls. As the band tunes up behind him, Iggy stares out at the audience before proceedings commence with 'one loud, repetitive riff that passes for a song and Iggy leaps into action, shouting the lyrics into his long phallic shaped mike. But the sound is so distorted you can only pick up the odd word.'[67] If Oldfield finds the music less than enthralling he is nevertheless taken by Iggy's performance, his physical presence:

> When there's a break, he turns round and shakes his backside at the audience in a lewd parody of the twist. He shakes his arms around wildly. He contorts his face. He prowls around the stage like a wild bear in a cage. He shakes his body like he's having a fit. He lies on the stage lasciviously, like a wartime pin-up on a fur rug. He holds himself with the mike stand. He falls off the stage.[68]

And all the time he is laughing at the audience. Microphone and equipment failure punctuate the show and Iggy fills dead space with his rehearsed improvisation of 'The Shadow of Your Smile', or berates those who have paid a solid £1 to see him, threatening cat callers. What you get from the band is a 'succession of riffs – one per number – with an odd solo thrown in. At the end of each number they just stop. Dead.'[69] Until the final tune the band have remained immobile. At show's end they become animated, coaxing a cacophony of feedback howls and screeches from their guitars and amps. And then it's over, no encore, 'no sympathy from the devil,' wrote Oldfield.[70]

The day after The Stooges' London gig, David Bowie gave his press conference at the Dorchester Hotel with Iggy and Lou Reed briefly in attendance. Asked by the NME's Charles Shaar Murray about his thoughts on rock becoming a formularized spectacle, a ritual, Bowie talked about stage craft and training and how so many bands had barely mustered a knowledge beyond that learnt at secondary school. Iggy, on the other hand, he said, 'has natural theatre. It's very interesting because it doesn't conform to any standards or rules or structures of theatre. It's his own and it's just a Detroit theatre that he's brought with him. It's straight from the street.'[71] Authenticity and artifice mix easily in Bowie's conception of The Stooges, just as they did in his Ziggy persona.

Ray Fox-Cumming, in his review of *Raw Power* in *Disc*, caught the idea of the primitive at the heart of The Stooges' ethos:

> Technically, *Raw Power* is a nightmare. Everything is lumped in and recorded together with each instrument doing its damnedest to get in a note edgeways. But while others are carefully separating everything out, perfecting mixes and making beautiful polite records, Iggy's got the excitement – yes, raw power.[72]

Not averse to a bit of cross-promotion, Mick Rock reviewed Iggy and the Stooges' album for *Club International*, for which, circa 1972, he was a regular photographic and editorial contributor. He was of like mind with Fox-Cumming. *Raw Power*, he wrote, is for those:

> who long for the days of yore when rock was an outlaw music; for those for whom the modern rock star is about as dangerous and sexy as Perry Como ...
>
> Nerve annihilation, total anarchy is what [The Stooges] are all about. It's as if the last ten years of increasing sophistication of layer upon layer of art and artifice in rock never happened.[73]

Rock thinks The Stooges are powered by a primordial surge that is rushing them into the future, which was how T. Rex were initially received. In the contra-pull of yesterday and tomorrow The Stooges create today: 'It's total rock 'n' roll but it belongs to the present.'[74] In the NME, Roy Carr similarly thought the album 'strips away the layers of veneer and commercial compromise that has – apart from a few rare occasions – defused the whole essence of rock ... As crude and perverse as a 42nd Street hard-core porn movie ... the first real rock album of the seventies.'[75] Iggy and the Stooges: third-generation rock 'n' roll by any other name.

Critical celebration of the album as a form of 'pathological gutter-level rock 'n' roll' had to be understood in the context of a prevailing counter move to take rock out of the street

Raw Power promotional advertisement, 'the first real rock album of the seventies'.

RAW POWER

Most rock groups would be better off listening to Iggy and the Stooges mixed by David Bowie

James Osterberg alias Iggy Pop, the committed pioneer of all the current diluted debauchery, the Master of Self-Immolation via his dementedly masochistic on-stage acrobatics, the very essence of mordant energy, returns after a protracted absence to ravage tender ears and upset musical literati. Despite the backstage presence of that discriminating connoisseur of the mixing console David Bowie, the rough edges remain intact as the reformed trio of Stooges provide a menacing wall of sound behind our hero's own brand of affirmative body-odour boogie. Praise Lucifer and pass the crushed glass in aspic.

"Raw Power celebrates Armageddon . . . In one searing blast it strips away the layers of commercial compromise that have – apart from a few rare occasions – defused the whole essence of rock.
. . . Iggy and chums play as if this was the first and last gig. Living for the moment, with no thought of the past or the present, they have come up with the first real rock album of the seventies."
Roy Carr, New Musical Express

Iggy and the Stooges, 'Raw Power.' Rock as it's meant to sound. On CBS 65586.

the music people

and put it into the concert hall.[76] Simon Frith's review in *Let It Rock* played *Raw Power* off against Mike Oldfield's *Tubular Bells*; 'brainy' versus 'gutsy' music but both, albeit in different camps, received as masterpieces.[77] Such 'violently' different albums raised the question of how rock can contain such extremes. Oldfield's album is an 'affectionate and funny Child's Guide to the Rock Orchestra'.[78] But for all the skill on display it lacks energy, he wrote – rock is body music and *Tubular Bells* has 'no sex, no violence, no ecstasy; nothing uncontrolled, nothing uncontrollable'.[79] *Raw Power* has all of those elements: it is high-energy, hate-filled, rude and crude. It is mean and magnificent as well as unmelodic, clumsy and mostly flat. 'For once, all this punk noise and contempt has got a focus – Nixon's America.'[80] And yet, 'it is just this exhilarating mindlessness that is frustrating; the simple music carries too simple a message ... *Raw Power* is a gesture and like all gestures it remains, however stylish, a little silly and a little sad.' Neither album, he concluded, is a masterpiece: 'one's too bright, the other too dumb.'[81]

In his review of *Raw Power* for *The Times*, critic Richard Williams emphasized Bowie's influence and, like Mick Rock, placed its appeal in the past – 'The music is simple rock 'n' roll which, in essence, could easily have been created ten years ago' – and then underscored its now-ness: 'it has a furious cutting edge which is entirely contemporary, plus a sense of imminent physical collapse which emanates from Iggy's own somewhat decadent persona.'[82] Like Frith he thought that Iggy was an extreme and, unlike 'Jagger or Cooper, he makes no sense in terms of intellectual analysis; his act is simply teenage insanity'.[83] Williams again made the point that Iggy was disdainful of 'the gap between the floodlights and the front row of the stalls, so carefully preserved even by Mick Jagger and Alice Cooper', and assaulted his audience.[84] There's a suggestion here, in the idea that Iggy consciously, premeditatedly violated the divide between stage and spectators, that he and The Stooges were less idiot savants, which is what Kent and Rock were promoting, than performance artists and, as such, they were more closely sympathetic to and aligned with the kind of dramaturgy Bowie practised than is generally acknowledged. Whatever the case, the binary between the visceral and the intellect, with Iggy associated only with the former, was a fiction.[85] Like Bowie, Iggy was adroit at moving between and within such abstract concepts. Just where along the fine art/popular culture continuum critics wanted to place Iggy and the Stooges could be debated, but that they were anything other than a quotidian rock show was not up for dispute. In early 1974, the *New Musical Express*'s monthly sister magazine, *Music Scene*, ran a short Mick Rock interview with Iggy Pop. Rock described Iggy as 'extreme'. 'The Ig', he said, 'is a monster,' to which Iggy responded, 'Yes, I'm a legendary figure.'[86]

In the cover story that introduced Bowie as the epicene star in waiting, Michael Watts celebrated the singer's ability to mimic others, such as Bolan on 'Black Country Rock' and Lou Reed on 'Queen Bitch', who he does to a tee, 'vocal and arrangement, as well as parodying, with a storyline about the singer's boyfriend being seduced by another queen, the whole Velvet Underground genre'.[87] Watts considered Bowie to be less an intellectual in his approach to songwriting and more intuitive,

responding to the world like Syd Barrett. If the Floyd man inspired Bowie to make his creative breakthrough, 'it's Lou Reed and Iggy Pop who have since kept him going and helped him to expand his unconsciousness. He and Lou and Iggy, he says, are going to take over the whole world. They are the song writers he admires.'[88]

In that same issue of *Melody Maker*, Richard Williams undertook what was probably Lou Reed's first published interview with the British media.[89] Williams covered the musician's background as a professional songwriter, producing genre tunes on demand, and his personal revolt against the system with 'The Ostrich', a song about an imagined dance craze for putting your head on the floor and then having someone step on it. Through the recording and promotion of that song, Reed began an association with John Cale that would lead to the formation of the Velvet Underground, 'in all its eventual legend-ary splendour', wrote Williams.[90] A band not yet two years in the grave, and from which a ghost entity would tour British halls in July, as Reed also played the circuit, had become fabled.

The end of the Velvets' five-year career meant Reed no longer had to work to escape the shadow Warhol had thrown over the band, or so he thought. He found, however, that the figurative monkey on his back that Warhol once represented had begun to shift to the band he had just escaped from. 'What about the group led by Doug Yule?' asked Williams. 'I don't follow 'em,' Reed muttered in reply.[91] The Velvet Underground MKII were little more than a hollowed-out effigy of the original

Lou Reed: the Chuck Berry of the 1970s,
UK promotional advertisement for his debut album.

and not worth bothering with but the excavation of the tomb, over which Yule's simulacrum lay, began in earnest in 1972 as Reed started to fire up his solo career, first with an album full of as yet unreleased Velvet Underground tunes and then in the latter part of the year with *Transformer*, produced by Bowie and Mick Ronson.

A retrospective piece by Williams, written for *Melody Maker* in October 1969, is often cited as being among the first British appreciations of the Velvets, at least in the weekly music press.[92] But in the same month, British electronic music pioneer Tim Souster, in the *Observer Magazine*, had compared the Velvet Underground's recorded output with the avant-garde experiments of La Monte Young, Terry Riley and John Cage, as well as considering the band's rhythmic affinities with The Who's *Tommy*.[93] Souster had rehearsed his ideas about the evolving link between serious music and pop a year earlier in 1968 in his lengthy review of *White Light/White Heat* for *The Listener*.[94] The Underground press had also latched onto the band as offering something unique within the transatlantic scene.[95]

Geoffrey Cannon had caught the Velvet bug early on and had published positive notices for most of their albums in his column for *The Guardian*. He began his September 1971 review of *Who's Next* by quoting 'Lou Reed, the leader of the Velvet Underground', who provided an insight into his and Townshend's approach to their art. Reed told Cannon that 'the 1965 Who electrified him into writing songs for the Velvets, which connected with the street lives of the kids around the jukebox, rather than with their fantasies – whether plastic or plausible.'[96] The target audience that The Who played to, and that Reed imagined he did, was the same one Bowie sought to find in 1972.

♀ ♀ ♀

All the Velvet Underground records were given contemporary UK releases; both Bowie and Mick Farren had secured pre-release or acetate pressings of *The Velvet Underground and Nico* album and had featured cuts from it in their respective band's repertoires. And, on their final jaunt around the States in 1968, the Jimmy Page line-up of The Yardbirds incorporated 'I'm Waiting for the Man' into their arrangement of Howlin' Wolf's 'Smokestack Lightning'. If not exactly high-profile, Lou's renegades were hardly hidden and lost from view in Manhattan's basements. Indeed, Michael Watts in *Melody Maker* reviewed *Loaded* on its British release in March 1971 and called it 'the most important album since *Tommy*'.[97] The following month, also in *Melody Maker*, and with a front-page tag using a picture of Reed, Andrew Lycett interviewed Sterling Morrison and Moe Tucker, a little after Lou had abandoned ship, and found them to be 'just plain folks' but still wilfully contrary with regard to prevailing trends.[98]

Reviewing *Loaded*, Fallowell recalled his chance discovery in 1967 of the first Velvets album, which he then forced on as many friends as possible; 'and an involuntary *cénacle* arose, the last word in dark sophistication'.[99] A cult formed of 'small groups of *dévots*', but it was not until 1969 that he encountered any reference to the band in a music paper (Williams's piece?).[100] The first album was his entrée into the world of pop that was more than 'tra-la-la-baby-baby'. It was 'moody and violent by turns' – a 'musical counterpart to the world of William

Burroughs, whose grim powers few would dispute'.[101] *White Light/White Heat* followed with 'Sister Ray', 'the toughest trip in rock music'.[102] With their third album the band had 'perversely mellowed', and with their forth, *Loaded*, they were playing 'mock rock' with 'broad splashes of kitsch'. Meanwhile, Lou Reed had 'withdrawn to a mental hospital . . . and may still be there'.[103] The Velvet Underground's 'corrosive energy' was now being channelled by certain German groups, like CAN, he wrote. But if Reed's band should 'disappear in a black tornado, never to be heard again, the Velvet Underground have already had enormous influence', he contended, 'if little widespread acclaim'. They may not have competed with the pre-eminent English groups of the day, but the Velvets were early on a potent mythical embodiment of a peculiarly European romantic disposition for New York's seamy side.

The deluge of critical appreciations properly began in late 1970 with *Zigzag* reprinting a three-page article by Lenny Kaye that had appeared in *New Times*; *Friends* provided a two-page review of the band at Max's Kansas City; and a reprint of a *Fusion* interview with Sterling Morrison was run in *IT* in February 1971. The next month *Zigzag* gave two pages over to Geoffrey Cannon's further ruminations on the band, and he was still meditating on the topic in October for *Time Out*. That particular issue of the listing magazine had The Velvet Underground MKII as the lead attraction on its cover. Under the heading 'The Janitors of Lunacy', Cannon's piece began: 'No American rock band has been so nearly buried alive in a coffin of mythology and mystifying twiddle-twaddle as the Velvet Underground,' which became more or less the opening for any number of appreciations of the band that followed. To supplement all this journalistic activity, the band's MGM back catalogue was reissued, including a double LP compilation with a woeful Warhol pastiche for a cover. The reissues were widely advertised and, on the whole, positively reviewed, notably by Richard Williams.[104]

Reed arrived in London late in December 1971 looking to restart a career that had stalled sixteen months earlier when he left the Velvets towards the end of the *Loaded* sessions. As he laid down the tracks for his debut solo album, Williams reported he was attempting 'to regain the directness of the sounds of his adolescence . . . "I just like rock 'n' roll," Lou Reed says.'[105] He was recording in England because 'we thought it would be interesting to get out of the New York thing . . . also we were very impressed with the sound of certain English records. It was a certain sound we were looking for, and we listened to a lot of records made in different studios.'[106] Perhaps he saw Marc Bolan's shucking of the Underground's hairshirt for the habiliment of the glittering pop star as a valid model? Even if T. Rex was not part of his reasoning for coming to Britain, he was, like Bolan, a tireless proselytizer on behalf of rock 'n' roll. Morgan studios in Willesden, northwest London, was chosen, not just because of its reputation (Rod Stewart and the Faces were regular clients) but because 'We knew we'd be isolated . . . like nobody comes into the studio here, there's no great parties going on. It's just making a rock 'n' roll album.'[107]

Reed was working with producer Richard Robinson, who had two hard rockin' Flamin' Groovies albums under his belt, *Flamingo* and *Teenage Head*, and was someone who had been a long-standing advocate of the Velvets in his other role as a rock journalist. But if the idea was to flash out, to strike new ground, they had pulled together a strange assortment of British musicians to help them achieve their aim. Steve Howe (guitar) and Rick Wakeman (piano) were from Yes, Caleb Quaye, who'd been backing Elton John, was part of the West Coast influenced band Hookfoot, and then there were professional session men Les Hurdle and Brian Odgers on bass and Paul Keogh on guitar. Except for drummer Clem Cattini, none of the musicians had any pedigree playing rock 'n' roll, whether first or second generation. Cattini had been Joe Meek's in-house percussionist and had laid down the beat on recordings by most of the formative British rock 'n' rollers, including Johnny Kidd and Billy Fury. In his review of the album, Lester Bangs thought the drumming inept.[108] It isn't, but it is basic, Scott Asheton style in fact. Maybe Reed and his producer were after that Gary U.S. Bonds drum sound, though it's doubtful anyone else at the session had ever heard 'Quarter to Three'.[109]

The arrangements are too busy, there's no air in the recording, the sound is full but to no purpose. And having four guitarists in play without one decisively taking the lead and creating an identity did not help matters. Andrew Weiner in *Cream* called the album a 'disorganised sequence of dimly remembered gestures'.[110] That this was a problem was as much as admitted when 'Walk and Talk It' and 'Wild Child' were released as a single in a seriously remixed form that brought the bottom end up so that the drums were now supported and the tiringly hectic muso licks, all panache and no style, downplayed. There was a lesson to be learnt here. Reed and Robinson should have listened harder to what Bolan and Tony Visconti had achieved with *Electric Warrior*, which was a masterclass in revealing the tension in a song, allowing for moments of respite so as to better dramatize the point when a song needed to be pushed hard or even just bent a little out of shape. Reed did, however, take the experience of his failures in Willesden into the *Transformer* sessions and, with Bowie and Ronson, found more sympathetic collaborators. Though it had nothing much in common with Bolan's take on rock 'n' roll, the three produced an album that had serious sonic affinities with T. Rex circa 1971.

In June, with the debut solo album released, Roy Hollingworth picked up where Williams had left off and interviewed Reed, back in New York, for *Melody Maker*. Reed was rehearsing with a new band, a Manhattan country rock group. Splendid, easy people, Hollingworth reported, young too: the guitar player still had a brace over his teeth. Reed said that they are 'a pretty straight-ahead rock 'n' roll band'.[111] A few American dates had been organized, and then shows in Europe and the UK, with sessions for a new album with Bowie and Ronson also in the mix. The rehearsal Hollingworth watched featured a number of songs from the Velvets' back catalogue and choice cuts from the solo album. Any residue of 'mystery' that still surrounded the Velvet Underground, Reed suggested, was solely due to the fact that they were from New York; 'we'd have been famous four years ago' if we were an English band, he said.[112] Right now he rated the Stones, The Kinks and Bowie. An Anglophile by inclination or need, Reed had his lines on sexual ambivalence rehearsed for the British media circus that was to follow. But whether or not he was willing to stick to the script and take direction was another matter altogether. Reed told Hollingworth that when he wrote up the interview he should describe him as a 'bisexual chauvinist pig', which wasn't quite the same line Bowie had been reciting.

When Bowie took the first part of his Ziggy Stardust tour to Sheffield on 7 June he had put in 33 performances since the Toby Jug gig on 10 February, and he had eleven more concerts to do before the tour climaxed at the Royal Festival Hall on 8 July. James Johnson's review of the Sheffield gig for the NME noted the influence on Bowie of the Velvets, Dylan and Warhol and that he encored with a 'rousing version' of 'I'm Waiting for the Man'.[113] In the same issue of the weekly paper, Tony Stewart interviewed Reed: 'Once he wore black, tinselled clothes and was a human screen for movies. He sang and wrote about evil characters; sometimes happier ones. But always the unlikely. A mystique and sinister aura surrounded the band Lou Reed led and directed: the Velvet Underground.'[114] The discussion between Stewart and Reed followed the same lines as Reed had fed to Williams, and he again reiterated that his solo work 'is rock 'n' roll'.[115] The next week NME announced that Reed was set to join Bowie at the Royal Festival Hall.[116] In his interview with Hollingworth, Reed had been full of praise for Bowie: 'He's the only person around. Everything has been tedious, rock 'n' roll has been tedious, except for what David has been doing. There's a mutual empathy between us. That's hard to find these days.'[117]

The intertwined stories of David Bowie, Iggy Pop and Lou Reed coalesced at the Dorchester Hotel when Bowie held a press conference that followed a gig in Aylesbury (to which a select group of American critics had been flown over to witness) and early morning shows by The Stooges and Lou Reed at King Sound that same weekend. Speaking to NME's Charles Shaar

Murray, Bowie said that the main influence on the 'rock 'n' roll things that we write, they would definitely be in the Velvets bag . . . more so than Chuck Berry, the archetype'.[118] Lying around was a tape box of recent Mott the Hoople sessions Bowie was working on, including a cover version of 'Sweet Jane': 'I've got Lou singing it at the moment. I've got to put Ian on, but he doesn't know the lyrics yet.' The Flamin' Groovies were also covering the song as part of their live set and would have featured it in their King's Cross show supporting Iggy. Reed briefly made an entrance while Murray was listening to the demo with Bowie, who had said Reed's new material was a departure from the Velvets and 'will surprise a lot of people'.[119] Murray had attended Reed's weekend show:

> With his short hair, livid make-up and velvet suit, Reed has an enormous manic presence – the kind of vibration only given off by especially blessed (or cursed) souls. He sings out of the corner of his mouth in a vaguely Dylanesque sneer virtually innocent of pitching or tonal coloration.[120]

But the set was short and the young backing band couldn't bring to the older numbers the 'demonic energy of the Velvets'.[121] He was wearing the same black velvet suit with rhinestone flowers running down the sleeves and trouser legs that he had donned when he joined Bowie on stage at the Festival Hall. Slightly overweight (as many commentators cruelly noted), he appeared like an inversion of blond-haired Gram Parsons in his white Nudie suit. Geoff Brown reviewed the show for *Melody Maker* and reported that the DJ had played Detroit's (Mitch

Ryder) version of the Velvet's 'Rock and Roll'. Just over an hour later, Reed played the song as an encore. Two weeks after the show, Atlantic released the Velvet Underground's *Live at Max's Kansas City*, which was warmly received, not least because it gave reviewers an excuse to once again proclaim the myth and the legend of Reed's old combo.[122] Whether or not Reed received the plaudits he deserved when he was an active member of the Velvets, he was now receiving serious recognition from critics and his peers alike. Except, that is, from Marc Bolan: 'Lou Reed? I've only heard several tracks at parties. I never liked the Velvet Underground,' he told Michael Watts, 'The singer always sounded like a bad copy of Dylan to me.'[123]

'I've heard about these bands who've been influenced by me,' Reed said to Nick Kent, 'but I don't see it. I send them questionnaires asking them if they understand parts of my work, and they write back "No", So ...'[124] Murray eventually got an interview with Reed. After dismissing Alice Cooper – who 'really doesn't make it as a drag queen . . . I mean he's so ugly. Iggy, now Iggy's really very beautiful, and so's David' – he addressed the new-found adulation being given to his old band:

> 'What I was writing about was just what was going on around me', says Reed. 'I didn't realise it was a whole new world for everybody else. Everybody else is now at the point where I was in 1967. Makes me wonder where they'll be in five years' time. Come to that, makes me wonder where I'm at now.'[125]

The fact was that within a few months, like Iggy and Mott the Hoople, he would be riding in Bowie's charabanc. If he had first Warhol and then the Velvet Underground dragging him down, as 1972 came to an end he had acquired another helper/ encumbrance, Bowie. According to Ian Hoare's review in *Let It Rock*, Bowie had given *Transformer* a 'flash, sumptuous production' and he is left only to imagine what 'Walk on the Wild Side' would have been if it was played by the Velvets.[126] It's all too lightweight, he thought, 'the matinee idol bit just doesn't seem to come naturally to [Reed]. If only he'd never heard about Bowie.'[127]

Cream's Andrew Weiner thought that Reed could be a Chuck Berry for the 1970s. He didn't mean that he could take things back to 'essential rock 'n' roll'; rather Reed had the potential to 'go forward from "Sweet Jane" and "Wild Child" and deal with the Seventies on their own terms'.[128] Eight months later the NME was calling Reed 'the Sinatra of the 70s'.[129] Whichever, Chuck or Frank, Reed was too encumbered by his past to be any kind of meaningful synonym for the '70s – that would need someone far more canny at throwing off old identities and slipping on the new. Or maybe Reed was just too subtle in showing his hand; despite his declaration that rock 'n' roll had saved his life and the later self-made claims to be a rock 'n' roll animal with a rock 'n' roll heart, Lou Reed never did cut that rock 'n' roll album he kept promising. He preferred to pillage his own back catalogue than walk backwards towards the 1950s like so many of his contemporaries.

Because they were recorded in London, and with involvement from Bowie, both *Transformer* and *Raw Power* were delivered with amplified vernacular inflections, respectively New York and Detroit accents. The two discs carried within them the sensibilities of Reed and Iggy's hometowns, distilling the milieu of Max's Kansas City and the Grande Ballroom. Unlike Reed's Velvet Underground recordings and The Stooges' two Elektra albums, the new records appeared less as authentic dispatches from the clubs and streets of Manhattan and the Motor City than as guides for the British tourist with a romantic investment in the mythology of American rock 'n' roll. If only in the case of *Transformer*, the process of distillation was also one of sanitization that made this New York version rather more appealing to those with a sensitive disposition who may have been disinclined to listen to the Velvets. *Disc*'s Ray Fox-Cumming loved the album; he thought it

> the best I've ever heard bar none . . . Great care has been taken never to offend . . . *Transformer* is a peep into a world that most of us would rather not experience first-hand, but it is presented with such humour and sympathy, without ever wallowing in the sadder aspects, that it's hugely enjoyable. A very stylish masterpiece.[130]

That was not what Richard Williams, Mick Farren, Nick Kent and others had found in the Velvet Underground's catalogue.

Iggy Pop and James Williamson began their stay in London at the Portobello Hotel, located in the heart of the Underground. They didn't renew their booking – Iggy felt the rooms were too cramped. Later he said he didn't like the English hippies who congregated in the area, just as he rejected Bowie's suggestion that local residents, the Edgar Broughton Band or Twink, back him and Williamson.[131] Furthermore, Iggy had checked out the West London competition, Third World War, and 'didn't think they were as forward looking as the Stooges already were'.[132] The pair moved on to the Royal Gardens Hotel, not so far away from the Portobello, situated next to Kensington Park, where they plotted their moves and Iggy got his Wild Thing jacket at nearby Kensington Market. Their next abode was a house in St John's Wood and from there to Seymour Walk, off the Fulham Road, where they were joined by the Asheton brothers and photographed by Mick Rock.

Looking back at his time in London, Iggy recalled the influence the places he stayed at, and the parks he walked through, had on his songwriting: 'Search and Destroy' was conceived as he paced around Kensington Park; 'I'm Sick of You' was inspired by the murphy bed he slept in at the Royal Gardens; 'I Gotta Right' was summoned up from the strolls around the St John's Wood cricket ground.[133] When not practising in the basement of the house in Seymour Walk, or partying, Iggy recalled spending his time traversing West London, mapping a psychogeography of the city out of his daily *dérive* that was less about chance encounters with characters and events than taking the opportunity, as he walked the city's pavements, to reimagine the sidewalks back home:

> England's very different to what I'm used to, very slowed down. I'm super-homesick for New York, Miami, or even Detroit. Y'know, the ocean, goin' to a movie late at night. It's not jus' cars and stuff, it's the feel. The feel over here's real weird.[134]

His own personal soundtrack to these perambulations was no doubt scored by British bands such as T. Rex (evident on 'Your Pretty Face Is Going to Hell' and 'Raw Power'), the Stones and early Led Zeppelin, but especially The Yardbirds' 'Happenings Ten Years Time Ago', which was pilfered for 'I'm Sick of You'. It was the band's earlier single, 'Heart Full of Soul', from 1965, which Iggy had particularly loved as a teenager and which, as he drifted through London, was refigured and then remastered as a glass shard of rock 'n' roll – 'Search and Destroy' featured a street-walking cheetah armed with a heartful of napalm. A figure capable of carrying with him the full weight of having to represent the Capitol's Thrill Kids and Fuck Girls.[135] For Iggy, as he told it to Mick Rock in 1972, London was a look-not-touch kind of place. He had noticed that there were 'a lotta nice girls in the audience' for the King's Cross gig, and he sees 'beautiful chicks walkin' around London, but I never seem to meet any'.[136]

As for Lou Reed's period in exile, Mick Rock reported that he was staying in Wimbledon, 'a smart suburb of London favoured by businessmen, film stars and respectable hoodlums, and hating it there. A man of shadows and cellar bars, a night-prowler, he needs the rootless, strung-out city for stimulation. Echoes of Baudelaire. A poet of pavements and splintered nerves.'[137] Reed spoke in similar terms to Iggy of his time in London in 1972, though a year later he now thought of the experience as something akin to a passing fad, the velvet suit, make-up and all: 'I only did three or four shows like that, and then it was back to leather. We were just kidding around.'[138] Maybe, but he was also putting air between himself and the whole glam scene. He was not prepared to live in Bowie's

shadow any more than Warhol's. He had not written a single
song while in London, he said to Michael Watts, as if the city
had done nothing but deplete him. Watts put it to Reed that
if he had worked on any new numbers they would not have
had a 'different perspective to what he composed in New
York'.[139] Reed agreed, but also pointed out that 'elements of
life found in New York also existed in London' though he
'personally found things a little slow-paced there towards the
end of his stay'.[140] Reed was shrewd enough to know that
whatever currency he carried it had been minted in Manhattan,
and Europe's cities, Berlin as imagined on his next album,
were for him always just versions of one of New York's Five
Boroughs.

For himself, Iggy imagined America anew as he walked
around parts of London, and saw within his homeland a speed
and immediacy of life that hadn't previously registered with
him. In contrast, English rockers, like Ian Hunter, driving down
American streets found an allure that was at odds with the inten-
sified images of alienation The Stooges mustered on *Raw Power*.
In Los Angeles, promoting *All the Young Dudes*, Hunter mused:
'So here I am on poetic Hollywood and Vine. How the hell can
you write about the corner of Wardour and Old Compton? The
people who named British cities, towns and streets want a kick
up the arse . . . "I left my heart . . . in Watford", etc.'[141] Under-
mining such romanticism, visitors to Hollywood learn there is
nothing much there beyond a set of road intersections. What
gives the street names resonance is the idea of the Golden Age
of the movies and its glamorous stars. It was that myth to which
Hunter responded when he imagined America. He was doing
much the same as every British rock 'n' roller from Vince 'Brand

New Cadillac' Taylor on down. As an actual place, Hollywood was about as interesting as Shepperton and a lot less fascinating than Soho's street corners.

The fantasy could be bought at Paradise Garage, which sold, for the first time in Britain, vintage American denim jeans and jackets. Parked outside the shop was the owner's yellow Mustang car customized with tiger stripes and carrying the licence plate 'FOK5D'. Teddy Boy regalia was later vended out of the same space at 430 King's Road, renamed Let It Rock, by Malcolm McLaren. Elsewhere on the King's Road, The Emperor of Wyoming sold cowboy gear and Granny Takes a Trip signified its fealty to American iconography in one of its many store front designs and in its line of clobber, like the Nudie-inspired black velvet bolero jacket and trousers, with beaded and appliqued rose design down the arms and legs, as worn by Lou Reed and, with their own individual trimmings, by Marc Bolan and Al Kooper. Then there was Tommy Roberts' Disney T-shirts and prints and the Pop-art stage sets and window displays used in his Mr Freedom store in Kensington; or the oversized Warholian sardine cans and baked bean tins used to display goods in Biba's food hall.

Post-Carnaby Street, after the Victoriana of a psychedelicized Underground, West London reimagined itself in fashion magazine spreads as a kind of arcade filled with 1950s Americana, a whirling kaleidoscope of coke bottles, cheese burgers, pinball machines, cars that looked like rockets, punk hoodlums astride m'cycles aping Brando and Dean (as filtered through the yearning fantasies of Kenneth Anger), Marilyn Monroe ever present, and bootlace ties and fluorescent socks. And always, there was rock 'n' roll on the jukebox.

The legendary phantom of Rock Lou Reed in concert

Sept 24 Apollo Centre, Glasgow
     25 Palace Theatre, Manchester
     26 The Gaumont, Southampton
     27 De Montfort Hall, Leicester
     28 Empire Theatre, Liverpool
     29 City Hall, Sheffield
     30 City Hall, Newcastle
Oct   3 The Odeon, Birmingham
     5/6 Rainbow Theatre London

On record

Transformer LSP 4807   LOU REED SF 8281
PK 2095 P8S 2095

Watch for his "BERLIN" new album   HS 1002

A haunting: Lou Reed in a Granny Takes a Trip velvet suit.

In June 1973, Nick Kent was still not entirely convinced by
Lou Reed's solo material, but if *Transformer* made listeners go
back and check out the Velvet's catalogue then all to the good
and, in the meantime, it made 'exquisite muzak for King's Road
boutiques'.[142] Back in the first decade of the twenty-first century,
Adam Ant's guitar-slinger extraordinaire, Marco Pirroni, curated
a trio of compact disc compilations that featured the music
you might have heard, alongside 'Walk on the Wild Side', as you
wandered about Biba, dropped in at Granny Takes a Trip and
leaned on the jukebox in 430 King's Road. *Biba: Champagne
and Novocaine* is a collection of mostly contemporary music:
'Make Up' by Lou Reed, as if to prove Kent's observation, and
tunes by Roxy Music, Bowie, Cockney Rebel and the New York
Dolls. Older sounds are also in the mix, with Hoagy Carmichael,
Marilyn Monroe and Edith Piaf, and Tiny Tim and Dr Buzzard's
Original Savannah Band linking the present with the past.
Granny Takes a Trip: Conversation's Dead, Man, has a more
eclectic assortment of styles: the blues, pre-war and postwar,
some soul, a Velvet Underground track – 'Venus in Furs' – The
Byrds' '8 Miles High' and The Ethiopians' 'Train to Skaville';
its nostalgia much less arch or camp than that found on the
Biba set. *Sex: Too Fast to Live Too Young to Die*, the more
popular spins on McLaren's jukebox, is, in contrast to the other
two CDs, a panoply of cultish rock delights: The Creation, Count
Five, Vince Taylor, Flamin' Groovies, Alice Cooper, The Sonics
and Screaming Lord Sutch. But no Lou Reed, McLaren no doubt
deeming him too obvious, too chic, not at all seditious, even if
he did wear a Let It Rock T-shirt; and there is no Iggy Pop either.

Sixteen months or so after The Stooges' King's Cross gig,
Nick Kent was asked for his view of the coming year, 1974.

Typically, he evoked the idea of the Punk Messiah's teenage followers overrunning the wasteland: 'hordes of deranged mutant-youth' springing up 'from the suburbs primed on Iggy Pop and wearing Keith Richards death-head face-masks to assassinate John Denver, James Taylor and Carly'.[143] Iggy never did find that delinquent audience, the one he must have fantasized about after he attended one of the T. Rex Wembley shows in March 1972, the one Lou Reed said The Who had earlier found, but Kent's image of malevolent youth in face masks had been playing out across the nation's cinema screens in Stanley Kubrick's *A Clockwork Orange*.[144]

4

KILL ALL YOUR DARLINGS: DAVID BOWIE RUNNING WITH THE THRILL KIDS AND FUCK GIRLS

The four of us were dressed in the height of fashion, which in those days was a pair of black very tight tights with the old jelly mould, as we call it, fitting on the crutch underneath the tights, this being to protect and also a sort of design you could viddy clear enough in a certain light, so that I had one in the shape of a spider . . . Then we wore waisty jackets without lapels but with these very big built-up shoulders ('pletchoes' we called them) which were a kind of mockery of having real shoulders like that. Then, my brothers, we had these off-white cravats, which looked like whipped-up kartoffel or spud with a sort of a design made on it with a fork. We wore our hair not too long and we had flip horrorshow boots for kicking.[1]

Alex, A Clockwork Orange (1962)

In 1971, Keith Richards gestured towards the appeal the violent pose held to those enthralled by rock 'n' roll:

I was just into Little Richard. I was rockin' away, avoidin' the bicycle chains and the razors in those dance halls. The English get crazy. They're calm, but they were really violent then, those cats. Those suits cost them £150, which is a lot of money. Jackets down to here. Waistcoats.

Leopardskin lapels ... amazing. It was really 'Don't step
on mah blue suede shoes.' It was down to that.[2]

Richards was making a connection between music, violence
and fashion: an association with a long history and one that
he had helped write the Stones into. *A Clockwork Orange* had
funnelled a similar set of references to those he listed and, in
turn, the Stones also burrowed into Anthony Burgess's version.
Describing the bond that existed between himself, Jagger and
Andrew Loog Oldham, Richards said: 'There was a time when
Mick and I got on really well with Andrew. We went through
the whole *Clockwork Orange* thing. We went through that
whole trip together. Very sort of butch number. Ridin' around
with that mad criminal chauffeur of his.'[3]

The idea of the Stones as droogies had been propagated
by Oldham as early as 1965, three years after the publication
of the novel, when he used Nadsat, Burgess's confected teenage
argot, in his liner notes for the band's second album, imploring
any fan, without the necessary loot to purchase said disc, to
rob a blind man and give him the boot just for the kicks.[4]
Oldham even tried to obtain the film rights to the novel, but
Burgess had already sold them on. His attention then turned
to an adaptation of Dave Wallis's *Only Lovers Left Alive*, but
that also went undeveloped.[5] Even without such film roles,
the Rolling Stones more than successfully claimed the space
previously held by first-generation rockers who had used styl-
ized violence and an aura of menace to attract an audience of
teenage mutineers.

As 1971 evolved into 1972, those who cared for the heat
and danger of rock 'n' roll used Stanley Kubrick's just-released

adaptation of Burgess's novel as a touchstone and flashpoint for their imagined teenage rampage. Kubrick's view of British youth was formed not only by Burgess's vision of 1950s British street gangs with affected American accents but the more recent cults of Mods and Rockers, bikers and Suedeheads. He was also looking ahead at what the near future might hold for the next cycle of hoodlum cultures, as others were doing.

A photospread accompanying a story on teenage cults in a 1971 edition of *Men Only* magazine featured a young couple listlessly hanging out on Brighton beach. She's dressed in silver stiletto-heeled shoes, slim-hipped in tight green satin trousers and a blue cord jacket covered in embroidered patches. He is wearing black boots, straight-legged leopard-print strides and, in some pictures, a studded leather biker jacket or, in others, a satin bomber with an image of a tiger on the back. Both are worn over a white T-shirt, reproduced on which are a pair of cartoon braces that frame the word 'SKINHEAD'. His hair isn't cropped, though; he wears it long and greasy and pulled back behind the ears in an exaggerated rocker style. His hairstyle will be echoed a year later by Bryan Ferry on the inside cover of the first Roxy Music album (circa 1973, Roxy's Andy Mackay and Chris Spedding also combed their hair just so), and in his silver pants and plastic and faux-animal fur jacket with the leopard's head, Iggy Pop looked every bit like a running mate of these two Thrill Kids.[6]

The boy and the girl are at the cutting edge of early 1970s teenage fashion, all satin 'n' grease 'n' leather, but they are featured as part of a fantasy with a 1989 August bank holiday setting: eighteen years on from the now of the photographs. The story used an imagined Shock! Sensation!! headline from the *Daily Mirror*: 'FUCK GIRLS HIJACK 80'. Men numbering fourscore have been 'raped' by 'fuck girls' who pounced on them as they lay on the 'uncomfortable shingle' of Brighton beach 'wanting nothing more than to soak up the sun'.[7] After the cultism of the Teddy Boys, Mods and Rockers, hippies and skinheads, following the revolution of Women's Lib, the Fuck Girls are the new teenage commotion – the 'Iron Maidens who preached sexual aggression rather than equality through liberalisation'.[8] They are the future teen fad enabled and given shape by an ever more permissive society. Before them, in 1975, the Thrill Kids had been the rage. Their cry had been 'outrage the bourgeoisie'.[9] They snubbed conformity, 'an ageless prerequisite of the young, inconveniencing their elders who'd had their youth in the traumatic Sixties and Seventies'.[10]

The fantasy of the Thrill Kids and Fuck Girls is a replay of the media's moral panic over the day's youth movements that was given a particularly prurient spin for the readers of a soft porn magazine. What tied all the cults together – past and future – was 'sexual depravity, strongly linked with a death wish'.[11] In 1972, as Bowie took hold of the pop imaginary, pushing ahead of Alice Cooper and T. Rex while dragging Lou Reed, Mott the Hoople and Iggy and the Stooges along with him, his rock 'n' roll messiah, Ziggy Stardust, confirmed third-generation rock as violent under the glamour and promiscuous in attitude. Bowie's rise would be a giddy ride fuelled on the fantasy of a teenage wasteland overrun by Thrill Kids and Fuck Girls. It was a speed trip in which he was being ably abetted by critics looking for similar kicks.

In January 1972, Jaynie (no surname given) reported for *IT* on a T. Rex concert that had left her, after she had gone face to face with the new teenage monsters, 'horrified':

> A frightening audience of 11–17 year old crop-heads, complete with mini-skirts, braces and chewing gum. The females of the species bopped together on the dance floor and the males wandered around in gangs eyeing them up. The rest of the audience consisted of 30-ish greaseys with thin ties, grey suits, chiselled faces and oily hair. Wouldn't wish that crowd on anyone.[12]

The audience, she wrote, got what they wanted, which was Bolan. The Underground 'idealism left from the "good old days"' of Tyrannosaurus Rex had vanished and was now replaced with his 'self-adoration':

> Marc, wearing a silver lamé jacket and glitter on his cheeks, flaunted himself outrageously, tempting the chickies to hysteria by leaning 'sensually' to within inches of their frantic fingers. He had a potential riot force under his control and could have used it to direct them into something worthwhile – make them THINK.[13]

If the fans were incapable of thinking for themselves then the new generation of rock critics would do that work for them. For many of these scribes, David Bowie's *Ziggy Stardust*, whatever else it might be, was a conscious reflection of the relationship between star and fan of the kind Jaynie had witnessed at the T. Rex show. 'Sometime between *Hunky Dory* and *Ziggy Stardust* David Bowie decided to be a star,' wrote Simon Frith in his end-of-year appreciation of the latter album. 'Bowie's stardom isn't a means to fame and fortune, it's the end itself,' he wrote.[14]

Previewing the January 1972 Lanchester Arts Festival (LAF), *NME*'s Tony Stewart made a curious comparison of featured performers Roland Kirk and David Bowie; they were from different worlds, he admitted, but both are musically brilliant and delightfully whimsical.[15] On the previous page, Danny Holloway had given *Hunky Dory* a rave review and then on the page adjacent to the LAF preview he wrote up his visit to Bowie's home in Beckenham where he listened to tapes of *The Rise and Fall of Ziggy Stardust* with the singer, who had recently lopped off his 'Lauren Bacall' locks and now had cropped red hair.[16] Three pages featuring Bowie, on each one a different version.

With Holloway, Bowie talked over the controversy around wearing dresses, which he shrugged off: 'I'm still very much a teenager. I go through all sorts of fads.'[17] Immediate plans included a few select dates using the same band that had appeared on the just-released album. But now he was intending to 'rock on stage' like The Who, only well-rehearsed. Comparisons with the theatrics of Alice Cooper were to be avoided. Holloway thought he would become an international star but when he asked Bowie if he is likely to become a cult figure, 'his only reply was: what kind of cult would I develop? Gay lib? Spaced-out queen?'[18] The piece is illustrated with a shot from the 'Starman' promo session; the new image is being pushed hard. Big times lay ahead, but first he was scheduled to play the Fox at The Toby Jug, a pub venue in Tolworth, Surrey.

The Spectator's pop columnist, Duncan Fallowell, penned a critique of *Ziggy Stardust* and his report on the climax of the tour started by asking if the 'world was ready for the rock review as art?'[19] If others were ill-prepared for rock as a form of burlesque – staged at Margate's Dreamland with a teenage wasteland for a backdrop – Fallowell thought Bowie was not only primed but ahead of the curve:

> He has created a drama and a style, plotted by his *Ziggy Stardust* album, then cast himself in the leading role. It is no longer merely a stage act, it is true. David Bowie *becomes* Ziggy Stardust, the dreamland rock star, a natural Mae Presley for the eighties. Hence the songs are not poses but poignant, sometimes desperate, statements about living in a lurid wasteland where fantasy and reality are indistinguishable. All the horror and beauty of it are trapped in a sequence of brilliant tracks fusing myth and life. Bowie could well be our first genuinely mixed-media personality, which may give him more problems than he realises.[20]

And he'll be bigger than Bolan to boot, he wrote, 'certainly more durable, because his mind is more interesting and the quality of his music from haunted ballads to hard rock 'n' roll is immeasurably richer'.[21]

Simon Frith had thought *Ziggy Stardust* was 'the most moving statement of the rock star mythology since Nik Cohn's *I Am Still the Greatest Says Johnny Angelo*. Bowie like Johnny Angelo is a fan-tasy.'[22] Nick Kent had also made a link to *Johnny Angelo* in his review of the album for *Oz*.[23] It was somewhat inevitable then that the most significant critic of the second-generation rock era would interview Bowie. Cohn began his autumn 1972 piece for *Harpers & Queen* by discussing the infantilization of the pop audience now dominated by 'puberts' – eight- to fourteen-year-olds. Bowie's success rested, he wrote, on the 'pubertal avant-garde' for whom he is a figurehead.[24] With his half-starved physique, make-up, dyed hair, bisexuality, his songs about junkies, queens, Warhol, alien invaders and rock 'n' roll suicide, he would seem to be poorly aligned to be the 'kindergarten messiah', however,

> What he is doing, in essence, is dressing up at being naughty, thumbing his nose at teacher. He isn't dangerous but he's brazen and provoking, and it's precisely this pride in his own peccadillo that gives him his force. Every tic and twitch of his psyche is transposed in gloating detail: no dare is refused.[25]

Cohn thinks him talented but not the genius the trade press is calling him; nothing he has done has yet matched the marvellous 'Space Oddity'. 'He's good at mood,' he wrote, 'but his melodies are predictable and his lyrics, much vaunted, slip slackly from instant message to instant dream to instant bitch. By far the best of him is his presence, his physical style.'[26] The two meet for tea at the Ritz, but Bowie in full 'schlap and tat' is refused service so they convene elsewhere. Cohn finds Bowie beautiful, seemingly bright and potentially funny but like most rock performers inhibited by the thought of interviews, so 'nothing new was said.'[27] Bowie can't explain his appeal, he just wants to be a star:

Not a Superstar or a Rock star or any kind of star in particular; just a star, period.

And what was a star? He didn't know, he couldn't define it, but he could recognise it by instinct. Then he paused, looked coy; 'a star is me,' he said, fluttering his lashes, and suddenly it was.[28]

Cohn doesn't say whether they talked about his novel *Johnny Angelo*, but it is difficult to imagine him or Bowie not registering with each other the similarities between novel and album as others had done, though it was far from a required reference point. In an essay for *Cream* on Bowie's career to date and the just-released *Ziggy Stardust* album, Ian MacDonald ignored or missed the Cohn–Bowie connection and instead drew attention to the emergence of a critical consensus over a conceptual link between The Who's *Tommy* and *Ziggy Stardust*. Though both albums featured (as did Cohn's novel) messiah-like figures who are first embraced and then violently rejected by their followers, against the grain, MacDonald argued that the similarities were superficial. The significant difference, he noted, was that the point of view was fixed in *Tommy* whereas in *Ziggy* positions were constantly changing, switching from first to second to third person. In Bowie's version the star and fan are folded into one another. It is uncertain whose arms are outstretched and who is watching who as Bowie constructs an image of co-dependency built on the idea of star and fan each desiring the desire of the other. The album's narrative (if such it can be called) similarly switched back and forth in time. MacDonald claimed it was fragmented, inconclusive, where *Tommy* was coherent and certain of its message. Essentially, he contended, Townshend and Bowie thought differently about their fans (or in the latter's case the audience he sought in his pursuit of stardom).

Bowie aimed, MacDonald wrote, for an audience in their late teens and early twenties, a 'suburban middle-class lost generation, Home Counties variety'.[29] It was Bowie's knack of addressing *and* identifying with this audience, expressed through a shared sense of alienation, that made him such a compelling artist. His recent work, he thought, was 'an extreme statement of alienation, and the move most likely to widen the gap between parents and children since "My Generation"'.[30]

If *Tommy* was something of a ready-made touchstone used in order to place *Ziggy Stardust* into a now familiar context of the concept album, rather than the new implied in the idea of Ziggy as a rock revue that Fallowell had proposed, and if *Johnny Apollo* was too esoteric for most fans (if not critics), a more immediately discernible influence on Bowie, one he was happy to not only acknowledge but actively promote, was Stanley Kubrick's *A Clockwork Orange*. The film's January 1972 London opening at Warner West End, Leicester Square, was widely advertised in the Underground press, the film's distributors clearly conceiving of the papers' readership as a key audience for the film: 'It's based on the novel by Anthony Burgess and stars Malcolm McDowell; he's a young tough into rape, ultra-violence and Beethoven' ran one tag line.[31] Whether or not the film resonated with post-school and undergraduate audiences, its influence on Bowie was present right from the get-go.

As it comes down to us today, Michael Watts's January 1972 interview with Bowie, 'rock's swishiest outrage', is all about the revelation, orchestrated or not, of the singer's bisexuality.

The piece, however, was neither essentially focused on this aspect nor entirely took his confession at face value. It had ended on a caveat not to 'dismiss David Bowie as a serious musician just because he likes to put us all on a little'.[32] Watts also highlighted the fact that Bowie had recently become a father and the impact he felt. Bowie said that his child will have to face new challenges as he grows up, he will become 'a new kind of person in a way', who, as part of a 'media saturated generation', will be lost, by age twelve, to his parents.[33] Watts summarized: 'That's exactly the sort of technological vision that Stanley Kubrick foresees for the near future in *A Clockwork Orange*. Strong stuff. And a long, long way away from campy carry-ons.'[34]

The Guardian's review of Bowie's Festival Hall show in July described him as being dressed like a 'Harlequin meets *Star Trek* ... he has a painted white face, a haircut from *Clockwork Orange* and moves like a marionette.'[35] Six months later Charles Shaar Murray was repeating the *Star Trek–Clockwork Orange* contraction in his NME report on Bowie's U.S. tour.[36] After rejecting *Tommy* as an adequate reference point, Ian MacDonald was more comfortable with the ready-made connection between Bowie and Kubrick, though he didn't take it too seriously:

On one level, *Ziggy Stardust* is a blueprint for the moonage youth culture that would theoretically extend between now and the world/time of *A Clockwork Orange*. Those who found Kubrick's film shallow and evasive need have no apprehensions about Bowie's use of it as a book-end; songs like 'Five Years' and 'Rock 'n' Roll Suicide' evade nothing, and 'Moonage Daydream' and 'Star' are exhilaratingly tangible as backdrops for the speculative fiction of the Spiders from Mars. And, although *Clockwork Orange* throwaways come up here and there, they serve only as distant trig-points in the main map.[37]

Bowie's lyrical and costume references to *A Clockwork Orange*, the use of the film's soundtrack as the herald for his imminent arrival on stage, the imitation of the droogs' vacant stare in the close-up photographic portraits of Bowie, Ronson, Woodmansey and Bolder on *Ziggy Stardust*'s inner sleeve – these were all indices for the idea of youth, points of assembly and identification with his audience, which Bowie intended to fully exploit.

Explaining to *The Guardian*'s readership the phenomenon that Bowie had become between the release of the album and the year's end, Martin Walker, like others, latched onto the star's self-avowed bisexuality and how, for a Manchester gig, he had drawn to him a 'parade of queens to celebrate the crown prince of Glam Rock'.[38] But, he continued, 'Bowie's audience is wider than that, so much wider that he and the Glam Rock movement have become a sociological phenomenon of major significance for those who still use the flagging phrase, "the Youth Movement".'[39] Why this mattered, he argued, was the idea that Glam was bringing back to music a shared culture.

Once there had been a 'youth coalition' for pop music but it had split even within certain classes such as that represented by students, some listening to 'country rock' by The Band or James Taylor, while others preferred a 'cerebral, electronic moon-rock' played by Pink Floyd. Other groups of youths such as skinheads and 'young blacks pushed their own reggae sound'.

But Glam, he surmised, is fusing these groups back together with figures including Rod Stewart – 'bovver-boy hair and high heels, the new Flash Harry'.⁴⁰ Marc Bolan, who 'upped and out of the underground', now has his 'face silk-screened on to pillowcases as the teenyboppers heart throb'.⁴¹ What these two, and others, shared with Bowie was an appreciation of camp; the glamour of the 1950s filtered the image of today's super-star who offered 'exotic cheap thrills'. Bowie 'knows them all, all the sectors of the culture. He used to be a mod in the early sixties, flashing around South London like Marc Bolan, all the new clothes and the dancing alone. You had to be cool in those days.'⁴² But Walker's new coalition of students, skinheads and Black youth was fanciful, as Pete Fowler pointed out in his seminal 1972 essay 'Skins Rule'.⁴³ Walker thought that in Bowie's play with fantasy and reality – starmen and soldiers fighting in Belfast – he was proposing a rapprochement between youth's factions, but his act was *about* those divisions; the drama of *Ziggy Stardust* took place in the space between reality and fantasy. Third-generation rock was defined by the frag-mentation of the audience.

What was certain was that, at age 25 in 1972, Bowie, along-side Marc Bolan and Rod 'The Mod' Stewart, had a history that placed him in an earlier tranche of the baby boomers. The new stars of third-generation rock were not teenagers, however much they fixated on youth, wrote for a teenage audience and self-identified as teenagers. In the summer of 1974, while holed-up in a New York hotel room, Bowie and Bolan amused themselves by repeatedly screening *A Clockwork Orange* – 'it reminded us of our childhoods,' said Bolan, who was born in 1947.⁴⁴ Looking back from the viewpoint of 2002,

Bowie said that 'you have to kill your elders . . . We had to develop a completely new vocabulary . . . The idea was taking the recent past and re-structuring it in a way that we felt we had authorship of. My key "in" was things like *Clockwork Orange*: that was our world, not the bloody hippy thing.'[45] Even if he had never considered himself to be a hippie, like Marc Bolan had, Bowie's rejection of that identity would have bewildered those who witnessed his Glastonbury set in 1971. Bowie was rewriting his biography, and in 1972 he had said 'his music is for the *Clockwork Orange* generation'.[46] It was his audience of teenagers that owned the film, he was just riffing on it.

Covering a Roxy Music tour of the provinces in spring 1973, Bob Edmands described the audience at the Guild Hall in Preston as mostly consisting of long-haired students untouched by King's Road glamour, their 'drabness' enlivened only a little by the presence of 'three girls in Clockwork Orange bowlers and braces, all of them eleven if they're a day'.[47] As master of ceremonies of his rock revue, Bowie sought to channel these teenagers' frustrations, their sense of alienation, their potential for violence, their un-curtailed energy and make it the subject of his show.

In preparing Mick Ronson, drummer Woody Woodmansey and bass player Trevor Bolder for their parts as Spiders from Mars, Bowie took them to see Kubrick's film, which had been the inspiration behind his and Freddie Burretti's costume designs for the coming tour.[48] When Cohn interviewed Bowie he found him to be brazen and provoking, 'positively flighty', but not at all dangerous.[49] Bowie looked to change that perception, he was out to create the effect that he had so keenly felt in the stance and performances of the first-generation rockers, subsequently reasserted by the Stones and The Who. In a 1964 NME interview with the latter, the reporter noted 'there's a sort of vicious strangeness about these four beatsters from Shepherd's Bush.'[50] A little over ten years later, the NME's Max Bell, writing a piece for *Club International* on the current state of the rock scene, laid out, once again, the idea that popular music had fragmented post-*Sgt. Pepper's* but, he added, that there had always been the continuity of two 'inspirational factors … sex and violence – in no particular order'.[51] With *Ziggy Stardust* and *Aladdin Sane*, Bowie worked those two factors as hard as he was able in order to produce his own kind of vicious strangeness.

The overt and implied references that Bowie made to Kubrick's movie were part of a strategy to find and exploit common ground with his fan base of fifteen-year-olds born in 1957. Among them were the kind of kids who over-identified with McDowell's character Alex and his droogies. Their mid-teen fantasies of casual sex and ultra-violence were played out, much like Bowie did with Ziggy, as a performance of style and attitude: dressing up in a white boiler suit, Doc Martens and a bowler hat (nicked from their school's drama department). Trevor Hoyle captured this aspect of the allure of *A Clockwork Orange* in his novel of disaffected youth, *Rule of Night* (1975). It's the story of a group of working-class council-estate kids who lurch from one unskilled job to another. In between their moments of fitful employment, Hoyle plots their endless drifting around Rochdale and excursions to Manchester and Luton, watching them getting drunk and blocked between the chance encounters that give vent, in spasms of gratuitous violence, to their balled-up anger. At a Rochdale–Blackburn game a group of interlopers are spotted:

Five lads were coming along the cindery dirt path towards them, walking in single file. Their heads were shorn and their trouser-bottoms ended just below the knee, leaving several inches of sock exposed; they wore scarves in their belts, which Kenny recognised as Bury colours; Bury were playing Swansea at home, so why they should be here he couldn't fathom – unless they'd been barred.

The one in front wore a bowler hat several sizes too small for him and had make-up on his eyes. Kenny thought: Another bunch of yobboes been to see *Clockwork Orange*.[52]

Inevitably a fight ensues, fictional worlds colliding with the real one.

Bowie filtered the violence in such teenage rituals and projected back to his audience of juvenile delinquent wrecks their own particular assertion of selfhood. Earlier in the novel, before the Bury droogs kicked merry hell out of Kenny, Hoyle reproduces (or creates) a *Rochdale Observer* news story headlined 'Jealousy motive of *Clockwork Orange* attack', a report of proceedings at the town's juvenile court. Three fifteen-year-old boys were on trial for attacking another youth; 'The father of one boy said he had not noticed the vicious streak in his son before, and the father of the other boy said he could not understand this "Clockwork Orange-type thing".'[53] The public sphere, Bowie understood, was a highly mediated space where image and reality are inseparable. His Ziggy Stardust was no less of a refracted image of the contemporary and a manifestation of its reality than Kubrick's film.

American critic Ron Ross read Bowie's gestures towards teen violence as having a cautionary purpose:

> For all his glitter and loaded lubricity, Ziggy is a warning as clear as a red light, but after midnight, traffic signals are optional anyway. Such futuristic teen tunes as 'Moonage Daydream' and 'Hang On To Yourself' reduce sex, love and kicks to a merely mechanical expenditure of energy, dovetailing trendily with the violent fantasies of *A Clockwork Orange,* but it's all right. As a matter of fact, it's a gas.[54]

A song written immediately post-*Ziggy Stardust*, and considered for the follow-up *Aladdin Sane*, 'All the Young Dudes' was presented by Bowie to Mott the Hoople. It was a gesture seen as a gift from a fan to a band on the verge of dissolution. There is no doubt a deal of truth in that but it is also a case of Bowie using Mott to appropriate the aura of a gang that he felt a group like Ian Hunter's droogies exuded. The B-side to 'All the Young Dudes' was 'One of the Boys', and Hunter told the NME that 'David liked this a lot.'[55] It was a Mott original that celebrated male bonding and delinquent tendencies of the kind Bowie barely, if ever, conveyed in his songwriting. But it was now one he was busy reflecting in his self-made hall of crazy mirrors that was Ziggy Stardust.

Around the release of Mott's third album and during a tour they were undertaking of the States, Allen Levy, in the New York music and arts magazine *Changes*, in July 1971, wrote that he liked the band well enough but found their albums and identity to be all over the place. Live, however, they made total sense, especially after he had witnessed them win around an initially hostile audience:

> They played a loud brand of basic rock that got to the audience so that, for a while, it forgot that masturba-tory surliness that has become the mark of New York rock. At one point, Ian jumped into the audience and offered the mike to anyone who would sing with him the 'Shake it, baby, shake' riff from 'Whole Lotta Shakin' ... there were few takers, but then one kid grabbed the mike and sang, a trifle off-key and a trifle behind the beat, but, what the hell, he was having fun and while he sang and imagined himself to be a rock 'n' roll star, it was nice to remember that one time, yes, rock had been a party.[56]

Mott the Hoople were accessible, touchable, knowable. The intimate relationship the band had with its audience was what Bowie wanted, but there was more to it than just that. Reflecting on Bowie's influence on his band, Mott's guitarist, Mick Ralph, said:

> I think Bowie realises that he never did basic rock 'n' roll very well, and that was part of the attraction to him in working with us ... He told us that we had a certain empathy with our audience which he liked, that we really were the old village hall rock group writ large, and that people seemed to be afraid of us because our image was merciless.[57]

An element of danger, of fear, must exist within an attraction if it is to be truly, delectably, desirable; whether found in a lover, a fairground ride, or a rock 'n' roll band. If a band is to produce any kind of frisson between itself and its audience there must be a sense of apprehension in the relationship: this mad love between fan and star was what Bowie wanted to generate with his Ziggy drama.

Some eighteen months or so after the release of 'All the Young Dudes', Ian Hunter looked back on that moment in time:

> I never asked Bowie why he took such an interest in us, but I was told by numerous sources that his image of us was that of Mott being the only true punk band ever in England, and that *Brain Capers* had turned him onto this. And I'd agree with those sentiments exactly, even though the word is over used. I mean, when I read Marc Bolan saying he's a street punk – y'know, don't make me laugh! But if that label was affixed to me, I'd go along with it because it's true.[58]

'All the Young Dudes' asked Hunter to assume the point of view of a teenage narrator *and* a rock 'n' roll star singing to that teen. Hunter was 33 years old when 'Dudes' was released as a single in July 1972 and still striving after stardom. When asked how old he was he'd say, 'I'm twelve years of age and I'll stay that way until I'm suddenly sixty-five.'[59] Hunter was perfect casting for a song that was an ode to the juvenile in one's older self. At the song's start the young protagonist recalls a night spent with Billy, full of amphetamine jive, who rapped on about killing himself and the pointlessness of living beyond the age of 25. The song then introduces Wendy, who's been caught shoplifting from Marks & Spencer, and Freddie, who has a bad case of acne, before turning to a TV presenter who is freaking out over juvenile delinquents. But, when you've got T. Rex and you're a dude, who cares anyway?

The term 'dude' had little or no currency among Bowie's home audience in 1972; it was not a part of their appropriated American argot, yet he used it for his very British teenager to emphatically self-categorize. Beyond any novelty value, the old masquerading as the new, the colloquialism helped to avoid an unwanted identification with one or another of the day's youth cultures, yet still suggested an ideal male camaraderie – the us against them of teen fantasy. Bowie's use of 'dude' carried that breadth of meaning and it also worked phonetically as a substitute for droog, which would have chimed with any fifteen-year-old. 'All the Young Droogs' slips the emphasis away from the stars on Freddie's face and sweet cross-dressing Lucy, who had a kick like a mule, and pushes the song towards unalloyed images of masculine ultra-violence. Using 'dude' instead of 'droog' kept Bowie in the picture, and the threat of becoming lost behind Malcolm McDowell's leery smile was avoided, excluding the possibility of the song being forever tied to its moment through Burgess and Kubrick.

What mattered to Bowie was the effectiveness of the image of youthful alienation, Mott's 'mercilessness', figured as third-generation rock posturing, that he built into 'All the Young Dudes': estrangement from the TV presenter, from those over the age of 25 (with their Beatles and Stones and all their second-generation revolution stuff) and disaffection with their more immediate urban situation. Bowie was not simply amassing cross-cultural reference points, he was using them. In this matrix, *A Clockwork Orange* served, as MacDonald suggested, not as the whole picture but as one of the many distant trig-points on the main map that was *Ziggy Stardust*.

When demoing 'All the Young Dudes', Bowie had sung the verses, assuming the point of view of the dude, and Hunter had taken the chorus, assuming the role of the rock star. In the finished version Hunter took both parts. In the song's coda he is the rock star calling to his audience even as he addressed an individual – I want *you*. I want to relate to *you*. He directed the friends of the guy with the glasses to bring him to the front: 'I want him right here,' he commanded. Like 'Rock 'n' Roll Suicide', 'All the Young Dudes' suggested the bogus promise of intimacy between star and fan: give me your hands, turn on with me, you're not alone and you are wonderful – was how Bowie played it out on the final track of *Ziggy Stardust*, and Hunter did something similar but not the same with 'Dudes'. Rather than fade out at the end, Mott's main man finished his appeal on a note of ambiguity, asking 'how'd it feel?' But to feel what? To be singled out for the star's attention? To carry the news? To be a star? To be a dude? Whatever the answer sought, the question broke the spell of the star's messiah-like hold over his audience; it brought doubt, fear even, into the equation.

In a sprawling and confused conversation with William Burroughs on the genesis and the concept of Ziggy Stardust, Bowie, wearing *A Clockwork Orange* T-shirt, explained the story dealt with the idea that the 'older people have lost touch with reality and the kids are left on their own to plunder anything'.[60] But their acts of ransacking, he seemed to say, leaves them with precisely nothing, and so there is no news for Ziggy to communicate. This is what '"All the Young Dudes" was about', Bowie said; 'it is not a "hymn" to the youth as people thought. It is completely the opposite.'[61]

Writing in the wake of *Aladdin Sane* and the May 1973 Earl's Court concert, *Let It Rock*'s Dave Laing echoed the thought that Bowie communicated nothing much at all and then turned that idea against the star:

> take away Bowie's image, and there's nothing left. The image itself is dense with weird and wonderful things – myths of inner and outer space, intimations of bizarre sexuality – but somehow they never lead anywhere except down the hole in the centre of the record. It's partly because he's too knowing. He knows everything that has been said and every lick that made a top ten hit, but ends up communicating nothing.[62]

Debating with Laing, Simon Frith countered that rock purists missed the point, the most obvious of which was that rock had always been about business, glamour and entertainment, not even Bob Dylan was immune. That Bowie makes this the topic of his art does not therefore make him a lesser artist:

> *Ziggy Stardust* is the loving creation of a genuine rock addict and the purpose of the Bowie show isn't to give pop a falsely glamourous glow but to point up the reality of the continuing star/audience relationship. Since 1967 and peace and love, rock has been about faking a community, as if Jimmy Page, by being scruffy, became a man of the people. But smoking dope together

in a field doesn't turn an audience into a society and it's this pretence that Bowie rips apart.[63]

In his *Creem* column, Simon Frith added that *Ziggy Stardust* is 'not really about being a rock star, it's about being a rock fan', which was about the sharing of secrets.[64] The first of these was that under the glitter, Bowie, like all fans, was truly a provincial. The clues to unravelling the mysteries of this suburbanite were all there on the album, 'right down to the message to Marc Bolan' that he was yesterday's man.[65]

The Rise and Fall of Ziggy Stardust and the Spiders from Mars had a marked English accent and appropriate settings that ranged from Heddon Street, W1 – under the K. West sign – onward across Shaftsbury Avenue and up Wardour Street to the Marquee, where a band rips out 'Round and Round'. All this before a Monday-morning coming down, and the first train back to the suburbs, Hemel Hempstead perhaps. Passing through the market square, minding the milk floats on the way home and, over a rushed breakfast, reading yesterday's copy of the *News of the World* with its stories of events in the Falls Road in Belfast and the economic melt-down after the postwar promises of Nye Bevan's welfare state. In contrast to the suburban humdrum, even if leavened by a weekend's cosmic crazy jive, Bowie's next album, *Aladdin Sane*, was decidedly American in its location and pronunciation: from New York to Los Angeles with Detroit in between. Bowie told Charles Shaar Murray the album had been written in the States: 'The numbers were not supposed to form a concept album, but looking back on them there seems to be definite linkage from number to number. There's no order; they were written in various cities.'[66]

In the New World, Bowie did the Tiger Rag with Shakey, got Hollywood high while watching video films at the drive-in, hung out with all the ravers in the Motor City, sedated himself downtown-style on quaaludes with Billy Doll or got smacked up on snow white with the Rev. Alabaster. All much more sexy than crashing in the Grove with the Pink Fairies on mandrax. In this mythical America, Bowie dances at the New York disco, twisting and turning on the cut-throat slashes of Ronson's guitar. 'Watch That Man' aka 'Suffragette City Redux', the Bo Diddley-esque 'Panic in Detroit', the ravaged and wrecked 'Cracked Actor', the Iggy-inspired 'The Jean Genie', and 'Let's Spend the Night Together' – the Rolling Stones' petrol fumes sucked through the New York Dolls' carburettor – were all executed with a combined fury only hinted at on side two of its predecessor. The released torque in these songs suggested that Bowie and Ronson were capable of keeping pace with the Thrill Kids and Fuck Girls of the day, even if the album's other tracks, 'Time', 'The Prettiest Star' and 'Lady Grinning Soul', gestured towards alternative interests and distractions.

'The Jean Genie' was as much a Mod anthem as any John's Children's 45, smashed and blocked, but it was not anywhere near as parochial – Leatherhead suburban so to speak. Like Nik Cohn, who had substituted the Goldhawk Road for Brooklyn and put Shepherd's Bush Mod colloquialisms into the mouths of the dancers in *Saturday Night Fever*, Bowie's subject is transatlantic: a continuation of that dialogue between Britain and America that had found new life with The Beatles and the Stones and was now jabbering on in his rapport with Iggy Pop and

Lou Reed. Like a thousand American garage bands before them, The Stooges revered The Yardbirds' 'I'm a Man'. This very English, Marquee-honed vamp, a psychotic reaction to the Chicago blues of Willie Dixon, Muddy Waters and, most of all, Bo Diddley, that rushed like a fumbling adolescent to its jerky climax, cast a spell so wide and deep it can be felt on most every track across all three of The Stooges' albums. With his love letter to Iggy, 'The Jean Genie', Bowie paid homage to the power source The Stooges derived their energy and inspiration from, barely deviating from its template. He was taking on the heat and the flash of The Yardbirds while showing Iggy and Williamson that he, too, could walk their razor's edge.

After *Aladdin Sane*, which fully established Bowie as a rock star rather than one who, prior to the release of *Ziggy*, had existed only in his imagination, the idea of the pop messiah

Hoodlum razor boys: David Bowie and his Spiders.

delivering to his fans the news, empty of meaning beyond the McLuhanite idea of the medium is the message, took the form of *Pinups*, a covers album of 1960s singles by the likes of The Who, The Yardbirds, The Kinks and The Pretty Things. Speaking to Charles Shaar Murray during the album's production, Bowie said: 'The future is very open-ended, actually . . . I can't tell you much about what I'm doing because I'm not really too sure yet. There's not much to add to what you already know.'[67] Continuing with the idea that he had no new news to impart meant that the context for *Pinups* was left to the critics to explain. It was poorly received, especially by those who had stood beside Bowie watching Pink Floyd at the Marquee in 1966 or had, at the time, bought a copy of 'See Emily Play'.

Ian MacDonald began his NME review by approving of Bowie's tacitly made claim that the golden age of rock had run from circa 1964 to 1967, 'when the acts who are on top of the pile today were laying the foundations of their careers, and before the university circuit had killed off the London club scene'.[68] But he thought that whatever aspirations Bowie had for this album were lost by his overly casual approach to the project, which had been hampered by playing to the rules of 1973 rather than 1963. With The Who's 'I Can't Explain' it was a case of 'amphetamine '65 to mandrax '73'.[69] If this track was unlistenable, as MacDonald thought, others were simply pointless ('who needs another "Rosalyn"?'), but Ray Davis's 'Where Have All the Good Times Gone' at least suggested how 'incredible the whole album might have been if it had been approached less casually'.[70]

Having attended the recording sessions, Murray thought *Pinups* would be a fun record, an 'affectionate look back at the rock of the '60s'. However, by the time he reviewed the album for *Oz*, he was basically in MacDonald's camp of thinking it was a failed experiment. At best, it had ended up as a 'charming piece of nostalgic self-indulgence': redundant for those who were there first time around but at least having some novelty value for those too young to have played witnesses to the halcyon days of rock, which would be those fifteen-year-old Thrill Kids that Bowie courted.[71] If Bowie was only aiming for the bittersweet taste of nostalgia, *Pinups* was by anyone's reckoning a failure, but that misreads its intent, which was murderous, not wistfully sentimental and respectful. *Pinups* was an album made with divine abandon, not throwaway casualness as McDonald thought; it was conceived as a set of deadbeat anthems for the 'don't bring me down' generation of young droogs who were fated to live in the faded lustre and broken promises of first- and second-generation rockers.

There is nothing affectionate about *Pinups*; it is a crime scene. The titles are like the splash lines on the cover of a True Detective pulp magazine. The songs themselves are the equivalent of the limbs and torso of an exquisite corpse, a surreal and marvellous fusion that in its rearrangement of perfect pop moments reveals the past to be less an age of youthful carefree innocence than a *danse macabre*. The Scene Club, the Marquee, the Ricky Tick were the locations for squalid crimes, not innocent pleasures. The pin-ups are not the pop stars of yesterday but victims and suspects arranged on a board so that Bowie can better show his fans the evidence and the scope of the investigation.

Bowie's critics stood before this imagined pinboard much like Dana Andrews's detective stood before the portrait of

Gene Tierney in Otto Preminger's 1944 film *Laura*. Andrews's character had fallen in love with a corpse, his ardour for the impossible object of his desire so fervent that it seemed he was able to call her back from the dead. *Pinups* echoes *Laura* but Bowie knew, even if his critics didn't, that there can be no recall from the past that can fill the hole in the present, certainly not nostalgia. The critic's desire for the lost object of their youth cannot be denied so, like an occultist, Bowie conjured up its spirit form and left them to stare morosely at his pinboard. When he had not given them the thing itself they tried to figure out just what crime had been committed. With the qualified exception of Lester Bangs in his review for *Creem*, they did not do a very good job of solving the mystery.

Like others, Bangs thought you could listen to the album with the ear of a jaded rock fan who was showing his age or as a naive kid discovering the 'chills and thunder' of rock 'n' roll. He was in the latter camp; the album was 'so good that it doesn't have the sickly reek of mouldy-oldie nostalgia, and that Bowie didn't find it necessary to camp the material up may be the highest tribute of all'.[72] But the album was neither nostalgia nor tribute; homage to his peers was not part of the currency Bowie was proffering and he wasn't, as Bangs had it, holding a screen up for his young audience onto which he projected the past's glories. Rather, *Pinups* is a flight from second-generation rock. Conceived as a fugue, its effect was to produce in its young listeners a dissociative experience, separating them from their older brothers and sisters, as 'All the Young Dudes' had agitated. *Pinups* provided a momentary loss of awareness; it was a dissembling of inherited identity, a breakdown intended to provoke a reset.

On the sleeve's insert Bowie is shown turning forwards with his sax erect, cocking a hip to the words printed down the side from The Kinks' 'Where Have All the Good Times Gone'. He is dressed for the 1970s in a box jacket suit designed by Derek Morten of King's Road emporium City Lights Studio that hints at the Mod style of yore as it pulls towards a soul boy chic yet to happen.[73] The style and stance refute any suggestion of inertia in his attitude or regression in his style: *Pinups* is not nostalgia, it is a closing of accounts. From here on in all bills are returned to sender.

When asked by Charles Shaar Murray whether a fourteen-year-old today could feel the same way about The Who as a fourteen-year-old had seven years earlier at the start of the band's career, Pete Townshend said he didn't think they would have the same response. Things had changed. Today's fourteen-year-old identified with Bolan, he said, or with minor geniuses like Steve Howe (a favourite of Townshend's younger brother) and musicians who have 'fantastic dexterity'.[74] The mutual sense of identification shared between The Who and their original Mod audience no longer mattered, he thought. Kids today were 'not interested when David Bowie, Elton John, Rod Stewart and Marc Bolan say "I was the archetypical mod." I've read every one of those people say that. It's quite possible they were.'[75] Townshend's point was that it is not having been an ace face, or even just a ticket, that mattered so much as being a keen observer of evolving youth culture, as he was. What was important was the ability to translate a teenager's experience and give it back to them in a form with which they could identify. As such, he respected Bolan because of what he was 'doing for rock 'n' roll' but The Who were working on a different level, or at least for a different, older, audience.[76] With *Pinups*, Bowie slipped in between The Who and Bolan and provided a set of 1960s vamps rewired to jolt a generation readying itself to step out from under the shadow of Mod and to slide past T. Rex.

The album's opener, 'Rosalyn' is lust unfettered, fuelled by Mick Ronson's slide guitar and Aynsley Dunbar's shuffle-skip drum pattern on its way to meet, at song's end, Bo Diddley's shave and a haircut . . . two bits. It makes a suitable start for an album aimed at teenagers, fast and leery, and one that challenged the ownership Bowie's peers claimed over authentic youthful experience and expression. For the most part, his contemporaries had long since left such primitivism behind, abandoning it for the finer arts. Fidelity to the originals, producing a perfect simulacrum of revered *and* forgotten icons, is not what Bowie covets; it is the originals' boastful bravado and youthful zeal that was based on nothing more than self-belief that he wanted to share with his young audience.

The flipside to the bravado was the feeling of desperation that lurks within a teenager's soul. Without hesitation, 'Rosalyn' segues into 'Here Comes the Night' by Them: a jilted lover follows his girl and her new boyfriend, watching them from the shadows, peering through windows as the lights are turned down; a creepy voyeur's tale told from a vantage point on the corner of Old Compton and Wardour Street.

On its heels, The Yardbirds' 'I Wish You Would' – Ronson's call-and-response guitar lick a mad gesticulation that meets, head-on, the death wheeze of Bowie's asthmatic harmonica – a hollow salute to Keith Relf who, along with Brian Jones, was one of London's most creative harp players. The track ends with a muted explosion that foreshadows the dystopic world of

Diamond Dogs or, more immediately, the entropic 'Shapes of Things to Come', the second of the album's two Yardbirds' covers. In turn, that tune doesn't so much conclude as stagger to its barely obtained finale, much like Jean-Paul Belmondo at film's end in Godard's *Breathless*.

In Bowie's hands, The Mojo's 'Everything's Alright', with its cramped 'Riot in Cell Block #9' opening, sounds like the theme for a TV cop show (echoed by the wail of a sax mimicking a police siren over the start of 'I Can't Explain' that follows and then closes side one). Bowie shrinks The Mojo's singer's *joie de vivre* into a fit of despair that is matched to the rasp of his saxophone (the harmonica and sax playing on the album is everywhere flat, inexpressive, consumptive; it lags behind rather than pushing a song forward). 'Everything's Alright' barely hangs together despite the lovin' man's repeated supplication to a girl to hold hands. The plea is unheeded, as if that familiar request, once made by Lennon and McCartney, now has neither truth nor meaning in its romantic sentiment. To underline the point, the recording concludes with a falsetto 'Oo-ooh'; an explicit reference to The Beatles. Nothing, not even the revered Fab Four, in *Pinups'* oneiric world of night and murder, is just alright.

Sandwiched between 'I Wish You Would' and 'Everything's Alright', Syd Barrett's reverie of childhood, 'See Emily Play', also has its innocence spoiled. His vision is corrupted and depredated by Bowie, whose rueful observations of Emily are squeezed dry by a goon squad's dirge-like chorus, which stomps over any hint of tenderness that might be recalled from Pink Floyd's original recording. The song ends by collapsing into a ragged coda of classical citations, a caricature of those with progressive inclinations – Pink Floyd post-Syd.

Mick Farren wrote that the early Floyd 'played music that sounded like a guitar solo by The Who, only it was a solo without any song to go round it'.[77] By the time they got into a studio they had found their song, but Pink Floyd remained just as indebted to The Who. In Bowie's take on 'Emily', any outstanding obligation to the Shepherd's Bush quartet is repaid on the Floyd's behalf when, during the instrumental break, Ronson quotes Townshend while Dunbar flashes on Keith Moon. Like Pink Floyd, Bowie too had dues owing, though he was not about to make good on them.

Bowie had already copped much from The Who, and had followed their lead on his third single, 'You've Got a Habit of Leaving', released in 1965. It was an uninspired attempt to mimic them; certainly it didn't come close to evoking a similar response to what one reviewer experienced when witnessing peak-era Who:

> The Who have a kind of bizarre science-fiction appeal
> – electronically violent, deafeningly strident, all rather
> removed from reality. There is no other group on the
> current scene remotely like them . . . there was a sort
> of sensual excitement about the performance – this
> in spite of the group's doleful, deadpan expressions.[78]

Back then Bowie obeyed the lines that had been laid before, but now he was seeking to approximate The Who's violent, otherworldly strangeness and to claim it for his own audience, to repurpose it for them. In 'Anyway Anyhow Anywhere', under the breath of the song, he twice utters, as if he were casting a charm, 'I can do it for myself.' That muted declaration follows the interjection of a particularly desperate sounding 'I wanna go.'

In 1965, Bowie lived in the shadow cast by Pete Townshend; now he projected his own silhouette, as if it were a shroud, over the Pop art Mods, who with *Quadrophenia* were stumbling back into a past that *Pinups* was intent on sealing off and moving on from. Rather than attempt to speed away from its original audience and on to the teens of the mid-1970s, as he had done with 'Rosalyn', in remaking 'I Can't Explain' Bowie slowed it down, turned it into a burial march. He let the song relapse into the seedy world of the 2i's of late 1950s Soho, with a soundtrack supplied by Vince Taylor and Johnny Kidd. 'Shaking All Over' is this recording's internal quotation; a recognition of the fact that The Who not only covered the Pirates' signature tune but were a rock 'n' roll group before they were Pop artists or pop gods. The Who had once defined the teenage wasteland, named it even, but it was Bowie who now claimed dominion; Townshend, Bolan, Iggy and Nick Kent be damned.

After the stupefying version of 'I Can't Explain', which had no more life in it than a severed limb, the memory spasm of an amputee's jumpy stump, side two is kickstarted by 'Friday on My Mind' – zoom, zoom, zoom – with Bowie's vocal pushed to the point of psychosis. The Easybeats song gestured towards pill-fuelled weekends, which Bowie's cover more than confirms as he rushes it straight out of Nowhere and into the certain collapse that is to follow. The Pretty Things' 'Don't Bring Me Down' was always more than just a request, it was their philosophy, but being brought down is precisely the point of *Pinups*, otherwise, as a fugue for all the droogies – oh don't crash here – it can't serve its purpose.

If Bowie's rendering of The Mojo's tune could function as the soundtrack for a slideshow of Weegee's crime scenes – a tour through the Naked City – the soul torture expressed in 'Sorrow' is close to what James Stewart's character must have felt after he had twice lost the woman played by Kim Novak in Hitchcock's *Vertigo*. Song and movie are a tale of *amour fou*, love star-crossed and impossible. Desire is held within a vortex: a fetish of long blonde hair with a void at its centre into which Bowie and Stewart tumble.

Bowie's previous albums had an expansive soundscape, wide open, produced for high-end stereo systems. Riding high on Dunbar's galloping drum patterns, *Pinups* is all pinched and compressed, mixed for those little portable cassette players teenagers carried with them in 1973. For much of the album the gap between tracks is negligible to non-existent, creating either a surging rush or a crepuscular dissembling of one recording into the next. Following 'Anyway Anyhow Anywhere', for the only time, there is enough space to let the listener breathe before the band shunt into The Kinks' 'Where Have All the Good Times Gone!' The exclamation mark belongs to Bowie, absent (as is a question mark) from the original title. Bowie's punctuation a heightened indication apropos of nothing.

The negation of the positive, the refusal to simply comply with the rules or to show the deference to one's betters, or just to one's peers, is why *Pinups* was by far the most driven and obsessive of Bowie's early to mid-1970s albums. This is regardless of what the old-school murder squad of critics told their teenage readers in 1973 after they had stared long and hard and found nothing of note or interest, rhyme or reason, on the pinboard images Bowie had presented to them as

It's
F-F-Fumble
Free!

With Philips new instant-action cassette recorder, even the microphone is built-in.

After making recording simple, Philips now make it *instant*. With the N2211 battery cassette recorder.

You don't even have to fumble with a separate microphone. The special 'electret' microphone is built into the recorder, ready for instant action.

No need to bother with recording level. It's handled automatically. For perfect results. Nor clutter yourself up with a separate carrying case. The detachable shoulder strap makes life easy.

Controls? You get a professional-style sliding fader for volume. Instant pushbuttons for everything else.

The sound? We've controlled the motor electronically. To keep speed steady and not change a note. And we've added a loudspeaker that gives incredible output for its size.

You get a direct recording lead and blank one-hour Philips Compact Cassette. And a full range of sockets for Philips headphones, battery saving Philips Mains Unit and separate Philips loudspeaker.

You can even play any of the world's biggest range of ready-recorded tapes. *Musicassettes*. Over 2,000 already available.

Philips recorders are so popular, most dealers stock them. So... instant action! See a Philips dealer now.

PHILIPS
Simply years ahead.

New instant action: *Pinups* – Compact Cassette ready.

evidence of their over-zealous faith in the music of *their* youth. In turn, they said Bowie's crime was a lack of respect. The greater crime was that the critics believed their past was unique, exclusive, and demanded Bowie's and his audience's obsequiousness. If the critics had cared to look more carefully, to stare through the fetish, then they would have seen that on this pinboard Bowie had shown them they were peddling a fantasy, a set of lies even. Whatever its faults, indeed because of its faults, *Pinups* was a genuine teenage wasteland: dissolute and indifferent, empty of a care for sentiment or history's truths. The album moved in double-quick time and had flash with lots of that bravado Bowie craved; it was unquestionably the second best New York Dolls album of 1973.

5

FOR YOUR PLEASURE . . .
WE PRESENT OURSELVES: ROXY MUSIC
— THE TEENAGE LIFESTYLE CHOICE

*We don't associate sincerity in music with drabness in appearance
. . . Hearing is conditioned by what one sees. Presentation is integral
to how we think the audience hear the music.*

Bryan Ferry and Brian Eno, *The Guardian* (1972)

s Roxy Music, in 1972, emerged out of their rehearsal
space and into the limelight, the critical descriptions they
elicited were uniform and consensual. 'A first impression of
Roxy Music suggested a blend of neo-fifties rock and synthe-
sized weirdness, compromised by an uncertain, pretentious
stage image,' wrote John Rockwell in the *New York Times*.[1]
'Roxy Music have been popularized by their image: yet another
case of the glitter and make-up syndrome. They come on with
obvious reference to Sha Na Na and Dan Dare – in gold lamé
trousers, mock leopard skin, and Brylcream,' wrote *The
Guardian*'s Robin Denselow.[2] In sum, the band were reducible
to a set of retro gestures that rubbed up against futuristic sonics
and a sophisticated or pretentious (take your pick) obsession
with image. With Roxy, such simplifications were not a limita-
tion but a conceptual matter; and mannered repetition, achieved

with nuanced modification, playful and serious, defined them. Such things set the band apart before it eventually contained them.

'Let's start with the cover, shall we?' wrote Richard Williams in his liner notes for the super-deluxe edition of the first Roxy Music album.[3] Like the band, Williams was performing a repeat act. Some 45 years earlier, he had begun his original review of the album by also describing the sleeve:

> Kari-Ann stares, with lustful expectancy, teeth bared and surrounded by frosted deep pink lips. She reclines on a counterpane of silvery satin in a halter-necked swimsuit, built strictly for the boudoir. There's a pink rose falling from one hand, its colour exactly matching her toenails, which peep out from silver platform-heeled sandals. A gold LP nestles beside her.[4]

Roxy Music start as a pin-up, a recurring fantasy in the form of a sexualized commercial image; all surface glamour – a tease. The pin-up as fetish, like all others, serving to distract attention away from the emptiness of the offer. But the deliberate playfulness of Kari-Ann's to-be-looked-at-ness suggests subject and object are held in a loop of exchange: she is known and knowing – a common product and a work of art. 'Roxy Music is a concept which not everyone will latch onto at first,' wrote Williams in 1972, 'but which is as rich in performance as in promise, carefully calculated yet simply oodles of fun.'[5]

Post-*Tommy* was the era of the concept album; the idea of a band as a concept, a collection of related ideas, as opposed to some manifestation tooled through hard graft and talent, be that Led Zeppelin or Jethro Tull, was still a novelty among rock's third generation, who aimed to make the scene T. Rex then presently occupied. As with Bowie, a question about Roxy Music's authenticity would continue to be asked, but it did not much concern them any more than it did him. The key distinction they and Bowie worked on was not simply between authenticity and inauthenticity but more specifically pop as product, created, for example, in the mill of Jonathan King, and pop as art as extolled, say, by the Velvet Underground. What Roxy were doing was as distinct from The Piglets' 'Johnny Reggae' as an Andy Warhol print was from its original signifier, Heinz or Brillo. This conscious play with a Pop art aesthetic was hardly new: second-generation rockers, with The Who being *the* stand-out example, had worked out of the same virtual studio. But only Roxy Music, alongside Bowie's Ziggy Stardust and the Spiders from Mars (supplemented by his chorus of Lou Reed and Iggy Pop) at that moment in time – early summer 1972 – could be conceived of as such an art project.

Duncan Fallowell caught this idea in the coda to his review of Bowie's Rainbow gigs, at which Roxy played support. Of the latter he wrote:

> They look a bit like Bowie. Gold boots, tigerskin zippers, all that. According to a somewhat hectic press release they appear to have several degrees apiece. The music? Imagine a juke box the size of Didcot power station and Eddie Cochran jiving with John Cage and you could be half-way there. Their album *Roxy Music*, will put you in the picture far better than I can. They are going to be famous very soon.[6]

Cochran and Cage, respectively avatars of teenage rock 'n' roll rebellion and the avant-garde. That such a connection had been made earlier about the Velvet Underground did not go unremarked; indeed they were often cited as an influence on Roxy by critics and used as a role model by its members, all further helping to cement the idea of the New Yorkers as artistic forefathers to the now scene. Talking to Nick Kent, as plans were being made for their second album, Brian Eno said:

> We are actually using the Velvet's *White Light/White Heat* album as a fair example of what we eventually want. I'm not saying that we are going to sound like the Velvets in any way, it's just that we will probably use the same conditions they used to record the album. We hope to make it in a single afternoon.[7]

At the time (and probably since) no one linked Roxy to the pop of Jonathan King, Mickie Most or Chinn and Chapman. But connections were commonly made to 1950s pop, Shadow Morton or Duane Eddy, for example, which allowed for a degree of discrimination – the studied view of past pop moments that can recognize the exceptionalism of The Shangri-Las and The Ronettes and separate them from the dross – while holding tacky and superficial contemporary pop at a distance.

The downside of Roxy's particular alliance with the pop masterpieces of first- and second-generation rock 'n' roll was that it fostered a link to the day's revivalists. In the NME, Tony Tyler noted the Velvet Underground's influence and then likened Roxy to 'a cross between Hawkwind and The Wild Angels'.[8] With striking regularity, whenever Roxy Music was being discussed in 1972, the band were compared to Sha Na Na, America's leading rock 'n' roll revival troupe. The references disappeared, just as speedily, in 1973 when the band no longer needed to be so reductively categorized.[9]

As if to offer a more intriguing point of comparison, and to deaden the accusations of being revivalists, Ferry told *The Guardian* that Roxy wanted to emerge like 'a fifties science fiction movie'.[10] Still, their reporter worried about the band being caught up and lost in the crowded 'camp-rock bandwagon', especially given that what they were trying to do was to retain the 'freshness and immediacy of fifties rock 'n' roll (which musically speaking, was very simple) while still progressing into "art music"'. Their method is 'an outrageous mixture of styles part revivalist, part forties nostalgic, and part-electronic. The result ought to be a terrible mess, but it works: Danny and the Juniors meet Cornelius Cardew.'[11] This was in effect saying the same as Fallowell had with his choice of Cochran and Cage.

While lines of musical influence were being drawn up and evaluated, critics also found material for debate by mulling over the time the band members had spent in higher education – all those university degrees mentioned in that first press release Fallowell cited. Talking to NME's Ian MacDonald, Bryan Ferry told him about studying with Mark Lancaster under Richard Hamilton, 'the father of Pop art', in Newcastle: 'Everybody was into Andy Warhol and Roy Lichtenstein – the American Dream. That's what the single, "Virginia Plain", is all about: dreaming of going to New York and living in an attic and painting. The whole Warhol set up was fantastically attractive then.'[12] Referring to a painting of the same name he made in 1964, Ferry explained the levels of allusion in the single and the sound collage they designed for it to underscore certain motifs – a motorbike revving as the line about teenage rebels of the week is sung and maracas casting their spell when Ferry sings about Rio and Acapulco. All of which made Ferry into a kind of Shadow Morton figure who created pop for Robert Fraser's gallery rather than the hit parade.

Countering the suggestion that his lyrical conceits are 'oblique', Ferry told MacDonald that he was less interested in ambiguity than he was in juxtaposition in order to create shock and surprise in the listener. Drawing on this idea, MacDonald highlighted the 'weird mixture of styles' that had critics name dropping Ethel Merman alongside The Shirelles and The Marcels and 'the whole melange dressed up as camp nostalgia'.[13] Their most important 'musical references are to white rock 'n' roll', he wrote, such that the danger they represent, especially given the album's cover image, is that Roxy Music will be seen as 'Sha-Na-Na-with-a-synthesiser'. 'That would be rather awful,' Ferry replied, 'But I don't think a group so much into advanced music has ever used these old sources so obviously before. It's our adolescent streak, really.'[14] The 27-year-old Ferry, like Bowie, was, for effect, forever channelling his inner teenage self.

Having left Roxy, and preparing for the release of his debut solo album, Eno told *Melody Maker*'s Geoff Brown that he thought he might, perversely, be seen as a 'rock revivalist . . . because the thing that people miss when they do their rock revival rubbish is the fact that early rock music was in a lot of cases, the product of incompetence, not competence'.[15] And Eno, of course, set himself up as an 'incompetent musician': 'There's a misconception that these people were brilliant musicians and they weren't. They were brilliant musicians in the spiritual sense. They had terrific ideas and a lot of balls or whatever. They knew what the physical function of music was, but they weren't virtuosi.' This was in essence a version of what critic Tony Russell had called the 'divine carelessness' in first-generation rock 'n' roll, a concept Marc Bolan had intuitively and effectively mainlined. What made Eno different from earlier incompetents – Gene Vincent, Eddie Cochran – and from T. Rex, was that he was entirely self-conscious about his lack of ability, paradoxically pursuing the accidental and planning a chance encounter. Eno thought of mistakes not as an end in themselves, something that needed to be rectified, but as acts that had the potential to transform the quotidian.

The problem with over-conceptualizing, overthinking things, according to Eno, as rock music was increasingly prone towards, is that it can lead to sterility and self-absorption. But it might, he theorized, in his contradictory manner, be overcome by the embracing of random and accidental events, so that's what he aimed for. While flying over the English Channel, drinking champagne (what else?) with Ian MacDonald, Phil Manzanera discussed his failure to correctly play the solo on 'Chance Meeting'. In his pursuit of randomness, Manzanera's miscues or slip-ups were what Eno valued, as he also enjoyed, the guitarist said, 'taping one track and then sticking another one over the top without listening to the first one. And with "Chance Meeting" it was singularly appropriate ... we still make mistakes, we believe in them as much as the things we plan.'[16]

Due to Ferry's forced recuperation following a bout of tonsillitis, Roxy were undergoing some down time in the late summer and early autumn of 1972 – hence the flight MacDonald shared with Manzanera. In October, MacDonald once again interviewed Ferry, this time while the singer convalesced in a Swiss health resort. Photographed in monogrammed gold-trimmed black pyjamas alongside a bottle of champagne, Ferry distanced himself from the pop rabble: 'We're not a singles group really . . . I certainly don't want to find myself sliding down that Slade/T. Rex corridor of horror.'[17] If repeating oneself endlessly was Ferry's fear, it was a condition that could be overcome by announcing that remaking and remodelling was their art project, just like Warhol with his serial prints. Ferry said:

> I think the second album . . . ought to be the same numbers in the same order as the first, but done in a different studio. The cover would be Kari-Ann one year older, and trying to adopt the same pose. And each year we'd do the same numbers, and the lines would start appearing on her face, and the times of the tracks would be a few seconds out.[18]

This concept had already moved from theory to praxis on the B-side of 'Virginia Plain'. The Andy MacKay tune had originally been called 'First Kiss' and billed, by the band, as a 'teenage instrumental'.[19] To better suggest its step-by-step routine, it pre-planned format, it was retitled 'The Numberer'. For Roxy, third-generation rock, with all of its repetitions of past moments, was an assembly of used parts, a calculated act of restatement – pop conceived of as a maths problem or a musical version of paint-by-numbers. This was the base they worked on and then developed:

I tend to think of everything we do as an extension of our previous creations, I was telling someone yesterday that a novelist has one book in him. I believe I have two songs in me – a slow one and a fast one. I'm just writing extensions to those two songs, vaguely hoping they keep getting better.[20]

Pondering on this scenario of Roxy as both retrogressive and progressive, Nick Kent pulled them back into his particular world view: 'music has always come out strongest when harnessed to the old teenage culture-vandal image projected by Mick Jagger to James Dean to Attila the Hun. After all, who needs all that spiritual awareness guff when you can submerge yourself in the established drugs – sex – and violence syndrome.'[21] Kent asked if the line between T. S. Eliot musing over his Chinese takeaway on whether true art was dead and Little Richard at the pinball machine picking his nose and pouting out an incisive 'Awopbopaloobopbamboom' was even tenable. Perhaps, he thought, the conversation between the high and the low was always doomed to failure. The Beatles and mid-period Beach Boys had shown potential, he wrote, but mostly things got carried away as in the case of The Moody Blues, Yes, Emerson Lake and Palmer or Pink Floyd. Only the German band CAN and Roxy Music seemed capable of being 'interesting', that is intellectually stimulating and yet somehow still occupying space in Kent's teenage wasteland.

Eno was being touted as 'The Face of '73', and Kent wanted to know how he was dealing with the whole 'teenage idol superstar image'. Eno picked up only on the 'image' part of Kent's question. He said that the flamboyance in costume and gesture

Roxy Music – gay glamour. *Music Scene* (December 1972).

FIRST ALBUM BY ROXY MUSIC [ILPS 9200] OUT NOW

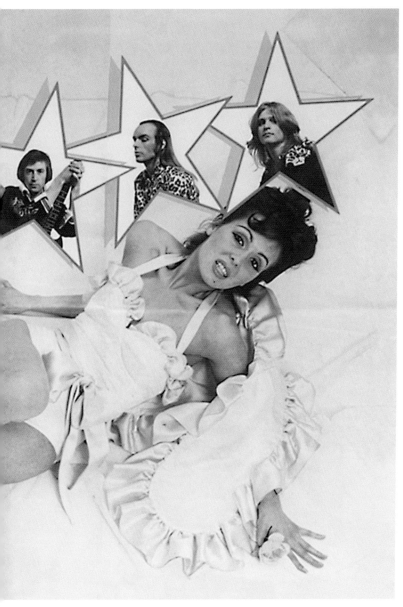

Starring Roxy Music: leopard spots and tiger stripes.
Debut album promotional poster.

Remake – Remodel: Marilyn Cole, Playmate of the Year (June 1973) and cover star of *Stranded* (November 1973).

New York Dolls on stage in Biba's Rainbow Room.

Pirelli calendar 1973. Kari-Ann is February's model.

was something that he had used to get himself noticed on stage whenever he emerged from behind his electronic gear, but now:

> Oh God. I'm really fed up with all this thing about glamour. We had to get a girl in to pose for the cover of the new album, which I thought was a drag because it's all becoming too stereotyped.
>
> Personally I'd prefer a nice unpretentious picture of the band wearing false beards and denims and standing around a tree with 'Support Ecology' on the back sleeve.[22]

Repetition could be a drag but drag was still preferable to dull authenticity. Eno had, anyway, he said, moved things along from an aesthetic based on chance to one underpinned by discipline:

> I came to this conclusion after listening again to the third Velvet Underground album. I'd always been intrigued by the Velvet's relationship with Warhol's factory, thinking it was tied in with their mutual love for the sinister, until it just dawned on me that the Velvet's whole approach to their music is identical to Warhol's approach to films. They believed that there should be no concept attached to art, that you don't have to consciously follow any specific patterns, that art just creates itself as it goes along.[23]

It is not entirely clear, at least as it is reported by Kent, what any of that had to do with discipline unless it was defined in terms of a meticulous attention to convention so that expectations can be better challenged or abandoned: 'There are passages in a Velvet's song when you expect there to be, say, a guitar solo and there isn't. The whole thing is just so obvious really.'[24]

Obvious or not, in an August 1972 edition of *Frendz*, Kent had more room to flesh out his ideas about Roxy Music. He had been unconvinced by the album but 'Virginia Plain' decided things for him: 'Roxy Music is a unique band. Hey! That's a pretty cool opening statement, right? And it's not really to say that they are good or bad, or valid or anything, beyond the fact that one would be hard-put to find another combo with that same vision or style.'[25] Placed against Elvis's 'Mystery Train', Bowie's rock 'n' roll comes across as 'bland and synthetic' even as he made up for such inadequacies by his 'calculated posing'.[26] Slade can rock with some sincerity but that only revealed there is a 'paucity of substance around', and Marc Bolan was 'shaping up to being little more than the third-generation Fabian in sexual drag and with artistic pretensions'.[27] Looking back, only the Velvet Underground and the Stones provided a 'true alternative dimension and insight'. Real rock bands both. 'And then there *is* Roxy Music', who 'come on like the lounge lizards of glam-rock':

There's none of the self-conscious macho of the high-energy boys. Their posing is tongue in cheek and at least acts as a refreshing Yang counterpart to Bowie's airy-fairy Yin seriousness. Where he uses mime-dancers, Roxy are aiming to bring on go-go dancers.[28]

Kent's piece is illustrated with panels from a girl's comic, the speech bubbles amended to feature lyrics from 'Virginia Plain'.

The article starts with him imagining a female-only space where the art of Noel Coward, Cole Porter, Michelangelo, Little Richard, Bette Davis, Aubrey Beardsley, Andy Warhol, Claudette Colbert, Dalí, Genet, Hubert Selby Jr, Billie Holiday, the Rolling Stones, the Beach Boys, Smokey Robinson, Bo Diddley and Elvis Presley all take second place to Roxy Music as 'Virginia Plain' belts out from the jukebox . . . 'she can feel the sweat rising from every pore of her lithesome frame, but it is too late to stop now. Total surrender' to the total collapse of cultural hierarchies is the high-stakes game that is being played. Roxy Music, Kent wrote, were finishing or following up on the attempts at Pop art that rock music had undertaken with The Who back in 1965 and that The Yardbirds flirted with on '"Happenings Ten Years Time Ago" . . . only this time around it will be done right.'[29]

In his album review column for *The Observer*, Tony Palmer first dismissed Bowie's *Ziggy Stardust* for being 'mannered and forced and loud to no purpose' and then did the same to Roxy Music for having similar faults in their 'attempt to evoke the sounds of the fifties using all the paraphernalia of the modern recording studio to cover up what the producers obviously thought were musical deficiencies'.[30] He then quoted Simon Puxley's sleeve note – 'rock 'n' roll juggernauted into demonic electronic supersonic mo-mo mentum – by a panoplic machine-pile' – for which he invited translations, and then finished his piece by heaping praise on the new compilation *History of Eric Clapton*.[31] You can bet Palmer knew the sincere from the superficial and just where he stood on the line that separated them.

Palmer remained fixed to the idea that Roxy Music, at least on record, were a parody of the 'more grotesque mannerisms of fifties rock 'n' roll', which, like their name, was 'intended to convey a revered, but tatty glamour'. But if he didn't think much of their first two albums, on stage, after watching them play at the Rainbow in July 1973, he thought they were 'demonic, sinister, apocalyptic, monstrous, dazzling, flashy – what opera might have been in the 1970s before it lost its nerve'.[32] While other 'groups have merely imitated the madness that was rock 'n' roll',

> Only Roxy Music seems to have caught the seediness quite so accurately. This it achieves partly through cari-cature – through costumes, for example, which are, for the most part, exaggerated versions of dandified Teds with various Frankenstein-like additions – and partly through a considerable skill in musical parody. Tunes that on disc seem fragmentary and faintly familiar take on new and more intelligible overtones when seen in the context of this sinister, leather booted performance.[33]

Like the band's name, Palmer thought the four go-go girls 'who pounced around' to be 'tatty' – that 'kind of tease is irrelevant and diminishing', he wrote.[34]

At the end of 1972, Roxy Music flew to the States for a promotional tour playing support to Jethro Tull, an unlikely temporary alliance between prog rock pomp and Pop art glam. Charles Shaar Murray accompanied the band to the airport. He was happy to report on Roxy as a kind of travelling fashion show: '"God", said Eno petulantly, "It's so cold in this office, my make-up's freezing".'[35] Eno looked 'elegantly wasted', Andy Mackay was wearing 'the most outrageously fluorescent green gangster suit imaginable' and Ferry was 'clad in a suave black overcoat and silk scarf . . . his hair a gleaming blue-black (like Superman's only not so curly)'.[36] It was all a wonderfully camp spectacle; a grand show at year's end played out in the theatre of an airport departure lounge.

♥ ♥ ♥

The sexual politics of Roxy Music's use of pin-up girls on their record sleeves and go-go dancers at their gigs has, by and large, been ignored. The band have avoided accusations of producing a prurient objectification of women, in part, because sexualized images drawn from commercial art have long been a subject of Pop art, which gave Roxy Music an intellectual and aesthetic alibi. Furthermore, when Eno was still with the band, Roxy Music took such obvious pleasure in dressing up in a blur of gender transgression that they easily confounded any ready-made charges of pandering to the male gaze. Michael Bracewell addresses the issue in his peerless book on the band, Re-Make/Re-Model (2007). In prepping his reader for Richard Williams's take on the first album's cover image as a challenge and an affront to rock's investment in honesty and integrity when it came to self-presentation, Bracewell writes:

> Within the masculine preserves of the rock music business, and its equally masculine press, Roxy Music brought with it a scent of artificiality – camp, even – all the way from the gay salons of Notting Hill. Antony Price's remark that 'fashion is nothing more, or less, than the seriousness of frivolity' seems to come in a whisper from Kari-Ann's parted, pouting and pearlized lips.[37]

Rita Hayworth in *Gilda* – Amanda Lear's role model.

The pastel pink and blues on a white background used on the cover of the first album was played as a contrast with *For Your Pleasure*, released a year later. The Vargas-style pin-up, an open invitation to the viewer to remove the gift wrapping, had transmogrified into the set of a crime film, a nightscape with deep glossy blacks broken by the white illumination of the Las Vegas skyline. Model Amanda Lear evokes the figure of Rita Hayworth in *Gilda* (1946), long black silk gloves and shoulders exposed. At the end of a diamond leash is a black puma, teeth bared at the viewer – vagina dentata or another variation of the leopard head on Iggy's jacket? On the left-hand side of the widescreen image that wraps around the gatefold, Ferry plays the chauffeur. His smile suggests he will be every bit the sucker for the charms of the femme fatale as Glenn Ford was for Hayworth and Burt Lancaster for Ava Gardner in *The Killers* (1946). The imagery rides just a little ahead of the wave of cultish enthusiasm and critical re-evaluation of 1940s Hollywood that by the end of the 1970s had become fixed and popularized under the term film noir.[38]

The spread inside the gatefold sleeve shows the five members of Roxy photographed, and sharply defined, against a white backdrop. Ferry is placed over the centrefold. Each has a guitar, less a musical instrument than a phallic trope, though the aspect is more akin to looking at a line of male impersonators than five versions of Jimi Hendrix playing with his Stratocaster. While the Roxy cover models ask 'What would you like to do to me?', *à la* John Berger's critique in the BBC series *Ways of Seeing*, the poses by the band members do not say, in masculine counterpoint, 'this is what I can do to you' but rather 'for your pleasure, we present ourselves'. Berger's programme was first screened in 1972 and was met with wide acclaim; its spin-off book has been an absolute staple in art and design course reading lists ever since. His accessible approach to art history and image analysis took place at a time when performers such as Bowie and Roxy were finessing and rewriting the codes of representation.

Roxy's use of female models was a post-Pop art response to the domestication of the pin-up that had once been the preserve of the garage wall or factory floor, but had shifted from those proletarian homosocial spaces to the exclusive interiors of art galleries and from there to the privacy of bourgeois homes. This movement was exemplified by the high-end production values, top glamour photographers and models that the Pirelli tyre company used for its calendars. These were essentially a marketing device, but one that had acquired some degree of cultural value or at least desirability. Creating an aura of exclusivity, the calendars were not sold in shops but distributed gratis; but from where and to whom? The Pirelli calendar for 1973 was photographed by Brian Duffy, who had regularly employed Amanda Lear, *For Your Pleasure*'s cover star, as a model. He had been responsible for the portraits – airbrushed by Philip Castle – on the sleeve of *Aladdin Sane*. In turn, Castle also worked on the 1973 Pirelli calendar, helping to realize the ideas for each month's pin-up that had been conceived by Pop artist Allen Jones. The cover star of Roxy Music's debut and Mott the Hoople's *The Hoople*, Kari-Ann, was Pirelli's model for February.

The slippage between the worlds of art, pop, fashion, glamour and commerce that Roxy and Ferry had creatively,

Roxy Music: for your pleasure … we present ourselves. Promotional poster.

humorously and intelligently pursued, finally folded in on itself once too often with the promotional video shoot for Ferry's 1975 solo single 'You Go to My Head'. Kari-Ann appears as the putative subject of the song, a ghostly memory, a haunting refrain. The video is set in a single location, a spacious, well-appointed living room, dominated by a large sofa on which Ferry sits. The pin-up image of Kari-Ann that adorned the first Roxy album sleeve is framed and hung above the room's mantelpiece. As Ferry sings about his lingering desire, Kari-Ann, in a pink shoulderless dress, throws lithesome poses in front of him. Ferry remains coldly unaware of her presence; she is a phantom he can't see or touch, only recall and imagine. The promo is like a parable of Ferry's career, an object lesson in solipsism – repetitive to the point of exhaustion. It can all be readily reduced to the martini glass and smouldering cigarette that he holds. His self-absorption absolute; a perfect expression of ennui.

Between *For Your Pleasure* and 'You Go to My Head', Ferry appeared on the cover of *Melody Maker*'s 1973 Christmas edition, dressed in a trench coat of the kind worn by Robert Mitchum in *Out of the Past* (1948). He holds again a martini and a Sobranie, and is encircled by five Playboy Bunnies:

> Bryan Ferry sets pop's Christmas mood – surrounded by Bunnies at London's Playboy Club, a setting highly appropriate for the guy whose mannered sexist image has dominated pop this year.
>
> Two years ago Ferry and Roxy Music appeared as late Fifties rockers who'd got mixed up with Star Trek. Now cocktail in hand, wrapped in a heavy gaberdine raincoat, Ferry is the elegant lounge lizard, a kind of modern version of the Sixties hip mod.[39]

Melody Maker's description of Ferry as a 'mannered sexist' is entirely apposite – he played the role of the louche connoisseur of female beauty as if to the penthouse born.

Michael Watts revisited the topic of sexism in his interview with Ferry published in the following week's edition of the paper. At one point their conversation turned to the session at the Playboy Club, and Watts asked Ferry if he felt any affinity with Hugh Heffner, 'After all, they're both selling stylish sex in different ways'.[40] The comparison amused Ferry, who confessed to always having liked pin-ups. How did he take to being called 'the sexist heir in the seventies to Mick Jagger'?[41] Ferry conceded to the idea if Watts was saying the 'sixties were more exuberant and reckless and the seventies are more stylised and considered'.[42] This was a response that Watts thought would not endear Ferry to women's lib. That set Ferry off, who then spouted a line of template misogyny: he hates those who knock beauty pageants and anyway, 'the girls love it don't they?'[43]

There is a playfulness, a sense of humour *and* an aesthetic integrity in the imagery used on the first two albums but by the third, *Stranded*, it had all become rather reductive, lacking the kind of applied, yet allusive, intertextuality the band had drawn from Pop art. Even if the seriality of the first five albums suggests a pre-planned coherence right down to the dominant colour variation for each sleeve – white, black, red, green and blue – Antony Price's contradiction in terms about the serious frivolity of fashion had been dropped for the simply obvious. Admittedly *Country Life*, with its punning title, was not without wit and with its use of non-professional models it carried a frisson of the risqué; *Siren*, however, was without wit or frisson, as was also true of *Stranded*. The model used on the latter sleeve was Marilyn Cole, *Playboy*'s Playmate of the Year 1973. The pose used in the magazine's double-page spread of Cole's oiled and sun-kissed body, garlanded with exotic flowers, stretched out and shot from overhead, is repeated for the LP's gatefold sleeve. It is all rather quotidian, as if Ferry had finally figured out that his core audience was not fine art graduates but apprentices and commercial design students who didn't much care for Richard Hamilton, or even know who he was, but did respond well to the playboy fantasy he had assumed.

In 1972/3 Roxy may have existed without much equivocation on their part within the glam and glitter scene, or what Fallowell called 'flounce rock', but their pose, like their peers', was rife in ambiguity.[44] In their survey of 'Gayness in Rock: Closets Galore' *Gay News* labelled Bryan Ferry 'a closet straight' while calling Bowie, who they considered to have an 'easy honesty' about his sexuality, 'computer camp'.[45] While not diminishing Roxy's appeal across the binaries of sexuality and gender, their ability to play strongly to the demographic of young males, outwardly heterosexual, was due in no small part to their dalliance with images of leisure and consumption, values that drew squarely on the same traits and tropes being sold in men's glamour magazines of the day: *Playboy, Penthouse, Club, Men Only, Mayfair, Knave, Club International* and so on.

In 1975, Pete Fowler undertook another rare look at rock's consumers, noting the radical divisions in fandom. He interviewed one section,

> the sophisticates, the smooth, smart and dapper follow-ers of Roxy and Bowie . . . The kids I talked to are all about seventeen, all Art Students and all specialising in Commercial Design (Advertising, Interior Design, etc.). They are not popular and are intensely disliked by the Man United boys – but they are the most fanatical followers of Roxy and Bowie lifestyle: or, rather, they are followers of *what they assume* Ferry and Bowie to be about.[46]

He asks three lads what they like in music, and one of them pinpoints Bowie and Roxy's futuristic aspects as a significant part of their appeal, and then continued:

> Really, though, I like the lifestyle, the whole Bowie/ Roxy image. It's very confined, but both of their images open your minds to what you could have. For them, it's

a kind of new world – superb colourful things, really bright buildings, cars really expensive, gadgets, everything, the women really fantastic, perfection itself.[47]

Like Bowie, Ferry was a good reader of his audience. A little after Eno had left the band he told Nick Kent that 'peacock feathers and sequins' were 'last year's thing'.[48] To which Kent posed the question, 'I mean, all this sedate sleaze and twilight zone Noel Coward-Lothario stuff is all very commendable, but can the kids relate to it all "in toto"?' Ferry responded:

It's a gamble really. You just have to work on both the subtle and the obvious, and attempt to balance the two in such a way that you can get to the whole audience. Actually, I think we're very fortunate in having these two very different audiences. I couldn't think of anything worse than having to play to those highly appreciative audiences who are always so aware of having to be cool and never going beyond that certain limit of polite applause. That would be such a drag.

But, of course, I want our 'finer points' to be acknowledged. I feel most critics have misunderstood us yet again, now that they're saying that we've become very sedate live. I think our act still has this very sleazy element to it.[49]

For both sophisticates and non-sophisticates in Roxy's audience, *Penthouse* had them all covered in its effusive review of their debut. It began, conventionally, with a description of the cover image. The reviewer then called the band:

a dated, camp, outrageous outfit of hard-line rock 'n' rollers, reminiscent of those crude, nostalgic nights at the Orchid Ballroom, Purley . . . To listen to, they're staggering. They have all the power and voltage of the heavy bands . . . but their connections with Pat Boone and early Presley introduce a lightness and sentimentality that the heavy groups never had . . . Their strength is that, apart from being impressive musicians, they have caught exactly the mood of today's pop. There is an increasing demand for a progressive treatment of kitschy songs, which is just what Roxy Music are deeply into.[50]

Penthouse's unnamed pop critic was back again the following year to review *For Your Pleasure*, which, with the exception of 'The Bogus Man' – 'a track of excruciating tedium: an endless riff' – fulfilled 'the beautiful vulgar tasteless promise of 1972'.[51] Nothing was written of 'In Every Dream Home a Heartache' – a critique of the empty world found in Bob Guccione's magazine and in any of his competitors' rags, but then glamour journals rarely indulged in such self-analysis. In October 1974, *Penthouse* ran a lengthy feature on Bryan Ferry; it is probably the most boring piece ever published on him. His music is barely mentioned, the reporter only interested in his sexual history and fantasies.[52]

Writing for the *New Statesman* in 1973 under the pseudonym Bruno Holbrook, Martin Amis surveyed the day's pornographic offerings from the 'grubbiest', *Soho International*, to the 'ritzier glossies', which included *Penthouse* and *Mayfair*.[53] Paul Raymond's titles, *Men Only* and *Club International*, he wrote, 'revert to a sophisticated version of *Soho*'s hard sell . . .

Instead of being implicit recommendations of the priestly life, like their tawdrier counterparts, these magazines actually *sex you up*.'[54] Onanism aside, the magazines all 'cheapen and dehumanise; although they may not be corrupting, they are corrupt.'[55]

Men Only and *Club International* were edited by Tony Power who, with art director Steve Ridgeway, sought to make the latter title, launched in July 1972, more responsive to, and engaged with, the voguish elements of aspirational men's culture, especially male fashion. Style features in *Club International* tended to avoid the more conservative high street brands that were the mainstay of *Penthouse*'s spreads and instead emphasized cutting-edge, bespoke or boutique designs. When the young photographer David Parkinson (responsible for the images that illustrated *Men Only*'s Thrill Kids and Fuck Girls fictional exposé) became the magazine's style editor he made astute use of the King's Road's emporiums, especially Malcolm McLaren's Let It Rock and John Krivine and Stephane Rayner's ACME Attractions. The story of Parkinson's chronicle of London fashion has been told by Paul Gorman, who makes a convincing case that his photography pioneered a whole 'new language of style' – punk (in the mode of the Westwood/McLaren) before the fact.[56] London scene-maker Chris Sullivan wrote that Parkinson's photographs in *Club International* 'literally changed my life. To this day I have yet to see a better fashion spread. It featured Malcolm McLaren, amongst others, modelling these superb American early '50s suits and hand-painted ties against period billboards and cars.'[57]

Mick and Sheila Rock also styled and photographed male fashion spreads for the magazine, one using Thin Lizzy's Phil

Lynott as a model. Beyond such pop-conscious sartorial items, the magazine proffered an often intriguing, and novel, engagement with contemporary culture. It did the usual thing of featuring celebrities, where, for example, it could mix up elements such as rock, sex and cars with a piece on Jeff Beck and his love of hot rods or a story on Keith Moon's fleet of automobiles, which included a small hovercraft. But it was at its best when the editorial favoured the outré, especially in the sexual sphere, such as a report, photographed by Parkinson, on a young transsexual, or a first-hand account of an Andy Warhol Super Ball.[58]

The pop culture stuff, however, is no more than marginalia in a magazine whose *raison d'être* was to supply masturbatory fantasies by way of agency-sourced images of nudes sunning themselves by the Mediterranean or of blonde Scandinavian models. More homegrown attractions were regularly provided by Israel-born and British-trained photographer Amnon Bar-Tur, whose figures, in a pornographic trope of dishabille that goes back at least to the *fin-de-siècle* Belgian artist Félicien Rops, are invariably wearing over-the-knee cotton stockings sourced, no doubt, from Mr. Freedom. Posed in coy, self-delighting abandon, teasing their blow-dried pubic hair or cupping a breast, the young women lounge around in Christopher Gibbs-styled bohemian chic interiors.

If the set designs and the stockings in Bar-Tur's spreads at least indicated a British and a somewhat contemporary *mise-en-scène*, other contributing photographers such as JP Smut, the collective pseudonym for Pete Smith and Jay Myrdal, suggested a more in-tune evocation of an Underground Freak sensibility, with spreads of hippy girls being 'natural', biker girls getting greasy and glam girls in silver paint and glitter.[59]

Illustrations were by some of the finest commercial artists of the day, including Mike Farrell, Brian Grimwood, George Hardie, Bob Lawrie and Bush Hollyhead. The last three were part of NTA Studio, which was to collaborate with Hipgnosis on many of their trend-setting album designs. In the first few issues, Hipgnosis directed not only the men's fashion spreads but provided various graphic elements that helped to elevate the magazine's overall aesthetic. Farrell had also worked on album sleeve design, notably on packages of Bo Diddley hits and compilations of 1950s golden oldies. Another regular contributor was Terry Pastor, who lettered and colour-tinted Bowie's *Hunky Dory* and *Ziggy Stardust* sleeves. Pink Fairies' confederate Jamie Mandelkau had his short story, 'Little Miss Sadie', illustrated by George Underwood. Underwood was Pastor's partner in the Covent Garden studio, Main Artery, and was friends with Bowie and Bolan. He provided illustrations for the debut Tyrannosaurus Rex album, *Electric Warrior*, Bowie's Philips LP and Mott the Hoople's *All the Young Dudes*, among many others.

'To get to Bryan Ferry you have to work through a lot of images' was how *Club International* began its interview with Roxy Music's singer.[60] He read the magazine, Ferry told Tym Manley, 'I love extravaganzas: showmanship is the core, if I may say so as one pin-up merchant to another.'[61] Such arch self-reflection from Ferry – an interview for a glamour magazine presented as a hall of mirrors, and an 'overlaying of images', was part of the whole Roxy Music package.[62] Ferry accepted the unreality of the images he worked with, wrote Manley, so as to better 'glory in the sheer style and presentation' of things.[63] 'After a gig I really like to go to the sort of club it's difficult to get into if you haven't got a jacket or tie on. Smart provincial clubs, the women you meet there have usually got more style. I prefer the straighter type of woman, she's usually a lot more bizarre, to me anyway,' said Ferry.[64] The Roxy fans Pete Fowler interviewed would no doubt have approved.

If Ferry acted out the part of an aspirational suburban lounge lizard with a membership card for a Harpenden country club or international playboy (whatever your preference), Brian Eno, pushing his solo career, heightened the stakes and played the role of an aesthete of pornography, a metropolitan connoisseur of life's rarer, erotic pleasures. Not for him *Club International* or *Penthouse*, but fetish magazines like *Search* or *Accord*, published by Illustrated Press/S.R.A. (Old Compton Street). He told the NME's Chrissie Hynde:

> It's a 'burning shame' that most people want to keep pornography under cover when it's such a highly developed art-form – which is one of the reasons that I started collecting pornographic playing cards. I've got about 50 packs which feature on all my record covers for the astute observer.[65]

Before going on to explain the distinction between his preferred forms of pornography and that peddled by *Penthouse*, which is a compromise, and explaining about 'burning shame' and 'golden showers', Eno said, 'There's something about pornography which has a similarity to rock music,' but beyond the fact that both might be said to be aimed at the groin, he doesn't much elaborate. He did, however, return yet again to the subject of the Velvet Underground, who he felt were the 'epitome of mistake filled music, and it makes the music very subtle and beautiful' and, without calling it out by name, he explained the impasse third-generation rock faced:

> I think bands like Yes and E.L.P., even the Floyd who everyone is saying are at the beginning of something new and exciting – the new rock tradition – are just tying up a lot of loose ends. They're finishing something off, which is a useful function, but not one which should be confused with breaking new territory.[66]

In the accompanying Pennie Smith photographs Eno plays the pornographer and Chrissie Hynde his model, which is a lot more fun than the image of Ferry adorned by bunnies. The subtext to all this diddling by Eno was that his music, his art, his erotica, unlike Ferry's, was not compromised; also he better understood pop and he had a sense of humour to boot.

Paul Gorman has captured the interplay in the early to mid-1970s between pop, porn, boutique and vintage culture in a series of blog posts, and a notable entry looks at how a 1950s necktie with an atomic print, which was part of Let It Rock's stock, took on totemic value. It was worn and modelled by Malcolm McLaren in a men's fashion shoot (the one that had such an impact on Chris Sullivan), photographed and styled by David Parkinson in 1973 for *Club International*, and subsequently used in a Bryan Ferry promotional image, circa 1973, of the singer surrounded by his creative design and backroom confederates, Nick de Ville, Karl Stoecker, Simon Puxley and Antony Price, who is wearing the tie.[67] Bryan Ferry then wore it on a 1976 promotional video filmed at Biba's Rainbow Room

Malcolm McLaren poses for David Parkinson in Let It Rock threads and atomic tie. Detail from *Club International* fashion spread (July 1973).

for his single 'Let's Stick Together'.[68] Images from the video were used on the cover of the album of the same name.

Typically, Malcolm McLaren kicked back. His vision of clothing, according to Nick Kent, tends to make him vehemently opposed to almost every other aspect of the rag trade. Rhinestoned 'Marilyn Monroe' or 'James Dean' sweat-shirts, for example, he considers 'horrifying', while the Tommy Nutter style of suit is condemned as utterly bourgeois. Mention Bryan Ferry and he almost bursts a blood-vessel. 'I think he is leading the kids astray. I mean, Andy Mackay comes in all the time and buys clothes for what I think are really "chic" calculating reasons. I think Ferry's stuff is too reserved, too English – I dislike how he puts it all together.'[69]

Like McLaren, Parkinson was something of a connoisseur of vintage artefacts and used his collection in any number of fashion shoots. In 1975, prompted by the loss of exclusivity, he sold his horde. Gorman writes, 'such was the singularity of his collecting zeal that Parkinson was prepared to go to these lengths' to avoid being identified with what he saw as mainstream.[70] For the photographer, Roxy Music were not style leaders, they were exploiters of a street-level avant-garde that they upscaled in their promotion of a phoney exclusivity of private club membership, sports cars, bespoke suits, and the company of beautiful women. All of this was a world apart in reality from their fans but a real part of that group's teenage suburban fantasies. Simon Frith caught this well in his overview of Roxy Music from 1974. Of Ferry he wrote:

The straightest account is on his solo album. His favourite songs, these foolish things, to remind him of . . . himself and his dreams, lone listening and private hopes.

The album was an attempt to confront the contradiction Ferry sees at the heart of pop art, whether films, music or pictures. The people who lived the dreams, provide them – the stars – know they're false; the people who get the dreams, consume them, the masses, know they're true. For Ferry dreamer becomes star.[71]

It had all been done before, was the message Ferry parsed. He sold variations on a theme that often appeared as no more than just a knowing wink, a louche gesture, a bored expression . . . a deathly suspension of pleasure.

The idea of Roxy Music, at least in the beginning, through the first two albums and Ferry's 1973 solo, *These Foolish Things*, was that they should represent both a sense of tradition, a pop heritage, and a simultaneous burst into the future, the kind of retro-futurism that Philip Castle's airbrushed vision of Vargas-style pin-ups adorned with polished steel-plated breasts evoke; the bygone/futuristic age of a 1950s sci-fi movie and glamour model allure – pictures of Lily astride a rocket ship to Mars. Roxy Music as a lifestyle choice was the concept; a band composed of a series of poses and a collection of gestures that had been made by the most discriminating of pop culture consumers. The success of Roxy's project can be measured by those bands and artists who followed a similar path and built for themselves and their fans private, exclusive, cultish worlds. Adam and the Ants, Dexy's Midnight Runners and The Smiths borrowed their template, but The Cramps took it further.

Maybe band members Lux and Ivy never listened to 'Virginia Plain' and its B-side 'The Numberer', or 'Pyjamarama' and its flip 'Pride and the Pain', maybe not even 'Street Life', coupled with 'Hula Kula', Roxy's first three UK singles. On the face of it The Cramps' particular take on primitive rockabilly and lysergic garage punk gives out a wholly different sonic vibe to what Roxy traded in, but on any decent jukebox selection the Roxy 45s are but a button press away from 'Garbage Man', 'Human Fly' and 'Goo Goo Muck'. Both bands made music that referenced the 1950s yet sounded so unlike anything else that it could only have come from some future world. Both toyed with the past's plastic detritus, the all-but-forgotten ephemera of a common culture, and out of it they made new art, perfect moments of monstrously beautiful pop. Roxy Music and The Cramps played rock 'n' roll that was best heard in King's Cross at a Scala Cinema all-nighter, their records spun in the intervals between sci-fi horror B-movies and abstract materialist avant-garde 16-mm films. Their audiences ever attentive to the catalogue of references, the slightest modification of gesture and mood, style and attitude, that the bands presented for their pleasure.

The glamour Roxy portrayed was always at its best when looking somewhat tired and wan like the posters in the Scala's foyer, sun-bleached and water-damaged. Or like the interior of the Rainbow Theatre, originally the Finsbury Park Astoria, which opened in 1930 and was once among the world's largest movie houses. When Roxy played there in 1972 and 1973 the foyers still had their Moorish gilt trappings and fountains. The relief representing a Mediterranean hillside village that surrounded the auditorium's proscenium arch continued to offer an illusion of escape from the humdrum world outside. On those streets that ran around the old cinema kids jumped off the number 29 bus, exited from the tube, and milled around checking out the action. As they waited for the doors to open they shared among themselves a brand of expensive cigarettes with a Russian name, just like the kind Ferry smoked.

6

LOBBING MOLOTOV COCKTAILS INTO THE OPERA HOUSE: NEW YORK DOLLS, SIXTEEN FOREVER

This is the story of the last rock and roll band. The New York Dolls.
There won't be another. They are the last of the propeller aircraft.
What follows will mean nowt.

Roy Hollingworth, *Melody Maker* (1973)

The New York Dolls were rock 'n' roll's valediction, at least that was how Roy Hollingworth framed things in his preview for the second British visit by the Dolls who, in the final week of November 1973, were *Melody Maker*'s cover stars.[1] As others did, Hollingworth loved the band unconditionally.[2] He said he would travel to Australia to pay witness, 'for they are the remnants of what it was all about'.[3] Expectations were heightened beyond all reason; the barely months-old band, with its small coterie of followers, who a year before Hollingworth had introduced to a wider public, had arrived in Britain trailing their just-released debut album and with two prestige gigs lined up at London's largest and swankiest boutique, Biba. They were undoubtedly the next big thing, and were now expected to fulfil all the promises Hollingworth had been given by them at the Mercer Arts Center sixteen months earlier. Yet here he was writing up what might best be seen as a requiem for both band and rock 'n' roll. Much like Sam Peckinpah had done for the Western with *The Wild Bunch*, the Dolls would be perceived as rock 'n' roll's saviour and executioner.

Rock 'n' roll had ended, Hollingworth had thought, when Lennon sang 'All I Want Is the Truth' and hereafter it would be all singer-songwriters and Tom Paxton numbers, but after seeing the Dolls he refused such an ecumenism. His 'no' to that consensus was unequivocal and, like the return of the repressed, rock 'n' roll was back:

> Here on this stage battles a baggage of balls and trou-
> sers and high-heeled shoes; and drunkenness and
> unwashed hair; and untuned guitars and songs that
> musicians would call a mess. But a rock and roll child
> would say 'God Bless You – You are so necessary!'
>
> Rock and roll is sex. And the Dolls played on. And
> they played sex. Non-stop.[4]

British expat Hollingworth was the *Melody Maker*'s New York correspondent and his initial dispatch on the Dolls had been made as far back as July 1972. In those early summer months they hadn't been the *last* rock 'n' roll band but they were the *best* in the world.[5] What he liked was their lack of manners. It didn't matter to him that they couldn't play very well, because instead of musical ability they had attitude and style in abundance: 'They pout, and swank, and shake their bums.'[6] And they are young: 'Not for them any attention to what old men are flogging off as hip. No class, little discussion, just stuff wild and unsubtle.'[7] He thought rock musicians were like footballers, as they matured they needed to become wiser, more canny in how they played, more eclectic, so that they might still hold the fan's attention, at least while they negotiated the years between the ages of 25 and 28. But after that even wisdom 'cannot match the impact of youth . . . And rock must be young.'[8]

To Hollingworth, the Dolls sounded like a cross between the early Stones (as every other article that followed on the band confirmed), The Pretty Things (Bowie's pin-ups) and The Deviants (their amateurish rendering of Bo Diddley rhythms perhaps or was it their similar refusal to kowtow to notions of good taste as dictated by their so-called peers?). The Dolls agreed with him on the influence of the Stones and the Pretties while adding The Kinks and James Brown to the mix, but swapped out The Deviants for the Pink Fairies. Whatever their touchstones, the legacy the Dolls refashioned was not that significant, Hollingworth thought; what was important was the fact that the band made you want to dance:

And the people at Mercer leapt up and down sideways, and went well crazy on the floor, as The Dolls music got louder, and sawed about the room. It's simple music, just rock, and blues, but it's played young, and played right, and played with monster arrogance.

They look young too. No lazy, bored 30-year-old in jeans, picking notes and their noses, but kids having a great time, playing heavy rock like it had just been discovered. They're going to make great singles are The Dolls.[9]

Just in case the reader had missed his message, misheard his sermon, Hollingworth concluded his piece denying any hype and reiterated 'they're just the best new young band I've ever seen. Yes, young.'[10]

The Dolls themselves said they were bringing back excitement to the scene, 'We knew we had PIZZAZ, we knew what we wanted to do.'[11] Like Nik Cohn in years past, as he blew in and out of the Marquee celebrating pop's youth, glamour, energy, sex and violence, delighting in the excess, the loud vulgarity of it all that found a focus, a burning summation, in the performance of flash delivered by The Who or The Jimi Hendrix Experience, Hollingworth found himself at the heart of the matter confronting the truth as he knew it to be: 'And whether you believe that or not, you're going to have to take notice of them ... The New York Dolls.'[12] Lou Reed had paid attention. In London that August he told Mick Rock about this New York band that was 'causing a few ripples called the Dolls. Something might happen with them, you know. I seem to inspire transvestite bands. They're very cute.'[13]

A little later, a vacationing Englishman saw the Dolls and reported back on the experience, this time in the men's magazine *Club International*. Dick Masters had travelled with friends to New York to take part in the second annual 'Everything Is Everything Costume Ball' organized by Tony and Laurita Cosmo. Staged in the grand ballroom of Manhattan's Hilton Hotel, the event purported to host the 'finest aggregation of freaks, fashions and friends ever assembled under one roof'.[14] It was a superball for superfreaks with a few of Warhol's old superstars in attendance; it promised to be a drag show for the ages, with strippers, jugglers, belly dancers, midgets, fire eaters and bands providing the supporting entertainment. Playing along-side the Dolls were their usual abettors Eric Emerson's Magic Tramps and Suicide.[15] Of the latter, Masters wrote,

> [they] created the most evil, menacing atmosphere I've ever felt at any sort of performance. He [singer Alan Vega] could only be for real . . . His moans and screams grew frantic as he lashed himself with the bicycle chain. Everyone watched in silence as he pulled out a knife and stabbed himself in the face and chest . . . he smashed the microphone into his teeth and leapt into the audience, lashing out at everyone who couldn't move fast enough.[16]

Violence remained in the air until midnight when the Dolls took the stage:

> Blending music of the early Stones and current Alice Cooper, they produced their own version of Fag rock. Camping joyfully around the stage, this five piece from Max's Kansas City enjoyed themselves tremendously and had everybody rocking and laughing again. Staggering and collapsing around the stage in their high heels, this energetic band lived the rock star-lifestyle without pretence. They were out for a good time and if you couldn't dig it then fuck you.[17]

Around the same time, Bowie, in town promoting Ziggy, caught a show by the Dolls. Witnessing the scene, Ed McCormack wrote it up for *Rolling Stone*: 'David Bowie, a brittle, powdered flake of hermaphroditic humanity, is watching the bodies writhing to the music of the New York Dolls in the Oscar Wilde room at the Mercer Arts Centre, a "subterranean Satyricon", for the second night in a row.'[18] The band play 'punky Stones-influenced rock and roll' in a 'funky transsexual style' while wearing the affected pose of looking 'sixteen and bored shit-less'.[19] Is Bowie threatened by the upstarts, McCormack asked; was he intimidated by a band that had been together for less than a year and who backstage pass lipstick to each other like other bands pass around a joint? With the Dolls making the scene, Bowie had become the 'elder statesman of the New Decadence'.[20] While their youth might have worried him a little, Bowie was quite capable, as he would show with Lou Reed and Iggy Pop, of purloining whatever he needed from whoever regardless of the competition they posed to him.

Bowie also fully understood the dynamic of exchange between performer and audience that McCormack valued.[21] After a November 1972 Mott the Hoople gig in Philadelphia, having introduced the band and helped with the backing vocals on 'All the Young Dudes', Bowie spoke enthusiastically to Ian Hunter about the New York Dolls. He loved their atti-tude, Hunter wrote, even if he was more convinced by Iggy.[22] Bowie appeared comfortable in whatever role he needed to assume, star or fan. In turn, after touring with the Dolls in support, Hunter told Nick Kent,

I think they are great in a way – Johansen has the right attitude as opposed to, say, Iggy who will never make it simply because he can't hold it together for more than half an hour a day. And Johnny Thunders is rock 'n' roll! Just like Keith Richard who to me is everything, visually, of what rock 'n' roll is all about. The clothes, the teeth – everything. And at interviews, he just has to say, 'I dunno' and its automatically great copy.[23]

The Bowie connection with the Dolls was reported on in the *New York Times*, though in this instance the article was concerned with the general trend in hermaphrodite rock. The bulk of Grace Lichtenstein's piece was on Alice Cooper's 'Ugh' factor; his 'epicene punkiness' disgusted her. On Bowie, who was set to play his New York debut, she thought he was 'the ultimate in self-conscious decadence'.[24] The final part of her trilogy of 'ugh' were the Dolls, who she watched at the Mercer: 'The music is loud and not particularly distinguished but the Oscar Wilde audiences adore it, especially the limp gestures of Johansen.'[25] She concluded with a cry of wild despair: 'Creedence Clearwater, where are you now that we really need you?'[26]

With industry veterans Marty Thau and Steve Leber on board as managers and with a small scrapbook of press cuttings, the Dolls headed to London at the beginning of October to drum up record company interest. Hollingworth continued to bang their drum:

The lovely New York Dolls will be arriving in England this weekend to start a twenty-date tour of the country – several of the gigs being with fellow New Yorker Lou Reed. This will be the Dolls' first experience of road work – their gigs in New York City being confined to just one or two places. Why start in England? . . . Well, they all feel it is happening there. Charisma label boss Tony Stratton-Smith has more than a mild interest in the Dolls – who are without record company.[27]

While in Britain they recorded some demos and played a few gigs, perhaps no more than three, but included among them was a prestigious slot on the Sunday-night bill at Wembley Empire Pool on 29 October. The London show was a sellout, with an audience in the region of 7,000. The Pink Fairies were at the bottom of the bill, followed by the Dolls and headliners Rod Stewart and the Faces. Without record-company backing there was little-to-no promotion around the band's presence in Britain – no interviews, no news stories to speak of – and, apart from listed support slots to Lou Reed in Birmingham and Roxy Music in Manchester, there were no adverts for their live appearances and nothing much in the weekly gig guides of *Melody Maker* and the NME.[28] If the visit had been intended to garner more than the interest of labels then it can only be judged as an outright failure. The band's lack of anything resembling PR meant that they were all but invisible to the nation's rock fans.

Nick Kent provided a brief review of the Wembley show, which he considered the best rock 'n' roll concert of the year so far. After the Fairies had reached 'quite awesome levels of sound' came the Dolls, '42nd Street's own version of Satyricon . . . What a band! Your own teenage cub-reporter was seen ecstatically preening himself to the sound of such-soon-to-be-classics as "Frankenstein" and "Personality Crisis".'[29] Mark Plummer in *Melody Maker* was not among the believers, 'possibly one of the worst sets I've ever seen . . . who really wants to know about "Pill City"? Wembley didn't for sure.'[30] Among those also inside the hall were the future Sex Pistols.[31] Glen Matlock remembered the gig as a grand spectacle and was particularly impressed by Thunders restringing his guitar on stage, tuning up as the audience booed, to which Johansen responded with 'Aww, fuck you guys.' The band lacked the stage craft for such a venue, but for Matlock it 'was a big eye-opener in terms of attitude. They really didn't give a shit.'[32]

Apart from the support slot beneath Status Quo at Imperial College on 4 November, with Mick Jagger apparently in attendance, it's uncertain which of the other shows listed on fans' websites they actually played. Arthur Kane recalls in his

New York Dolls backstage at Wembley. Left to right: Billy Murcia, Johnny Thunders, David Johansen, Arthur Kane and Sylvain Sylvain.

autobiography playing a pick-up gig at the Speakeasy, with Mick Farren heckling from the sidelines, but it's unlikely they did any with Lou Reed and certainly not the Roxy Music gig on 9 November, because two days earlier drummer Billy Murcia had died after being placed in a bath while unconscious.[33] Even this sad event caused little interest either in the UK or stateside; the Dolls were simply not yet that newsworthy. Instead, it was as if the whole visit, even the tragic end to the tour, was no more than a rumour. A few faint traces of evidence in the music press, a sole name-check in the tabloids and a news item in the *Kensington Post*, covering the Westminster Coroner's Court session that recorded a verdict of accidental death by drowning, was the grand total of documented instances of the trip.[34]

Murcia had met the model Marilyn Woolhead at the Speakeasy on Saturday 4 November and she had gone back with him and others from the group to their hotel in Holborn. On Monday, he phoned her at around 8 p.m. and she invited him to her flat in Brompton Lodge on Cromwell Road. When he arrived, half an hour to an hour later, 'He didn't seem absolutely sober, but he didn't seem that drunk,' she said.[35] She, Billy and James Owen, an actor, shared a bottle of champagne and they were then joined by Malcolm Raines, a milliner. Billy passed out on the bed, 'We tried to get him to move over and he didn't,' Marilyn said, 'So we tried to wake him up. I went and made some black coffee and the others put him in the bath.'[36] They failed to bring him around by slapping him, at which point she phoned for an ambulance. Owen and Raines tried to walk him up and down the passage, but his legs just dragged. Before the ambulance arrived they took him back to the bedroom and tried to dress him. Raines said, 'I felt for his heart beat and it felt to me as if it was beating.'[37] The two men denied Billy's head had gone under the water while in the cold bath and said they had kept it up as they tried to give him the coffee and held ice against his neck. After recording his verdict, Coroner Gavin Thurston said, 'By far the best thing to have done would have been to get an ambulance straight away and certainly not put a person in a bath of water.'[38]

Marilyn Woolhead was Miss Bikini 1964 and an ex-Bunny who had been arrested and fined in 1968 for credit card fraud. Accompanied by two men, and using her collection of wigs to vary her disguise, they hit 31 branches of Barclays Bank in one day. The trio made £775 at the bank branches and then the next day bought £297 worth of goods on a stolen card. She was fined £100.[39] Two years later she was caught up in an Italian sex and drugs story. When police raided a holiday villa, *The Mirror* reported, Woolhead and two other women and two men were found nude and semi-conscious in a 'bizarre room full of mirrors and coloured lights'.[40] In 1974, she married Led Zeppelin's road manager Richard Cole.

In her biography of the New York Dolls, Nina Antonia cites the *Kensington Post* report and the death certificate that referred to the alcohol and methaqualone in Murcia's system.[41] She repeats Arthur Kane's assertion that Woolhead was 'an international call girl with Mafia connections' and reports that there had been around fifty people at the apartment the night of Murcia's death, some of whom gave testimony to the police, but the *Post*'s account indicates only Woolhead, Owen and Raines as present.[42]

The line the story made between crime and rock 'n' roll, with drugs at the interstice, which might have played well as an echo of Donald Cammell's *Performance* (1970), didn't rear its head until years later.[43] Unlike the Iggy and the Stooges' King's Cross gig, the Wembley show, and wherever else the Dolls played, produced no iconographic images to fetishize and no eyewitness accounts significant enough to provide the basis for a mythology; even the four demos they recorded in Kent, a squall of buzzsaw guitar, and the best thing they had done in a studio up and until the sessions for their debut album, were inconsequential, not appearing until long after the band's demise.

♀ ♀ ♀

Back in Manhattan, with Jerry Nolan having replaced Murcia, *Melody Maker*'s Michael Watts, having taken Hollingworth's place as the paper's New York correspondent, caught one of their early January 1973 gigs at Max's Kansas City. He was less impressed than his predecessor. He thought their music second-hand and, as for their musicianship, he had seen better youth club bands. What they did have over other groups was a 'sense of themselves', which they communicated effortlessly to their young and 'small cultish audience', who were also self-assured – band and followers a mirror reflection of each other.[44]

Having left London behind as the 1960s dragged into the '70s, Underground notable Barry Miles also washed up in New York, from where he sent back reports for *IT* on the scene and its players. On 11 February 1973 he attended 'An Endless Valentine's Day All-Night Party' at the Mercer Arts Center. Playing from 10 p.m. through to dawn were the advance guard of Manhattan's 'fag rockers', glitterati that included Queen Elizabeth featuring Wayne County, Ruby and the Rednecks, Eric Emerson and the Magic Tramps, Alan Suicide and a 'hard rock, camp prissy 100% homosexual group in black tights posturing and imitating all of Mick's [Jagger] stage gestures and leaps': the New York Dolls.

> The lead singer wore a tanktop, diamonds and diamond rings while the one who modelled himself on Keith had a Rod Stewart hairdo only overdone and worn with a red satin Marc Bolan jacket. Second guitarist was very weird, pale white make-up and straggling curly hair he darts about the stage in tights, a mini skirt, toy gun and holster and a transparent top. The bass player is large, looks like Richard Brautigan with straw hair and a fetching white dress, he seemed very much out of it. The drummer was also in white top and make-up and all five balanced precariously atop outrageous platforms.[45]

Unlike Wayne County, Miles reported, the band didn't overly 'flaunt their homosexuality' though they did 'simper at times': 'These preening and posturing musicians actually play some pretty heavy rock, a number like "Jet Boy" really takes off.'[46] As much as the band fascinated Miles it was their audience that really caught his attention, mostly high school kids so dolled up he could barely, if at all, tell the boys from the girls. They too, like the band, tottered about on 3-inch platform shoes, as they sang along, showing familiarity with all the words, and danced to the music. 'The entire thing is almost some outrageous parody of the 1930s American glamour concept' from which 'Faggot-rock emerges . . . out of the closet and nothing could get it back in again.'[47]

Comparing the scene at the Mercer to the glitz and allure of Hollywood in its Golden Age made sense in the context of a post-Warholian New York with fast-fading memories of the Factory's superstars. Miles's own set of experiences meant he also likened the situation to the UFO club in 1967, the crowd's reaction as accepting of the Dolls as the Underground hipsters had been of Arthur Brown. When not doing a passing imitation of the Stones, the band remind him of The Move in the 'old days', just as 'loud but more soft and floppy'.[48]

Despite being unsigned, McCormack reported, the Dolls had built up a local following the like of which has not been seen since the Velvet Underground. He, Miles and Kent had all equated the band's audience to players in a production of the Satyricon, riffing on the Fellini film from 1969 with its hermaphrodite central character and steam-room aura of sexual dissembling.[49] It was a film Marc Bolan claimed to have seen twelve times.[50] Their crowd, McCormack noted, is essentially the same, night after night, which forced the band to improvise and become resourceful in altering their image to stay a step ahead of their followers, who appear like a room full of 'living art nouveau arabesques, they look like some decadent drawing by Aubrey Beardsley come to kinetic life as they dance through the Dolls' midnight set'.[51]

Looking ahead, and prompted by Bowie, the band dream of playing with David Cassidy and seducing his audience of fourteen-year-olds. They would have as much luck enticing that cohort as Iggy had. McCormack continued to keep *Rolling Stone*'s readers appraised of what was happening at the Mercer Arts Center in his 'New York Confidential' column and, like Miles, took in the Valentine's Day show:

Parading around in the lounge before the show were the usual collection of sexes and sub-sexes, all of them in their finery and tilted forward on enormous platform heels for that streamlined assembly-line proletarian decadent effect. One girl standing at the bar even had a live goldfish swimming around in one of her transparent plastic platforms.[52]

The band themselves no longer seem to interest McCormack, his attention drawn to the parade of freaks moving around in the Mercer's *Clockwork Orange*-styled Blue Room.

John Rockwell reviewed the band's first uptown engagement at Kenny's Castaways in February 1973 and made the now usual early Stones connections alongside the thought that they were bringing back a lost but 'essential ingredient of rock: outrageousness'.[53]

Any band that can inspire a gaggle of gyrating, squealing young women to feel as deliciously wicked as they apparently felt Tuesday night can't be all bad, and you'd be advised to check them out (the band and their fans) while they can still be seen in small clubs.[54]

In his bittersweet memoirs, Arthur Kane recalled the establishment of the special rapport between band and fans that followed their second gig at the Mercer:

The audience response to the show was what got us our 'permanent slot' gig every Tuesday night in the infamous Oscar Wilde Room (for seventeen weeks). That's where we, as real life living Dolls, became available for all fans in a place where they could actually meet their heroes in the flesh if they so desired. The New York Dolls became a band of the people that evening. We were all very accessible real human beings that you could talk to (and/or flirt with), not golden idols living in cellophane display cases.[55]

Like The Who and their Mod followers at the Goldhawk Road Club, Watford Trade Union Hall and on Tuesday nights at the Marquee, the Dolls and their audience formed a symbiotic relationship where the line between stage and floor no longer existed. This lack of a division was actually the case in the Mercer's Blue Room: 'The fourth wall, that invisible line, simply didn't exist,' wrote Kane, 'You could literally be standing next to someone who was busy performing.'[56] As The Who's popularity grew that codependence between band and fans diminished, and they became a simulacrum of a 'people's band'. Though they toured extensively in 1973 with Mott the Hoople, the Dolls never quite made it in tandem with their fans to those larger stages, so never had to figure out how to work a divide between themselves and their followers: success never reduced them to playing an impersonation of the New York Dolls.

In April, staying at the Chelsea Hotel, Nick Kent finally caught the band on their home turf, the dark side of town he called it, at Max's Kansas City. He wasn't sure whether or not he'd missed the ride and if the band had straightened out their kinks. He feared that what the Dolls had built their reputation on was now all in the past; the Fellini-esque had been cleaned up and sanitized, and the more 'outrageously demented' denizens of Max's had been driven away so it was no longer the 'absolute murk-pit of Babylon'.[57] Kent need not have worried. Eric Emerson, The Brats and Wayne County shared the bill, but they were just so much noise before the Dolls' entrance:

> 'THIS IS A song about the days when love was free, before all the boys burnt out their energy fibres and their girlfriends went to work in massage parlours.'
>
> A pause and then the kid in a lamé jump-suit, who looks like a sixteen-year-old Mick Jagger, starts up again: 'When-I-say-I'm-in-love – believe-I'm-in-love-L-U-V'. Wham!
>
> So what's a bunch of New York slobs doing trying to cut a talent like The Shangri-Las and damn near succeeding?
>
> Listen, bucko, these are the New York Dolls, the sweet-hearts of Babylon themselves, the band you're going to love whether you like it or not; these boys who cop the intro to 'Give Him a Great Big Kiss' (they leave that song for an encore) for their own classic 'Lookin' for a Kiss'.[58]

Inside Max's or out on the streets, fortunately for Kent, the scene is still strictly 'downtown Satyricon'.[59]

Malcolm McLaren's flyer for Too Fast to Live Too Young to Die —
David Johansen's talisman: 'Let it rock!'

Singer David Johansen strolls over to the plate glass partition which separates the studio from the control room, and scotch-tapes an advertising flyer he's just found to the window so that it faces the booth. 'Too Fast to Live, Too Young to Die', it reads, 'let it rock!' He spins around, the band launches full-throttle into 'Trash', an electric explosion that seconds his gesture with a vengeance, and without which his action would have been empty and melodramatic. In that moment it becomes perfectly apparent that the New York Dolls – far from being an easy target for anybody's labels – are in the midst of creating a category that doesn't even have a name yet.

– Ben Edmonds, reporting for *Creem* on the recording
of the Dolls' first album (October 1973).

The band's debut album was released in the States in the final week of July and in mid-October 1973 in the UK. The buzz around the band was such that NME and *Melody Maker* reviewed import copies in August. Both reviews noted that the Dolls divided listeners, but then, as Richard Williams argued in *Melody Maker*, those that dismissed the band had either not seen or heard them or simply did not understand the meaning of rock 'n' roll. The shared touchstones for Williams and Nick Kent at NME were the MC5's *Back in the USA* and Iggy and the Stooges' *Raw Power*.[60] The Dolls' album may not have the dynamics of the MC5, but the band possessed a 'pure teen consciousness' that the Detroiters lack, while their 'all dressed up with nowhere to go' attitude is a fine alternative to Iggy Pop's 'manic visions', wrote Kent.[61] The two critics differed, however, on the production. Williams thought that 'competence' over 'fire' had too often been producer Todd Rundgren's default position and, while the guitars sounded like 'a horde of Triumph Bonnevilles', the effect is only heard on a very good stereo; on a cheap mono player 'the album simply doesn't work.'[62] Kent felt Rundgren had performed miracles and presented a 'vivid document'. Both did agree, however, that the band's lack of self-consciousness was a decisive factor in their appeal; they may not be as funky as the Stones but they have it all in terms of 'sass, vulgarity, energy and fun', wrote Williams.[63]

The album was also reviewed while still on import by *Gay News*. Their music critic, Denis Lemon, had not yet seen the band but he had high hopes they would play Crystal Palace on the same bill as Lou Reed in September (they didn't). He had read all about them, knew where they played in New York and with whom, and he knew the titles of songs from their set list that had not been included on their debut. He had begun his review with some context on what lay behind the labelling of the music that bands like the Dolls played. Whether called 'glamour', 'glitter', 'gay' (which always 'brings out the moralising puritan worst in even the hippest critics'), or 'decadent' ('But to twist an old adage, "one man's decadence is another man's liberation"'), the labels are all suggestive of outrage based on the groups' 'rejections of stereotyped sexuality . . . As a result, gayness, bisexuality, drag or whatever are very much part of the newly found liberation . . . in contemporary music.'[64]

Of the Dolls' exaggerated appearance on the album's sleeve, Lemon thinks it 'no doubt shocking to some' but he finds 'their drag/make-up/transsexual image stimulating and adventurous, particularly as they avoid the tackiness and predictability so many *male feminists* (substitute your own label if that one offends you) settle for. The Dolls really are just a natural progression of the liberating trend started by Bowie.'[65] As for the music, 'it certainly isn't pretty; it's harsh and loud and dancers will need no encouragement to start shaking their hips.'[66] 'Liberty' is the key word in Lemon's lexicon when it comes to describing the Dolls, their music and their milieu. Following his review of the album he provided an extract from an interview with David Johansen, conducted by Ted Castle, which explained the singer's sexual libertarianism and, more broadly, what his songwriting responded to: 'Rimbaud used to write about the monstrous city and the effects it would have on the species. And here it is 1973 and everything is very fast and moving and I try to understand how people feel about it, how they relate to the environment.'[67] That *Gay News* provided a likely audience for the band was confirmed when the Dolls' record company, Mercury, paid for a four-page advertising supplement in the journal promoting both the album and their forthcoming Biba engagement.

Unlike their previous trip to the UK, the late autumn 1973 tour was heavily marketed.[68] Full-page adverts for the album began appearing in mid-October, competing for a reader's attention with Bowie's *Pinups*, Ferry's *These Foolish Things* and Reed's *Berlin*. By the second week of November, news stories of their Biba show began to appear.[69] By month's end the gigs and album were being sold with full-page ads for the single 'Jet Boy', and they made the covers of the weekly papers *Melody Maker* and *Disc*. They even made 'Tuesday Scene', the pop page of the *Daily Mirror*. 'Oh Horrors! Five Men in Pink Woollen Tights and Sequined Hot Pants' ran the story's headline, alongside a picture of the band with 'ruby-red lipstick and eye make-up'.[70]

The greater PR coup was their appearance on the premier British rock show *The Old Grey Whistle Test*. Without a hit single there was no chance of a slot on *Top of the Pops* along-side Sweet, Gary Glitter or Suzi Quatro where, like Bowie with 'Starman', they might have got the great British public to turn and face the strange. Instead they were met by the patronizing attitude of the *Whistle Test*'s compere, similar to that with which he had introduced Roxy Music a year earlier. History has given the last laugh to the Dolls and Roxy but Bob Harris was not alone in his supercilious response.[71] Earnest young corres-pondents to the letters page of the *Melody Maker* concurred wholeheartedly with him: 'I have never, at any level, seen such an amateurish performance or heard such an unmoving, mean-ingless row,' wrote Peter Moxon about the band's TV appear-ance.[72] *Melody Maker*'s editors were taken to task by another reader for having put the band on its cover. Pure gimmickry; a serious journal should not be hyping bands who have jumped onto the 'Pouff Rock' bandwagon.[73] Furthermore, wrote another irate correspondent, why had they shot Cat Stevens down in flames for wearing a 'barely noticeable swastika pendant' and given the Dolls front page coverage when Johnny Thunders had on a Gestapo-type armband?[74]

For their British television debut, Johansen had worn a black-and-white polka-dot blouse, and bassist, 'Killer' Kane, a jacket with leopard-print fur collar and cuffs; both acquired only days earlier from the ladies department at Biba. The two nights at the Rainbow Room at Biba's Kensington High Street department store, billed as a 'Grand Ball', represented the high point of the British fascination with the Dolls. *The Spectator*'s Duncan Fallowell wrote that the shows were 'electrical heaven mainlining the jugular and we were teenagers again, emotion-ally retarded punks strung out on noise like clothes on a line'.[75]

The store had opened in September 1973 (two months before the Dolls appeared on 26 and 27 November) and had made the most of the existing Art Deco designs that had been such a feature of the original building out of which Derry & Toms first traded in 1932. The Rainbow Room was the restaurant on the seventh floor with a neon-lit ceiling. That feature gave the room its name and was suspended over a dining area that seated five hundred and a dance space in front of the rotunda that housed the stage.

Visiting American Jymn Parrett, editor of the fanzine *Denim Delinquent* and Dolls' fan, described Biba as 'an entire department store devoted to decadence'.[76] The lavish and opulent goods and fittings created a spectacle of splendour, which was incredibly popular, attracting thousands of visitors a week who mostly spent time not money in the store; they were gawkers, unlike the audience that attended the Dolls' shows. Parrett described the attendees as 'being dressed to kill', as always for the band, 'but this being London, few audiences could rival these glittery obituaries'.[77]

Biba's founder, Barbara Hulanicki, recalled her encounter with the Dolls: 'Oh, they were fantastic. They came up in the goods lift and they were very quiet, never said anything, very sweet and nice. They looked amazing and so elegant, with beautiful shoes – sort of Jacqueline Onassis shoes, Italian shoes. I was so jealous.'[78] In an age of runaway inflation, miners' strikes, three-day weeks, fuel shortages and blackouts, Biba was the ultimate retail folly. Built on the most unstable of financial foundations, it was a cathedral to fashion and glamour, a hall of mirrors, which, like the Dolls, collapsed in on itself before the end of 1975.

New York Dolls backstage at Biba. Arthur Kane is being made up by the store's assistants, who wear the eye make-up that inspired *A Clockwork Orange*.

At the beginning of 1973, Michael Watts had written his less-than-enthusiastic report on the Dolls for *Melody Maker* and, after attending four more New York gigs, he had remained uncertain of their merits, but with Biba making his sixth sighting of the band he became something of an advocate, if not quite yet an apostle. He was now convinced 'that they're a great kick in the ass to the corpus of rock and roll'.[79] He recognized that there was never going to be a consensus over the Dolls; the scene itself was too split between those wanting to create 'an art form out of pop' and those who think 'it should all revert to awopbopaloobop'.[80] Nevertheless, 'rock and roll needs its anarchists and heretics, and the New York Dolls lob Molotov cocktails into the opera houses that some wish to build.'[81]

When Watts argued that the band were of the pop moment, its *now*, it was as if he had Nik Cohn on speed dial:

> The Dolls, with their crude musicality and exaggerated posturing, are the new children of pop, mimicking their elders and blowing rude noises; just generally letting out stuffiness. They make you feel sixteen again. You don't have to think about your response; you just respond . . . You think the band sound bad? Well, you should have heard them six months ago; they're getting better by the minute. You think they're taking off the Stones? I think they look fabulous, the best visual image since Mick and Keith first stepped out.[82]

Like Doghouse Riley – the detective who grew too tall – Nick Kent was back following the traces left by the exiles from 'Babylon Satyricon'.[83] He thought the two Biba gigs 'failed to approximate the feeling one can get from any real Dolls' performance when they are working within a suitably sleazy environment'.[84] His stance said as much about the need to play the exclusivity card as it did about the gig itself. His review of the Paris Olympia concert, which followed the Biba performances, was equally non-committal. Nevertheless, in between his thoughts on the shows in the British and French capitals, he caught perfectly the droll, or just incoherent, Thunders, here speaking about his relationship with fifteen-year-old Sable

Starr: 'We just . . . uh . . . livin' together, y'know . . . We ain't married or nuttin.' And Johansen's blousy immodesty, bad-mouthing all and sundry and telling tales: 'Hey, did you know I used to be a porn star? Uh-huh – well, let me tell you I was the biggest draw on 42nd Street. What films did I make? Oh, *Studs on Main Street – Bike Boy Goes Ape* – I was only sixteen when those were made and I was very naive. I was manipulated, so to speak.'[85]

In a news stub that looked back over 1972, *Rolling Stone* called the past twelve months 'the year for mascara rock'. This was a polite rephrasing of 'fag rock'; an equivalent of the British swapping 'glam' for 'poof'. The drag balls and bath house gigs, make-up, costumes, fey postures, camp gestures, bitchy asides, and those platform high-heeled shoes that ensured the band were always tottering into one another, meant the Dolls played the dissembling (and reassembling) of gender to its very limits. But things were not quite as definitive – 100 per cent homo-sexual – as Miles, subsequent to his first encounter with the band and their followers, had assumed.

Some eighteen months or so after *Rolling Stone* had left the closet door ajar, witnessing the Dolls at the Academy of Music in New York (after which he filed a report on androg-yny in rock), Nick Kent tried to close it: 'Both you and I know asexual rock was Last Year's Thrill (or was it punk rock?).' Alice, David and Lou, he wrote, are either pulling back on the act or have lost the plot.[86] Queen and Cockney Rebel are redun-dantly replaying the old roles and Kiss are boring and repulsive, 'nothing less than America's own Chicory Tip'.[87] Iggy Pop, however, is once again transcendent in Kent's cosmos, the only performer who 'can give this whole bloated AC/DC burlesque the finger with any conviction'.[88] But the reality was that Iggy was in full self-destruction mode in the Hollywood Hills and, however much Kent might will it, he was not coming down any time soon.[89] So the field is left to the Dolls: 'the best and the last of their breed, jack-knifing their way with style, across their aforementioned infinity of parodies that currently makes up the true substance of rock 'n' roll right now'.[90] Excepting Reed's *Transformer*, the truth is, Kent suggested, the displays of androgyny were never really about any 'gay consciousness' but instead were all about the pursuit of a teenage sensibility:

> The only way this whole rock 'n' roll mess can be salvaged and ultimately transformed into a feasible form again is if, as will happen, the whole schism blows itself up like some toad inhaling cigarette fumes and sometime after the ashes have settled, a whole new breed of teenage bands will sprout up slowly who will write songs about being self-conscious and suffering from acne and having nocturnal emissions and premature ejaculations and all the hideous things young teenage kids really have to go through.[91]

Despite all the play with gender boundaries, the Dolls always exhibited a decidedly non-decadent gang mentality that was a match with the Stones' at times thuggish stance. They could deliver in-jokes and wisecracks like The Beatles, and they displayed a volatility that only just fell short of The Who. On stage and off, the Dolls toyed wholeheartedly with the way boys taunt and flirt with each other, competing for attention, as they test the limits of fidelity to the gang. No band before (or since) has looked so comfortable flaunting a physical intimacy between themselves. In staged publicity photographs they cling to one another, Sylvain Sylvain slotted under a band mate's arm, embracing Johnny, or adjusting Jerry's floppy bowtie, stroking Arthur's hair. All the while Johansen pushed himself to the front or stood a little back to better get the limelight. Theirs was the theatre of the street gang, not the make-believe pose of the Dead End Kids, but of toughs played by Paul Muni, Edward G. Robinson or Jimmy Cagney. These actors played the part of city kids who took pleasure in parading around in bespoke suits (bought with ill-gotten gains), which were always, because they were punks and had no class, a little too flamboyant, a little too flash. Or it was the theatre of the street corner, as described by Nik Cohn:

> They were hooligans. They were kids with money and time to waste and nothing to do. They were bored and malcontent, and they formed themselves into gangs. Sometimes they only roamed the streets and brawled a bit and made noise; sometimes they got involved in real crime. But they didn't break laws for profit, or not primarily – the attraction lay in the excitement, the sense of action. The word 'kicks' was used a lot and it meant something, anything that made time pass.[92]

Cohn was detailing the culture of the Teddy Boy, but it stands in well for the Dolls, or youth culture, more generally: 'They had no concern with morals, politics, philosophies of any kind – Style was their only value and, about that, they were fanatic.'[93]

Mick Rock's Dream: Guy Peellaert's Rolling Stones meet the New York Dolls. *Club International* (March 1974).

Our rock expert, the gentleman who makes your magazine look as lovely as it does, insists that the Rolling Stones are the best band the world has ever seen. The above picture of the Stones is taken from Rock Dreams, *a nostalgic, amusing, wicked and beautifully put together pictorial essay by Guy Peelaert and Nik Cohn (Pan £1.95). Using a photomontage technique, the book takes pop and looks at it in a way it's never really been looked at before. The word that sums it up best, in my mind, is startling. It's almost bound to become a classic, which will be interesting because it's about the most transitory thing in the world. As Nik Cohn says in* Pop From The Beginning, *"the anarchists of one year are the boring old farts of the next".*

The top pictures, taken by Mick Rock, are of the New York Dolls. To quote Mick: "They bounce and pout and sneer on stage like all good teenage rebels should. But in spite of all this, one quality holds them apart . . . is their cuteness . . . Their upfront littleboy sexiness lends them a very approachable vulnerability. What they convey is the barely controllable excitement of the white middle-class youth lookin' for kicks. Not overwhelmingly original, it's true, but of perennial interest!"

That confluence between Teddy Boys and the Dolls was made manifest on their second visit to London when they rolled into 430 King's Road, Malcolm McLaren's Let It Rock emporium.[94] He recalled:

> Suddenly, a force-10 gale blew open the doors of my pathetic sartorial oasis, and in burst a gang of girly-looking boys looking like girls dressed like boys. Tiny lurex tops, bum-freezer leggings and high heels, this gang with red painted lips and rouged cheeks and hair coiffed high ran riot. They crawled all over the jukebox, destroying the neat racks of Teddy Boy drapes in their wake. Their tongues revealed they were not from the old country. The Uxbridge teddy boys were stunned into silence by the alien invasion – from Harlem? Dressed up to mess up, their shoulders became enormous in their new teddy boy clothes. I learned they were called the New York Dolls before they vanished.[95]

Boys to girls, girls to boys, or 'Doll-Men' as Arthur Kane called his bandmates, sexual ambivalence and gender uncertainty was the game even though things often swung away from the strange, especially when the band acquired celebrity girlfriends. David was coupled with Cyrinda 'queen of Max's backroom' Foxe, who had a four-page feature in *Andy Warhol's Interview* (four months after the Dolls had their page in the magazine). She had also been Bowie's lover and appeared in his promo film for 'The Jean Genie'.[96] And Johnny Thunders dated Sable Starr, the underage teen-queen of Rodney Bingenheimer's

English Disco. Arthur Kane was romanced by Stacia, the statuesque dancer with Hawkwind. She told *Club International*:

> I just flipped when I first saw Arthur. I made up my mind
> to get him and I did. At first we didn't screw at all, and
> even when we did it wasn't the most important thing.
> If Arthur got on the 'phone and said come over now.
> I would, but only if he asked.[97]

While in Paris with the Dolls, Arthur, who looked 'like he'd been run over by a truck load of Valium', asked Nick Kent about her: 'Hey. You know Stacia? . . . She's a nice girl, I met her in New York. She's kinda crazy right? I like crazy girls but the last crazy girl I was with tied me up while I was asleep and tried to cut my thumb off.'[98] However their gender was perceived, or their sexual proclivities and romantic associations were portrayed, the Dolls slotted easily into the context of pop's long fascination with the outré. The most striking visual realization of this is a piece in *Club International* where a promotional stub on Nik Cohn and Guy Peellaert's *Rock Dreams* is illustrated with an image of the Stones as crossdressing dominatrices that is set under four images of the Dolls shot by Mick Rock at Biba in November 1973. Of the Dolls, Rock said:

> They bounce and pout and sneer on stage like all good
> teenage rebels should. But in spite of all this, one quality
> that holds them apart . . . is their cuteness . . . Their up-
> front little boy sexiness lends them a very approachable
> vulnerability. What they convey is barely controllable

excitement of the white middle-class youth lookin' for kicks. Not overwhelmingly original, it's true, but of perennial interest![99]

Caricatures, but at least for the moment the Dolls had age on their side – 'The Stones have had their day,' Johansen told *Beetle* magazine, as he had told every other writer in 1972.[100] The press rarely failed to point out the Dolls' tender years, which, according to John Rockwell, writing in the *New York Times* in February 1973, ranged in age from eighteen to twenty.[101] Johansen was born in 1950, Sylvain and Billy Murcia 1951, Kane 1949, Nolan 1946 and the youngest, Thunders, in 1952. He alone could, up until July of 1972, legitimately state that he was still a teenager. On the other hand, Mick Jagger turned 29 in 1972. He was that old.

Throughout their short existence the band frequently expressed the desire to get Leiber and Stoller to produce their records but instead they ended up with pop maven Todd Rundgren and pop hang-over George 'Shadow' Morton, the architect behind The Shangri-Las. 'It really doesn't matter who produces us, we're still gonna make crazy records. The way Todd recorded us was the way we were playing then. Real frantic. The first album was made for mono. We wanted it to sound like a transistor radio,' Johansen told *Beetle* magazine.[102] He continued, 'Our sound is instantly identifiable. If you've never heard the song before and it comes on the radio, you know it is us.'[103] In their imaginations, the Stones were the map they followed and the road they travelled over, but the Dolls never truly left Gotham. They were urban America and the soundtrack they grew up on mixed the Stones with Brill Building pop. Johansen said:

> The thing that influenced me was the music I heard when I crawled out of the hole. The radio was probably on when I was born. The Red Bird records, Gary U.S. Bonds. He had wild untamed anarchistic sound, but it was right on time. Very cool. The Phillies stuff. I loved the Orlons in those days, the Chiffons, all the stuff that was happening.[104]

Though The Shangri-Las and The Ronettes are consistently evoked when the Dolls are being examined, there's little of the teen pop boy-girl melodramatics and the sonic bricolage of Morton or Spector in their ramshackle rock 'n' roll.[105] What they had is the kind of sass of Veronica Spector (née Bennett) or Mary Weiss, a cool, collected, don't fuck with me attitude. The two groups might have been the big sisters to the boys, certainly they were involved in their play with mirrors. Johansen's pout and microphone technique was as much Ronnie as Mick and Johnny Thunders's mane, an exaggerated rooster comb in the style of Keith Richards, just as readily doubled the bed hair of a recently aroused Ronette.

Girl group historian Charlotte Greig writes, 'The Ronettes were part of a female underground that still exists today: teenage girl clones who turn up to clubs to devote their whole evening to serious dancing, who know that when all kitted out in exactly the same gear – however seductive or outrageous – they were totally unapproachable.'[106] The Dolls had that same sense of dedication, only theirs was to the art of rock 'n' roll. They, too, were the self-defined in-crowd, the style steppers and setters – they were the gang who had all the moves, the flash ones who demanded and received respect.

For critics Greil Marcus and Mitchell S. Cohen, the girl group sound was still in the air in the early 1970s because it could be heard in any John Lennon vocal (going all the way back to The Beatles' covers of The Shirelles and The Marvelettes), in a Bette Midler parody and especially in the trash aesthetic of the New York Dolls, but it was also being relayed by Dave Edmunds, Bryan Ferry, 10cc, Roy Wood and Sha Na Na.[107] Looking back at the best of the records by The Chantels, Rosie and the Originals, The Crystals and The Ronettes, Marcus defined the phenomenon as principally Black, always urban, with a distinctive lead voice addressing teenagers. Above all it was a producer's art, a product put together in the studio:

> The oppression of the process has to be a source of much of the acute pain and desire these discs convey so powerfully . . . From one point of view, they're all about one girl's wish to be free, to break loose, and the impossibility of making it. But paradoxically, instead of smoothing out the emotions of the singers, as producers do so often, here they intensified them, because, well, that is rock 'n' roll. Or was. So personality came through with real force, and the singers lived, for two minutes, with all the life they had.[108]

The point of view is female; girl fantasies of boys rendered as impossible objects of desire. Beyond the conventional expression of desire for completion – girl and boy as a couple who have mum and dad's approval – the records expressed the girl's lust and her 'staggering demand for life'.[109] The simplicity of the song and its performance hid a world of deep-felt contradiction and unresolved aspiration.

The complexity concealed behind the veneer of simplicity and lurking under the cover of innocence and naivety is transformed when played as part of the soundtrack to Kenneth Anger's *Scorpio Rising* (1963); the allure of the macho posturing of his bikers filtered teen girl fantasies through the lens of a homosexual gaze. Bette Midler was doing something similar when she sang for the boys at the Continental Baths (in June 1972; still unsigned and with only a handful of gigs to their name, the New York Dolls also played this venue, but it was a one-off and they were not well received). Marcus was clear that Midler, at least initially, did not sing the songs as camp because 'girl group rock is part of her soul music, and the mad energy and excitement she throws into her favourites are her way of getting to their love, and their heartbreak, her way of blending experience with their innocence.'[110] In a lengthy introduction to Midler for the readers of *Rolling Stone*, Ed McCormack, who was also proselytizing for the Dolls at this point in time, would certainly have agreed with Marcus's view of how she channelled the girl group sound, but for all her vitality and 'energy akin to rock 'n' roll' she was not rock 'n' roll.[111]

Scorpio Rising re-ran the girl group sounds for a gay sensibility, with the director's subsequent production, *Kustom Kar Kommandos* (1965), doubling up on that mode with the Paris Sisters crooning 'Dream Lover' while a hunk in tight, pale blue jeans polishes his hot rod with a large powder puff. With *Mean Streets* (1973), Martin Scorsese overwrote that script, as the Dolls had been doing, and created a perfect urban soundtrack – The Ronettes, The Charts, The Shirelles, The Paragons, Little Caesar and the Romans, The Marvelettes, The Aquatones, Betty Everett, The Chantels, The Nutmegs, The Chips, Johnny Ace, The Shells and The Miracles – radiating out of jukeboxes and transistor radios; the sounds of the streets, bars and pool halls of Little Italy. In these scenes, Scorsese took back the songs from their queer appropriators, ignored the teenage girls who were the original intended audience, and gave them to the object of gay desire and a girl's sweet-teen fantasy, the doomed bad boy on the corner in the black leather jacket.

Marcus writes:

> The songs most often celebrated a shadowy male figure of wonderous attractiveness, but he took on a reality only as a function of the vitality, commitment, and musical invention of the girl singer . . . so mythical in fact, that when the Crystals meet him in 'Da Doo Ron Ron', even though he makes her heart stand still *some-body else* has to tell her that his name is Bill.[112]

Few songs step outside of this rulebook but one is 'The Boy from New York City', who, Marcus reports, has grown up to be a pimp. The shadowy boy as sexual procurer is surely the flip of The Shangri-Las' object of desire who is good-bad but not evil. The Dolls played that line, indeed sung it for all they were worth: 'what colour are his eyes?' 'I dunno he's always wearing shades', and how does he dance? 'Close, very very close.'

Leaving aside their cover of 'Give Him a Great Big Kiss', it was with songs like 'Bad Girl' that the Dolls showed their debt to, and a disdain for, the girl-group sound. They were not producing a homage to The Shangri-Las, as Bette Midler did on her 1972 debut, they were throwing the girl's innocence back into her face, laughing at her fantasies. In assuming the role of the shadowy male the Dolls reprised the part as the girl's tormentor, not her gentle lover, in black denim and motorcycle boots. They were the bad boy looking for a kiss, surveying the scene with a pimp's-eye view of the dance floor. In this they played out the same misogynistic hand the Stones had been dealing for the past ten years, but the Dolls did not have in their gang the kind of angelic naughty boy that appealed to that teenage audience of girls that their mentors once had in Brian Jones.

♀ ♀ ♀

Unlike Midler, no one ever accused the Dolls of not being rock 'n' roll but whether or not they were any good at it was another matter entirely. From 1972 to 1973 the band's advocates held the upper hand, but by 1974 their detractors took control of the narrative, especially in reviews of *Too Much Too Soon*. Dave Marsh in *Rolling Stone* and Ron Ross in *Phonograph Record* continued to support them, but one-time booster Nick Kent thought the production and songwriting under par and the whole thing was just 'too cute'.[113] Writing in *Gay News*, Phil McNeill laid it on the line: 'I feel like I'm in a time warp listening to this garbage, for apart from the Seventies macho guitar sound everything about it is ten years old.'[114]

For McNeill the Dolls now sounded as anachronistic as The Shangri-Las must have to teenage ears when 'Leader of the Pack' rose up the charts once more to number three in 1971. This didn't mean that teens didn't like it, they were buying it after all, but it was definitely old. The reissue was promoted with a cheap cut-and-paste animated film featuring drawings of girls who looked exactly like those in the comic section of *Jackie* (or any other contemporary teenage magazine) and a similarly updated Jimmy, who looks like a British rocker on a chopped Harley. Together, the sound and image compressed time.

The Dolls' stretch in the limelight was short, eighteen months maybe, but in that moment they were of their time even as their fans believed they transcended that moment and their critics thought they belonged to an earlier era. In a 1973 feature in *Sounds*, they were trailed as 'The Shangri-Las of the Seventies', the past as the present. Perhaps to counter such expected regressive constructions, David Johansen told his interviewer that the Dolls were absolutely about the contemporary, the now:

> The words, and the songs, are strictly scenarios of our civilisation at this late point of the century. The howls and the whistles that punctuate the tunes are the sounds of our streets, and the lyrics tell us what happens above them, on them, and under them. Whether the Dolls are cruising 'Looking for A Kiss', riding a 'Subway Train', or watching 'Jet Boy' up in the skies, they're telling us about how it is in New York City, USA, and how it's gonna be everywhere soon.[115]

Johansen delivers a brilliant piece of self-analysis – the New York Dolls, above, beneath and on the city's streets. But whether he knew it or not, this scenario is also a direct echo of what Pete Townshend was saying about The Who, circa 1965.[116]

Following the band's break-up in 1975, the man who had signed the Dolls to Mercury Records, Paul Nelson, penned a valedictory piece on them for the *Village Voice*. He loved the Dolls still, perhaps more than ever now that they were gone, but he could see their faults with an acuity that only hindsight can provide. He wrote that the Rolling Stones could have 'written "Bad Girl", the Dolls could never have brought about "Moonlight Mile": they lacked the smoke and duskiness.'[117] The Dolls' tastes were too New York to appeal to Middle America, too limited, whereas the 'Stones could encompass the broad human comedy':

> In the end, [the Dolls] rode on real rather than symbolic subway trains to specific rather than universal places, played for an audience of intellectuals or kids even farther out than they were; and, when they eventually met the youth of the country, that youth seemed more confused than captivated by them, and could no more imagine itself a New York Doll than it could some exotic palm tree growing in Brooklyn. The Dolls appealed to an audience that had seen the end of the world, had in fact bought tickets for it but probably didn't attend because there was something even funnier on television that night.[118]

Someone who hadn't been watching television was Malcolm McLaren. Before the Dolls had run riot in his store he had been an ardent rock 'n' roll revivalist, a romantic who saw in the 1950s a model of revolt from the quotidian that he might put to contemporary use. Observing the Dolls, he saw that his view of the past was a dead end. They were his epiphany, they made manifest the idea that ransacking the past did not have to be about parody, pastiche or homage. It could, if you so willed it, be a wholly transgressive ploy: a ploy every bit as larcenous as rock 'n' roll had been when it first entered public consciousness with Elvis, Eddie Cochran, Little Richard and Gene Vincent. The Dolls didn't borrow from those that had gone before; they stole and plundered and created a juvenile jive that was perfect in its aggressive refusal of the social facts of everyday life. They taught McLaren to play with culture, not revere it, an idea he ran with.

Regardless of their drug habits and internecine conflicts, what killed the Dolls and brought down their house, as certainly as the Mercer Arts Center had collapsed in on itself, was that they were seen as parlaying something second-hand, pre-worn, once-loved yet so easily discarded. That was the reality, even if, as McLaren knew, it was a gross oversimplification. The past is always with us, the new in pop culture is nothing but a marketing angle. The Dolls understood the way things were; they worked with what history had handed them and, in that short window of time allowed, they traded in a rock 'n' roll that stood tall with what had gone before and bettered anything that came after.

♥ ♥ ♥

If the girl group sound still resonated in 1972 it carried with it a definite necrophiliac taint; cult or camp it was a reanimation of a dead corpus. That year, Nik Cohn was, as he told it, holed up in New York with a one-time Teendream, Rebecca – in her thirties but she still looked about seventeen with 'pubescent bad skin, no breasts and infinity eyes; still went out in ponytails; still chewed gum, walked with a wiggle, necked on sofas, treasured pin-ups of Frankie Lymon'.[119] When the other members of the Teendreams had got married, turned to fat or hooking, Rebecca was left to spend twenty hours of every day in her bed and the rest of her time procuring drugs. Cohn is obsessed with her. She represented Manhattan and all that he loved about the city; its speed and its rage. At night she played him 'Angel Baby' by Rosie and the Originals, 'Tonite Tonite' by the Mello Kings, drowning him 'ballad after slow smooch ballad: "Every Night I Pray" by The Chantels, "Sixteen Candles" by the Crests and "Deserie" by the Charts, "The Ten Commandments Of Love" by Harvey and the Moonglows, "Goodnight Sweetheart Goodnight" by the Spaniels, "Lovers Never Say Goodbye" by the Flamingos, on and on far past dawn'.[120]

Cohn's delirious repast is an unexpected and beautiful entrapment. Pop for him had been split into two camps: revolt and love. His predilection had always been with rumbles, m'bikes, switchblades: 'outrage, excess, impossible gesture; first and last it was release.'[121] He had spurned soft kisses and sentiment but finally, at the grand age of 22, lying alongside Rebecca, his 'sickness swole', he gave himself completely to the fantasy of a teenage Madonna loved by a motorbike angel. Teen dreams promised eternal youth, he wrote, within them you could be sixteen forever: 'Nothing could age you, nothing corrupt you or turn you sour; nothing was dimmed, not ever.'[122] It was the mythos the New York Dolls peddled wholesale when they traded out of the Mercer, Max's and Biba. It was why so many of their original supporters thought they had the power to transport them back to their primal teenage selves.

Before long, Cohn is staying in bed all day with his make-believe teen dream Madonna while the real Rebecca is out working street corners, cruising St Marks to bring home the cocaine. In his narcotized state, he plotted to fly to LA to find Phil Spector, to give him his girl and then, warm in the couple's embrace, die.

Written a year before the publication of *Rock Dreams*, Cohn's article on the vocal groups sounds of the late 1950s, 'Rebecca and the Teendreams', published in the October 1972 edition of the British rock magazine *Cream*, told not just the tale of marvellous, fabricated, disposable pop songs master-minded by the likes of Spector, Shadow Morton, Leiber and Stoller, but also the tale of the listener ten to fifteen years after the fact. That person had aged and been corrupted by life, experience had soured his pleasures, for him the light had dimmed. Rock 'n' roll was now only a fever trance rinsed in coke; a fugue played for addicts, whores and pimps. For critics such as Hollingworth, the Dolls stalled that tale of rock 'n' roll's decrepitude, but behind the rumble and flash of their act there was something preternatural, vampiric – the old mas-querading as young as it fed on youth's energy and exuberance. In this version, third-generation rock was not a new begin-ning, it was rock 'n' roll's funeral with punk as its wake and obituary.

CONCLUSION: OH, I WAS
MOVED BY A TEEN DREAM

Gene Vincent played a short-tour of Britain in 1969 with backing by the Teddy Boy band The Wild Angels. A television crew documented the first four days of the singer's stay and told a story rich in the pathos of a middle-age too soon met brought up hard against a grubby British social reality.[1] While they wait for their hero in the airport arrival area a small gaggle of Teddy Boys kill time by pouring scorn on skinheads for not looking smart, what with their granddad braces, old jeans, cropped hair and all that. Their aggression towards others who don't share their sartorial taste is an insular and self-affirming act; the anticipated arrival of their hero no more than an excuse to gather together and promote their gang identity. 'You know, Gene Vincent is the greatest,' said one Ted. 'He's good you know,' confirmed another, 'but if he don't play for us he's a wanker.' All this delivered like fans of Nik Cohn's Johnny Apollo, just before they turn on him.

Soft spoken, polite and unassuming, Gene Vincent is in constant pain from his bad leg and a severe case of dyspepsia. To cap it all he's caught a cold. His hair is dirty and unstyled, he's overweight and dresses like the guy who sits in the corner

Backseat for the rock 'n' roll revival. Bush Hollyhead's illustration for
Club International (July 1973).

of the pub muttering to himself (or like Mark E. Smith, which
is much the same thing). He's only 34 years old. In two years
he'll be dead from a ruptured stomach ulcer, the heartburn
having killed him, his bad health aggravated, no doubt, by

having travelled with The Wild Angels in a Dormer van to play an Isle of Wight dance club. Guy Peellaert's image of Vincent as a punk with a switchblade in a leather jacket terrorizing the local constabulary is here just myth, echoes of records on a jukebox and an image of a man hanging onto a mic stand as if his life depended on it; a stance that would be reframed by Mick Farren right on down through David Bowie (on the rear of *Pinups*) to Ian Dury, Johnny Rotten and Joe Strummer.[2] Many others tried to grab that mic stand but most failed to reach it, clutching at air as they read Gene Vincent's name on the tail of his shirt.

No group missed that stand quite as spectacularly as Teddy Boy revivalists, the 'Super Sexy ... Ballsy Rock 'n' Roll Allstars', who played out their ascribed role in things over a seven-page photographic story published in 1972 in one of *Curious* magazine's many special editions. The band are depicted in various stages of undress in the company of two young women:

> Written and photographed by their manager, Waxie Maxie, this feature on the boys of an authentic Rock 'n' Roll group shows that they live up to their on-stage image off-stage. It's pure fantasy of course, and very funny – but isn't that what most music is about today: sexual fantasy and pure entertainment? The Rock 'n' Roll image of bicycle chains and knuckle dusters is hit in the eye with this. If music be the food – and fun – of love ... read on.[3]

These 'Ton-Up Teds in black shirts, long drape jackets, and blue suede shoes' had a new maxi-single to promote, *Rock 'n'*

Roll Allstars Play Party Rock. Released at the tail end of 1971, the disc features a medley of five golden oldies and T. Rex's 'Get It On'. On the latter, the Allstars' guitarist highlights the 'Peter Gunn' riff Bolan's composition was based on, as if to say, in a cocky put-down, 'look where he stole it from!' It is a depressing affair, wholly lacking in imagination, much like the photo story:

> He watched her crawling towards him on all fours, barking like a dog, eyes wild, and nostrils flared. Furiously he peeled off his stage clothes, and tossed the Teddy Boy clobber (Let It Rock, 430 King's Road, SW3) towards a chair, not bothering to notice that his Morley string vest and lime green socks fell into a bowl of dirty water.[4]

The band's idea of release, of letting rip, is pitched as an authentic response to the false consciousness held by others: 'The group's stage act moves you fast – like a dose of Andrews – but without the UGH! SHUDDER! CRINGE! effects of today's mind-dulling "rock" groups, who suffer from dandruff, smelly feet, and have lice crawling in their beards!'[5]

In 1972, youthful rebellion was not a shared and uniformly expressed endeavour. Within its own defined limits, its deadening insularity, it could be cringingly conservative, like Waxie Maxie taking refuge in his proletarian roots and misogynistic mindset, while the band he managed took one of the truly great singles of 1971, or any other year, and reduced its glorious sense of self-possession, sex and swagger into a mindless sub-Duane Eddy death twang.

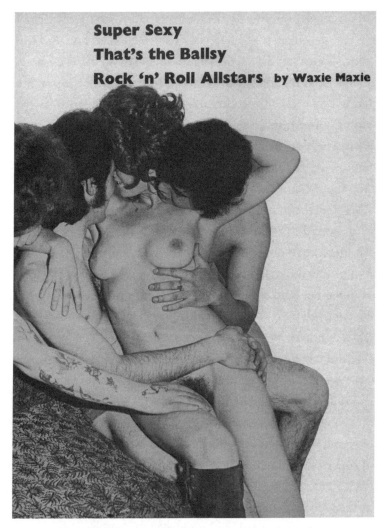

Super Sexy
That's the Ballsy
Rock 'n' Roll Allstars by Waxie Maxie

Ballsy: the Rock 'n' Roll Allstars in *Curious* magazine (1972).

The Rock 'n' Roll Allstars had one good gag in their pocket: they had played Red China to wild acclaim, so they said. Who could argue with that? The proof was on the front of their album sleeve, Chairman Mao in a Let It Rock drape and George

Cox creepers. But mostly the band were just a bad joke. Their type of revivalism was what Mick Farren had early on said was a dead end, a tawdry, sexless act of onanism. In its reactionary pursuit of authenticity, its refusal to contend with the present, Teddy Boy rock 'n' roll closed down options as readily as any Monday morning. But, at its most splendid, Nigel Dixon's Whirlwind, for example, it was as fabulous an expression of George Melly's revolt into style as can be imagined and, more than that, it spoke eloquently to those who wanted something other than the routine of everyday life. It had real value to those who aspired to make the juvenile jive of the youth club disco not just a temporary release but the whole of their existence. As a proposition, Teddy Boy rock 'n' roll was a living paradox of deference and impudence, conformity and rebellion, but the contradiction at its heart was one that could not be easily effaced or even held in abeyance for long.

Malcolm McLaren and Vivienne Westwood eventually understood that the future did not lie with Waxie Maxie and his confederates, which is why they got on a ferry and followed the New York Dolls from London to Paris at the end of November 1973. In France, the couple were part of the gallery of rogues celebrated in the French music press, including Eno, Nick Kent, and Michael Des Barres, who had joined the Dolls in their endless party.[6] When asked by his interviewer who among today's bands he admired, David Johansen turned to Malcolm for a prompt. 'Kilburn and the High Roads' was the answer that came back, not The Wild Angels, Shakin' Stevens and the Sunsets, Impalas, Houseshakers or any of the other revivalists who had been Let It Rock's most lucrative customers.[7] By then, 430 King's Road had already changed its name to Too Fast to Live, Too Young to Die and it would soon change it again, rejecting its 1950s associations altogether, to become Sex. The Soho porn connection, however, never quite quit, with *Curious* running a ten-page feature on the store in 1975 with Karen McCook (aka Susan Shaw aka Mona Solomon) modelling their clothes. Three years earlier she had been a cover model for *Penthouse* and had posed as a Bardot-like figure in leathers, leaning back on a chopper, with a Teddy Boy and his cut-throat razor at her side for the sleeve of the 1972 United Artists compilation of golden oldies, *Rock 'n' Roll Is Here to Stay*.

The best of third-generation rock plundered the past, didn't present it as an authentic artefact and used it to refigure the present. The golden age of rock 'n' roll was not 1956 but whenever Ian Hunter sang to the dudes and, anyway, it was Alex Harvey, born in 1935 (four years before Hunter), who best held the claim to be The Last of the Teenage Idols. Harvey was there for the unfolding of the first generation, worked through its second iteration (with a stint in the pit band for the musical *Hair*) and then, third time around, with The Sensational Alex Harvey Band (SAHB), he was at last a headliner and every sentient juvenile delinquent's hero.

Paul Gadd had also served time across all three generations, first as Paul Raven and then as Gary Glitter. Likewise his contemporary, born two years earlier in 1942, Bernard William Jewry managed a career that spanned the decades, first as Shane Fenton and then as Alvin Stardust. Others from that first generation of British rockers found space on the revival bandwagon: Billy Fury, Marty Wilde and Terry Dene. The latter was described on his 1974 comeback LP, *I Thought Terry Dene Was Dead*, as 'Britain's first mean and moody rock 'n' roll star'. He had disappeared from sight after National Service had interrupted his singing career, which, in turn, was cut short by a spell in a mental institution. For those Teddy Boys who thought Gary Glitter's resurrection shuffle was a joke in bad taste, and Terry Dene was still best left forgotten, at least these two hadn't appropriated their wardrobe like Mud and Showaddywaddy and shaved off whatever vestige of rebellion was left in a drape suit and a pair of crepe-soled shoes.

Though Teds held their own through much of the 1970s, successfully petitioning for their own radio show on the BBC and finding, after skinheads and hairies, new forms of opposition with the King's Road punks – McLaren's new customers – the rockin' scene was changing fast, working again to put a gap between the authentic and inauthentic. The transition can be seen with Charly Records' 1978 release *Rockabilly Rules OK?* The compilation featured on its cover an anonymous lad with an unruly quiff, wearing a donkey jacket, blue jeans and work boots – dandyism all but dead but street cred re-established. Youth style goes in cycles and, by the late 1970s and early '80s, there was something of a peacock renaissance with the Polecats, Stray Cats and Levi and the Rockats, all styled in pink peg pants by Johnsons (recently arrived in the King's Road after a long spell in Kensington Market).[8] The Polecats shook things up with spirited versions of 'Jeepster' and 'John I'm Only Dancing', which were as good a riposte as you could find to the Allstars' version of 'Get It On'.

While British rock 'n' roll vocal groups The Darts and Rocky Sharpe and the Replays, née Razors, brought back a bit of showbiz missing with the likes of Crazy Cavan 'n' the Rhythm Rockers, they in turned lacked the grand spectacle

The Last of the Teenage Idols ... Alex Harvey.

of their Atlantic cousins Sha Na Na and Flash Cadillac and the Continental Kids. The pizzazz evident in *West Side Story*, and channelled through those American bands, hadn't translated well into British revivalism. The Wild Angels' covers of songs from the stage production of *Grease* – 'Beauty School Dropout' and 'Greased Lightning' – show a band willing to step outside of a parochial authenticity in search of an elusive hit single, and they give the tunes some welly that was entirely lacking in the original cast recording and, subsequently, in the film's soundtrack. But there's little flair in the Angels' delivery, the drama of pop to them is as a foreign field.[9] Those who were less concerned with fidelity to an image of the 1950s, but did embrace its drama, like Alex Harvey and Mott the Hoople, put on a show and produced records that evoked the razzmatazz of Broadway.

You can hear the direct echo of musical theatre in Mick Ronson's 'Slaughter on 10th Avenue' and in The Sweet's rambunctious version of 'The Man with the Golden Arm', which features a lengthy drum solo that concludes with a Las Vegas jungle grind before segueing into a Burundi beat (anticipating Adam and the Ants and Bow Wow Wow), but it is best manifest in the sort of revue Mott and SAHB delivered, which made rock itself the topic of the show – an idea first registered with Bowie's Ziggy spectacle at the Rainbow that Duncan Fallowell had born witness to. It was evident on Harvey's 'Vambo' suite of songs played as a 'Hot City Symphony', but it would reach a kind of perfect summation with the two post-Bowie Mott the Hoople albums that hit maximized form in their live shows with the set piece of 'Marionette' running into the medley of 'Drivin' Sister', 'Crash Street Kids' and 'Violence'.

Truth be told, though, watching Mott the Hopple or SAHB had as much in common with seeing a Broadway show as *Tommy* had with opera, which was not much at all. Rock's theatricality was more akin to that found in a passing show or a carnival of freaks as portrayed by Guy Peellaert in his illustration for Bowie's *Diamond Dogs*, than a Broadway or West End extravaganza. In reality, much of it had the feel of an end-of-the-pier-style finale orchestrated by Ken Russell, with Portsmouth Teds scuttling about on the beach beneath its walkways: the film version of *Tommy* playing as the *reductio ad absurdum* of rock.

Before things had got quite that insular (and self-regarding), Pete Townshend discussed with Charles Shaar Murray the backwards glance of *Quadrophenia* and pop's recent historical and intellectual turn, of which he thought *Pinups* a particularly egregious example. The problem, he said, had been compounded by a critical cabal threatened by the onset of early middle-age. Townshend found fault with rock journalists who want their stars to stay young or to be their court jester, imagined as a noble savage, like Iggy Pop – the former not possible and the latter not desirable. The Stooges' singer appealed to the more jaded critics, Townshend said, because he thinks, as them, like an old man. His point was that Iggy was incapable of writing for an audience of fifteen- or sixteen-year-olds. That demographic, Townshend said, needed music that is cast with 'tight, integrated, directed, pointed frustration', much like that produced today by The Sweet (and he was not being facetious).[10] That said, he also felt The Sweet were a bit out of place time wise: 'They should have been around ten years ago.' But if The Sweet had been making the scene in 1963/4 they would have been a second-generation band, like The Who. What made them a pop band who were, contrary to Townshend's argument, precisely right for the times was that they had learnt much of their craft directly from The Who; they were strictly third-generation.

Setting aside their thirteen Mike Chinn and Nicky Chapman-authored top twenty hits, the band's signature album was 1974's *Desolation Boulevard* featuring 'The Man with the Golden Arm'. Housed in a Hipgnosis-designed gatefold sleeve with images of the four members of the band haloed and pasted onto a view looking down Sunset Boulevard (just like Ian Hunter in his suburban dreams of Hollywood and Vine), the record kicks off with 'Six Teens', which features a Bowie-esque cast of characters – Bobby and Billy, Julie and Johnnie, Suzie and Davey – all still stuck in 1968, which, at least for Billy, was out of date. The album ends with a cover of The Who's 'My Generation', a rendition that in its fidelity to the original is the converse of Bowie's 'I Can't Explain'.

As a single 'Six Teens' followed up 'Teenage Rampage', its title suggestive of a repeating theme of songs about the travails of adolescence, an endless summertime blues. But 'Six Teens' was not a direct continuation as 'Teenage Rampage' had been to 'Blockbuster!' 'Hellraiser' and 'Ballroom Blitz'. It was more indirect, less about the now than about yesterday. As a youth club anthem it worked well enough, but as a dance number it was not much better than 'Drive-In Saturday'. It lacked that drop-shoulder sway and stomping beat of its predecessors. Instead what the band and Chinnichap produced was a wry comment on the 1960s teenage dream that no one had yet woken up from, a deep slumber that third-generation bands couldn't

The Sweet on Desolation Boulevard.

pull free from any more than they could from producing Eddie Cochran rehashes.

The figure of Cochran returns with 'Turn It Down', the album's third track, which has the familiar authority figures shutting out teenage pleasures, calling the noisome kid a 'punk' and demanding he dial down the volume of that god-awful sound. The track features Steve Priest doing a David Johansen set of motormouth asides, 'don't give me no lip' kid (and its verses provided a blueprint for Eddie and the Hot Rods' 'Teenage Depression', released but two years later). As much as the album's lyrical themes are confined by past expectations, which is to say the conventions of teen anthems, then so too are the main influences on the music. After Mick Ronson, guitarist Andy Scott showed on 'Solid Gold Brass' and 'Turn It Down' that he was the era's best Jeff Beck interpreter, while his composition 'Lady Starlight' has an arrangement which, like the songs of Big Star or Badfinger, stands in thrall to the grandeur of 1960s pop.

The Sweet's core business had been parlayed through lessons gleaned in a bedroom posing in front of a mirror with Cream,

Small Faces and The Who as the wannabe rock star's soundtrack. *Tommy* is the band's secret text; they were keen students of its vocal harmonies. But it is not a simple case of pastiche or plagiarism; they build on The Who's arrangements, much like Queen had done. The reverberations between them and Freddie and the boys is particularly noticeable on 'Medusa', but The Sweet were never going to make a highbrow concept album, or bother parodying opera, which is why they end the album with a fairly straight cover of 'My Generation', a fulsome celebration of being sixteen forever. The track concludes with the sound of the band larking around, having a giggle as sonic slices of tympany, church bells and a hammered piano finish off what the feedback hadn't quite managed to conclude. It is the perfect end, reiterating the lock-grooved hold earlier generations had over the contemporary scene and then bringing the house down rather than worrying over the predicament, much in the vein of the New York Dolls.

American third-generation rock thoroughly absorbed the iconography of Leonard Bernstein and Stephen Sondheim's musical, albeit heavily filtered and focus corrected. They did so by reference to things such as Irving Shulman's 1947 novel *Amboy Dukes* and Bruce Davidson's photo essay *Brooklyn Gang* (1961), which found a kind of culmination of sorts in Richard Price's 1974 novel *The Wanderers* – all sound-tracked by Dion and the Belmonts, Gary U.S. Bonds, The Coasters, The Crystals and, of course, The Ronettes and Shangri-Las – a potent mix of the reality of street life and pulp romanticism. Dave Marsh put it this way:

It's a great temptation to view Ronnie Spector as a rare and precious treasure that we once held but somehow slipped away. After all, so many of us fell in love the first time we heard her sing – 'Be My Baby', 'Do I Love You', 'Walking in the Rain', or one of the half dozen other great singles she made as Veronica, lead singer of the Ronettes, with producer (and later husband) Phil Spector, from 1963–1965. And since 1965, as Ronnie acknowledges, nothing has quite measured up to the magic of those moments.[11]

As third-generation rock took hold of the imagination, Dave Marsh was hurting; the music he loved, its innocence above all else, was being 'curdled into cynicism'.[12] He believed that rock 'n' roll could save lives; it had certainly shaped his: 'we had nothing; rock lent us a sense that we could have it all.'[13] But rock, over the course of the 1970s, had betrayed itself, lost its heart and become a stone cold product: 'Asking who was fake and who was real used to be half the joy of the thing. Losing that option was our own fault, of course, but that doesn't make it hurt less. Rock saved my life. It also broke my heart.'[14] What gave him back hope that such a vitality could be retrieved were the recordings and performances of Bruce Springsteen, within whom the 'great promise of rock and roll' was at last fulfilled.[15]

Even if he led the pack, Springsteen was not a lone wolf in the project of pumping life back into American rock 'n' roll as corporate hands squeezed it dry. His home town boys, Southside Johnny and the Asbury Jukes, shared his vision. On their sophomore album from 1977, with the perfect third-generation title, an answer of sorts to all that British 1950s fakery, *This Time It's for Real*, the ten-piece band line up under a streetlight outside the Pussycat Theatre, a strip club. Though it is dark out, at least four of them are wearing shades and all but one has on a satin jacket with the band's name emblazoned on its rear. The album is dedicated to Jerry Leiber, Mike Stoller and 'Pammy Popovich's silly daddy'. Like with Springsteen, there's an acute sense of street-corner knowledge and gang loyalty with roots dug deep into the neighbourhood's cracked sidewalks. The band as a soul brotherhood is best visualized in the image of Springsteen leaning on Clarence Clemons on the sleeve of *Born to Run*; the bonds formed early are the ones that will define you.

Brownsville Station's *School Punks* album, complete with a cover version of Gary Glitter's 'I'm the Leader of the Gang', is like a caricature of the poses Springsteen and Southside Johnny are flawlessly pulling off.[16] The cartoon version was better presented by The Dictators and then delivered to perfection by the Ramones. That 1950s street-punk stance forms the spine of the imagery that drew together the bands that played at Max's Kansas City and CBGBs in the second half of the 1970s: Mink DeVille, Blondie, The Heartbreakers, The Cramps and Robert Gordon as the standouts. But it was there too in lesser efforts by The Tuff Darts, Wayne County and Cherry Vanilla: just wanting to play so the kids could dance, as Johnny Thunders would sell his post-Dolls schtick with The Heartbreakers. It was also a club scene where the relationship between band and audience was at its most intimate, which is to say, honest. These were all instances of a flight from rock's overweening ambition and the reckless pursuit of ever bigger numbers in record sales and attendance figures; and the failure to leave the previous two decades behind.

Yet, compared to what Bolan, Bowie, Roxy and the New York Dolls had achieved using similar materials, and finding themselves in a similar set of situations caused by the uncertain end of generation two and the extraordinary lionization of generation one, generation three (the late New York version) seems less a new wave than a dead end every bit as futile as that in which Britain's Teddy Boys found themselves trapped, even if the American bands played it with a passionate attitude that matched such an end-of-days scenario, and did it too with undoubted style – because, what kind of chump could deny the Ramones?

Writing to the *Melody Maker*'s 'Mailbag' at the end of December 1973, Hemel Hempstead resident, Mick Johnson, picked up on the hoo-hah that surrounded the Dolls' recent UK visit. The critical backlash the band had faced was as narrow-minded as that which created the generation gap in the 1960s, he thought, but something had changed: 'Gone is the revolutionary violence of the early sixties. No longer will society be shocked by the outrageous Stones. How come no one has told the Dolls yet? It is impossible to recreate the excitement of yesteryear. New kicks have to be found.'[17] The Dolls served up a trash aesthetic that said generation one and two don't rate much more than as junk, so who cares that the latest iteration is no better? Let's just dance. But as Simon Reynolds writes:

> their camp and cavalier refusal to take anything seriously – is what held them back from being the Sex Pistols. The Dolls *didn't* mean it, man. Johansen didn't have Johnny Rotten's puritan streak of righteous wrath. Rotten could do sarcasm, but there was nothing ironic

about the Sex Pistols. When Rotten sang about being society's 'flowers in the dustbin', he wasn't saying, 'We're trash and proud of it'; he was railing against the wasting of youth's precious potential.[18]

Were the Pistols then the new kick the commuter from Hemel was looking for? In their careering rush into no future, the Sex Pistols, like the Dolls, could make you feel that intense experience in which others before had revelled. They could even make it appear as if it was for the first time – because they played it as if it would be the last time. Whatever Rotten's attitude belied, the Pistols, as much as anyone, knew they were peddling a morbid form, old thrills in new threads – no more tomorrows.

As for The Clash, they, like the Pistols, had figured out that third-generation rock had never really got going, the weight of the legacy it carried on its back was still dragging things down, so each night, throughout 1977, they killed Elvis, The Beatles and the Rolling Stones. But who believed in that as anything more than a bit of theatre, another bit of business in the White Riot's passing show? Certainly not the Subway Sect, who, as a support act, simply turned their back on the audience and declared 'We Oppose All Rock and Roll'. But however much punk tried to suppress the music's past, the repressed returned. By 1979, The Clash had stopped all attempts to murder the object of their desire with its own mirror image and had joined with Springsteen, albeit with a suitably Anglicized accent, in resurrecting rock 'n' roll so it might, if you could just persuade yourself to suspend disbelief for a moment, live again. The album *London Calling* was their rebel truce with the music's past, the masterpiece and true end of third-generation rock 'n' roll, lover's rock even. Its 29 tracks were a totem for all that had been experienced and witnessed in the 23 years since 'Heartbreak Hotel', one final line in the West End Story that said, 'Balls to you daddy. I ain't never coming back.'

NOTE ON SOURCES

What started out as a research project undertaken in the British Library (BL) reading rooms ended up, due to COVID-19, online and with daily care packages sent by eBay sellers. My primary source material was the UK music press, which has been digitalized but was taken offline some years back due to an ongoing dispute over authorship rights. Accessing hard copies, or microfilm, can still be done at the BL for all the major publications, *Melody Maker*, *New Musical Express*, *Sounds* and so on, but their holdings of less mainstream journals are often incomplete. *Zigzag* doesn't start until issue eight, for example, and the final five issues of *Frendz* are missing. The BL has only a few issues of *Cream* and some of those have been cut up, but it does have a complete run of *Strange Days* (all four editions). Complete runs of *Oz* and *IT* can be accessed online at https://ro. uow.edu.au/ozlondon and www.internationaltimes.it.

A major gap in the BL is the lack of American music publications, but I was able to access *Rolling Stone* through the now archaic technology of a CD-ROM I own and I have acquired a sizeable collection of *Creem*. *Rock Scene* and *Star* have been scanned and are available online at https://rockscenemagazine.com.

Though I miss the illustrations, advertisements and marginalia that accompanied the original pieces, Rock's Backpages is an absolutely essential resource: www.rocksbackpages.com.

REFERENCES

INTRODUCTION

1 Steve Mann, 'Alice Cooper Third Generation Rock', *Frendz*, 4 (23 June 1971), pp. 20–21; Jamie Mandelkau, 'Alice Cooper', *IT*, 106 (16–30 June 1971), pp. 10–11.

2 Alice worked the idea not only in London but in American interviews: 'Our music is . . . high energy . . . That's what third-generation rock is . . . look at us, the MC5 and The Stooges – it's all high-energy music.' *Hooka Magazine*, republished in *Zigzag*, 22 (1971), pp. 13–14. He also makes more or less the same points in Elaine Gross, 'Where Are the Chickens', *Rolling Stone* (15 October 1970), p. 18.

3 Nik Cohn and Guy Peellaert, *Rock Dreams: Under the Broadwalk* (London, 1973), np.

4 Ibid.

5 Ibid.

6 Ibid.

7 Ibid.

8 Paul Gorman's blog has regularly shared images from *Curious*, see www.paulgormanis.com, accessed 2 November 2020.

9 Dai Pusher-Davis, 'Rudy Valentino', *Curious*, 19 (May 1971), pp. 39–40.

10 Richard Allen, *Suedehead* (London, 1971), p. 27.

11 Barney Hoskyns, *Glam! Bowie, Bolan and the Glitter Rock Revolution* (London, 1998), p. 11.

12 Ibid.

13 Jerry Hopkins, 'Beatle Loathers Return: Britain's Teddy Boys', *Rolling Stone*, 103 (2 March 1972), pp. 1, 14, 16.

14 Ibid., p. 14.

15 Ibid., p. 16.

16 Paul Gorman, *The Life and Times of Malcolm McLaren: The Biography* (London, 2020), p. 131.

17 Ibid., p. 136.

18 Ibid., p. 150.

19 Ibid.

20 Iggy was delivering the annual John Peel Lecture (October 2014).

21 'Forward into the Fifties', *Daily Mirror* (30 May 1972), pp. 14–15.

22 Ian Hunter, *Diary of a Rock 'n' Roll Star* (London, 1974), p. 7.

23 Mick Farren, 'Once It's Started', *Oz*, 48 (Winter 1973), pp. 12–15.

24 Mick Farren, 'Bedsitter Loving', *Club International*, iv/7 (July 1975), pp. 20–22.

25 Mick Farren, 'Back to That Teenage Heaven', *Club International*, iv/9 (September 1975), pp. 50–52.

26 Jonathon Green, 'Blood, Sweat and Sheer Imagination in the Porn Trade', *IT*, 153 (May 1973), p. 7.

27 'The Deviants', *Zigzag*, 5 (September 1969), pp. 28–9.

28 Mike Clifford, 'Mick Farren and The Deviants', *Beat Instrumental* (January 1969), pp. 29–30.

29 Quoted in Nik Cohn, 'Ready Steady Gone', *Observer Magazine* (27 August 1967), pp. 12–16, 19.

30 Nik Cohn, 'Pop Scene', *Queen* (8 May 1968), p. 28.

31 Quoted in George Tremlett, *The David Bowie Story* (London, 1974), p. 111.

32 Mark Plummer, 'Silverhead Savage', *Melody Maker* (6 June 1973), p. 39.

1 ROCK 'N' ROLL UNDERGROUND

1 Mick Farren, *Give the Anarchist a Cigarette* (London, 2001), p. 34.

2 Mick Farren, *Gene Vincent: There's One in Every Town* (London, 2004), p. 21.

3 Mick Farren, *Watch Out Kids* (London, 1972), np.

4 Mick Farren, 'Back to That Teenage Heaven', *Club International*, IV/9 (September 1975), pp. 51–2.

5 Farren, *Anarchist*, p. 228.

6 For a much more positive assessment of The Deviants' output see Seth Wimpfheimer, 'The Deviants We Got Garbage!', *Fuz*, 2 (Autumn 2000), pp. 2–11.

7 'Easy Rider with Arthur Lee and Richard Williams', podcast (23 August 2019), www.rocksbackpages.com, accessed 5 August 2021.

8 Rich Deakin, *Keep It Together! Cosmic Boogie with The Deviants and the Pink Fairies* (London, 2007), p. 75.

9 Jenny Fabian, 'All Change', *Queen* (5 February 1969), pp. 58–64.

10 Ibid.

11 Ibid.

12 Charles Nicholl, 'IT, *Oz* and All the Others', *Daily Telegraph Magazine* (28 September 1973), pp. 60–66.

13 Ibid.

14 Ibid.

15 David Huxley, *Nasty Tales: Sex, Drugs, Rock 'n' Roll and Violence in the British Underground* (London, 2001).

16 Nicholl, 'IT', *Oz*, p. 63.

17 Pat Long, *The History of the NME: High Times and Low Lives at the World's Most Famous Music Magazine* (London, 2012), p. 74.

18 The commercial importance of coverage of the music scene and the political backlash to it in the Underground press is discussed in Nigel Fountain, *Underground: The London Alternative Press, 1966–74* (London, 1988), pp. 80–85.

19 Martin Cerf and Ben Edmonds, 'About the Author: Dave Marsh', sleeve notes accompanying *Jan and Dean Anthology Album* (1971).

20 Ibid.

21 Ibid.

22 Sarah Malone, 'We Want the World and We Want It Now!', *Strange Days*, 2 (Autumn 1970), pp. 10–11.

23 Ibid.

24 Ibid.

25 Fountain, *Underground*, p. 51.
26 Mick Farren and Edward Barker, *Watch Out Kids* (London, 1972), np.
27 Ibid.
28 Ibid.
29 Jonathon Green, 'Light Yourself a Candle', *IT*, 134 (27 July–10 August 1972), pp. 14–15.
30 Ibid.
31 Ibid.
32 Ibid.
33 Ibid.
34 Ibid.
35 Charles Shaar Murray, 'Watch Out Kids' review, *Cream*, 16 (September 1972), p. 42.
36 Mick Farren, 'Rock – Energy for Revolution', *Melody Maker* (3 October 1970), p. 31.
37 Cited in John Carding, 'He Not Busy Being Born Is Busy Dying . . .', *IT*, 127 (6 April 1972), p. 16.
38 Farren and Barker, *Watch Out Kids*, np.
39 Mick Farren, 'How "Free" Is a Free Festival?', *Cream*, 21 (February 1973), pp. 10–11.
40 Farren and Barker, *Watch Out Kids*, np.
41 Ibid.
42 Mick Farren, 'Letters', *Friends*, 14 (18 September 1970), p. 13.
43 Ibid.
44 Ibid.
45 'The End of the Summer', *Frendz*, 12 (14 October 1971), p. 21.
46 Arthur A. Pitt, 'The Underground Music Is Dead Long Live Pop', *IT*, 72 (28 January 1970), p. 13.
47 Mick Farren, 'Do Gooders Suck', *IT*, 4 (27 February–13 March 1970), p. 7.
48 Mick Farren, 'If the Underground Is Dead, Then God Help Us All', *IT*, 73 (12–15 February 1970), p. 17.
49 Ian, 'The Importance of Not Being Earnest', *Zigzag*, 12 (May 1970), pp. 5–7.
50 Ibid., p. 45.
51 Ibid.

52 Steve Mann, 'It's All Wank', *IT*, 2 (20 November–3 December 1970), p. 11.
53 Ibid.
54 Ibid.
55 Ibid.
56 Ibid.
57 Ibid.
58 Eddie Briggs, 'Edgar Agin', *IT*, 93 (3–17 December 1970).
59 Geoffrey Cannon, 'Third World War', *The Guardian* (16 October 1970), p. 12.
60 Ibid.
61 Ibid.
62 Ibid.
63 Anthony Haden-Guest, '3rd World War: A Long Way from Pepperland', *Friends*, 22 (22 January 1971), pp. 14–15.
64 Ibid.
65 Ibid.
66 Ibid.
67 Mick Farren, 'Third World War at the Northern Polytechnic', *IT*, 100 (25 March–8 April 1971), p. 21.
68 Mick Farren, 'Third World War', *IT*, 103 (6–20 May 1971), p. 19.
69 Steve Mann, 'Alice Cooper Third Generation Rock', *Frendz*, 4 (23 June 1971), pp. 20–21.
70 Ibid.
71 Ibid.
72 Mick Farren, 'Alice Cooper *Killer*', *IT*, 121 (13–27 January 1972), p. 19.
73 Nick Kent, 'The Politics of Flash', *New Musical Express* (6 April 1974), pp. 20–21, 39.
74 Ibid., p. 21.
75 Ibid.
76 Nick Kent, 'Alice Cooper: The Killer Comes to Town', *Frendz*, 32 (28 July 1972).
77 Ibid.

2 DIRTY-SWEET

1 Simon Frith, 'Letter from Britain: Life's a Gas, I Hope It's Gonna Last – Notes on T. Rex', *Creem* (July 1972), www.rocksbackpages.com, accessed 9 November 2020.
2 Ibid.
3 Ibid.
4 Ibid.
5 Nik Cohn, 'Pop Scene', *Queen* (8 May 1968), p. 28.
6 Ibid.
7 Cited in *The Real Marc Bolan: A Record Mirror Special* (London, 1972), p. 7.
8 Cohn, 'Pop Scene'.
9 Ibid.
10 Cited in Cliff McLenehan, *Marc Bolan, 1947–1977: A Chronology* (London, 2002), p. 68.
11 Cited ibid. (eBook edition, 2019), np.
12 Cited ibid., p. 74.
13 Cited ibid.
14 Nick Logan, 'Last of the Great Underground Groups', *New Musical Express* (19 December 1970), p. 2.
15 Ibid.
16 Ibid.
17 Ibid.
18 Ibid.
19 Ibid.
20 Ibid.
21 Ibid.
22 Ibid.
23 Keith Altham, 'Sounds', *Club* (December 1971), p. 23.
24 James Johnson, 'Took Talks', *New Musical Express* (15 April 1972), p. 11.
25 Ibid.
26 Ibid.
27 Michael Watts, 'T.Rextasy', *Melody Maker* (22 January 1972), p. 5.
28 McLenehan, *Marc Bolan*, p. 107.
29 *Frendz*, 17 (23 December 1971), np. With T. Rextasy in the air, in autumn 1972 the NME gave its centre pages over to an

interview with Took: Charles Shaar Murray, 'Steve Took –
from Bolan Boogie to Gutter Rock', *New Musical Express*
(14 October 1972), pp. 20–21.

30 'Bolan Booms with Cosmic Rock!', *Melody Maker*
(6 March 1971), p. 1.

31 Ibid.

32 Susan Male, 'Mail Bag', *Melody Maker* (22 July 1972), p. 16.

33 Tony Norman, 'Under the Influence Special', *New Musical
Express* (23 December 1972), p. 26.

34 Ibid.

35 Pete Frame, 'Meanwhile down in the Bolan Alley', *Zigzag*,
21 (1971), np.

36 Ibid.

37 Chris Welch, 'From Elf to Electric Warrior', in *Bolan:
The Rise to Fame of a 1972 Super Star – In Words and
Pictures. A Melody Maker Special* (London, 1972), p. 9.

38 Watts, 'T.Rextasy!', p. 14.

39 Ibid.

40 Ibid.

41 Ibid.

42 Nick Logan, 'Slade, T. Rex and Faces – The Mini Phenomenon:
An Analysis', *New Musical Express* (19 February 1972),
p. 15.

43 Ibid.

44 Cited ibid.

45 Cited ibid.

46 *New Musical Express* (25 March 1972), p. 1.

47 Tony Tyler, 'Reviews That Incredible Wembley Concert',
New Musical Express (25 March 1972), pp. 18, 27.

48 Ibid., p. 18.

49 Nick Logan, 'Marc Bolan: Takin' Care of Business',
New Musical Express (29 April 1972), pp. 6–7.

50 Cited in *New Musical Express* (30 September 1972), p. 5.

51 George Melly, *Revolt into Style: The Pop Arts in the 50s
and 60s* (Oxford, 1989), p. 117.

52 Richie Yorke, 'Bolan and America', *New Musical Express*
(6 May 1972), p. 11.

53 Mark Wesley, 'The Bolan Interview', *New Musical
Express/208 Special* (10 June 1972), pp. 26–7.

54 Roy Hollingworth, 'Will America Learn to Love Marc Bolan?', *Melody Maker* (23 September 1972), pp. 9, 44.

55 Ibid., p. 44.

56 Richard Cromelin, 'Still Hard for Marc . . .', *Melody Maker* (28 October 1973), p. 45.

57 'T. Rex Militants Freak Out', *Creem* (October 1972), p. 8. T. Rex's first *headline* tour of the States took place in February 1972, followed by a longer tour in September/October. Their third tour in July/August 1973 had them paired with Three Dog Night. A representative example of the critical reaction the band received from American critics is reproduced in Cliff McLenehan's Bolan chronology; not all of it is bad, but the majority was decidedly negative. Don Hickman for the *New York Times*, reporting on a Carnegie Hall show at the end of the first tour, essentially summed up the consensus: 'Mr. Bolan is a performer who builds an illusion of style with an almost total lack of substance . . . One is constantly aware of the mannerism rather than the music, of the self-consciousness rather than the total, energetic performance. And the ego behind it all – underneath his white satin and lamé suit Mr. Bolan wore a T-shirt with a picture of himself printed on the front – was first humorous and then simply disturbing.' (McLenehan, *Marc Bolan*, p. 117.)

58 Cromelin, 'Still Hard for Marc . . .', p. 45.

59 Cited in McLenehan, *Marc Bolan*, p. 162.

60 *Beat Instrumental* (February 1974), p. 10.

61 'What's On', *New Musical Express* (10 June 1972), p. 12.

62 In November 1972 the NME carried a Bolan interview that was printed towards the back of the paper; six months earlier it would have run on the front page. Bolan takes a pop at the competition, especially Bowie: 'Really, I've always thought Mott the Hoople were bigger than David. When you're talking about him, you're only talking about one record so far.' There was a good deal of truth in how Bolan saw things at that point in time; Bowie self-evidently had not experienced anything like the chart success T. Rex had recently enjoyed, but Bolan's lack of generosity does him no favours whatsoever. He comes across embittered

at the attention given to others as if it is at a cost to him.
(James Johnson, 'Saucy Words and a Lot of Ooooeee . . .',
New Musical Express (11 November 1972), p. 40.)

63 Roy Carr, 'Looks for the Next Superstar', *New Musical Express* (1 July 1972), p. 15.

64 Ibid.

65 Charles Shaar Murray, 'Teenage Teardrops', *New Musical Express* (22 July 1972), pp. 8–9.

66 Ibid.

67 Ibid.

68 'Gasbag', *New Musical Express* (29 July 1972), p. 39.

69 Charles Shaar Murray, 'David at the Dorchester', *New Musical Express* (22 July 1972), pp. 18, 31, 44; Murray, 'David at the Dorchester', *New Musical Express* (29 July 1972), p. 12.

70 Danny Holloway, 'Marc Bolan', *New Musical Express* (5 February 1973), p. 23; Holloway, 'Marc Bolan', *New Musical Express* (12 February 1973), pp. 1, 6, 25; Holloway, 'Marc Bolan', *New Musical Express* (19 February 1973), p. 25.

71 'Gasbag', *New Musical Express* (19 February 1973), p. 36.

72 Ibid.

73 Charles Shaar Murray, 'Looking Back: Where Now, Elemental Child?', *New Musical Express* (28 April 1973), p. 44.

74 Ibid.

75 Ibid.

76 Ibid.

77 Ibid.

78 Ibid.

79 Ibid.

80 Ibid.

81 Ibid.

82 Ibid.

83 Charles Shaar Murray, 'Hello. I'm Marc Bolan. I'm a Superstar. You'd Better Believe It', *Cream*, ii/1 (May 1972), pp. 26–31, 47–50.

84 Ibid., pp. 26–31.

85 Murray's view on T. Rex remained the same right through 1972, ending the year with a 'snide', to use his own term, response to one of their Christmas gigs. Charles Shaar Murray, 'Uneasy Action', *New Musical Express* (30 December 1972), p. 18.

86 Michael Watts, 'Lock Up Your Daughters, Iggy's Here', *Melody Maker* (1 April 1972), p. 10.

87 Sylvain Sylvain with Dave Thompson, *There's No Bones in Ice Cream: Sylvain Sylvain's Story of the New York Dolls* (London, 2018), p. 122. 'What [the New York Dolls] heard in the music of Marc Bolan and T. Rex . . . was the same glitter-clad car crash of fifties riffs, Stonesy grooves and seventies sexuality that they'd been aiming for in their sound.' Walter Lure with Dave Thompson, *To Hell and Back* (Lanham, MD, 2020), pp. 29–30.

88 Nick Kent, 'Too Pooped to Pop, Too Old to Rock', *New Musical Express* (16 June 1973), pp. 8–9.

89 Nick Kent, 'Superhype as Art?', *Cream*, 17 (October 1972), p. 41.

90 Michael Watts, 'T.Rextasy', *Melody Maker* (22 January 1972), p. 5.

91 Ibid.

92 Richie Yorke, 'Bolan and America', *New Musical Express* (6 May 1972), p. 11.

93 Danny Holloway, 'The Bolan Story – Final Part', *New Musical Express* (19 February 1972), p. 16.

94 Ibid.

95 Ibid.

96 Logan, 'Marc Bolan'.

97 Roy Hollingworth, 'The Marc Bolan Interview', in *Bolan: The Rise to Fame of a 1972 Super Star – In Words and Pictures. A Melody Maker Special* (London, 1972), p. 32.

98 Norman, 'Under the Influence Special'.

99 Roy Carr, 'Jagger', *New Musical Express* (20 May 1972), pp. 16–17.

100 Danny Holloway, 'Singles', *New Musical Express* (16 September 1972), p. 15.

101 Ibid.

102 Ibid.

103 Danny Holloway, 'Singles', *New Musical Express* (25 November 1972), p. 23.
104 Tony Visconti interview, *New Musical Express* (15 April 1972), p. 14.
105 Logan, 'Marc Bolan'.
106 Tony Russell, 'Reviews: Wild Angels and Brett Marvin and the Thunderbolts', *Cream*, 4 (August 1971), p. 46.
107 Ian MacDonald, 'Shangri-Las', *New Musical Express* (27 January 1973), p. 14. See also, Bryan Ferry's choice of The Crystals and The Shirelles in 'Whatever Turned Me On', *New Musical Express* (26 August 1972), p. 6.
108 Dave Laing, 'T. Rex: Bolan Boogie', *Cream*, II/3 (July 1972), p. 38.
109 Ibid.
110 Ibid.
111 Chris Welch, 'From Elf to Electric Warrior', *Bolan – Melody Maker Special* (1972), p. 7.
112 *The Real Marc Bolan: A Record Mirror Special* (London, 1972), p. 23.

3 EX-PATRIA

1 Simon Frith, 'Letter from Britain', *Creem* (September 1972), pp. 32, 62.
2 Ibid.
3 Ibid.
4 Ibid.
5 Ibid.
6 Ibid. Ian McDonald later echoed Frith: 'So it is that, in a period in rock's development in which hardly anyone really knows what his role is and the map showing The Way Out is lying crumpled in a puddle on some windy festival site a man like David Bowie – who not only knows what he's doing but *why* he's doing it, becomes rather important.' (Ian McDonald, 'The Prophet without Honour', *Music Scene* (December 1973), pp. 12–13.)
7 'Are Those Iggy Stooge – Judee Sill Rumors True?', *Creem* (September 1972), p. 19. *Creem*'s reports on the British scene were always some good weeks, if not months, behind the

action. The description of Iggy Pop in London is from an image in *Melody Maker*, 1 April 1972, four months prior to *Creem*'s street date.

8 The following month the magazine published a more comprehensive overview of the u.s./London scene, and gave a head's up to the Groovies' presence among the contenders ('Exiles in Piccadilly Circus', *Creem* (October 1972), p. 20).

9 'The Psychedelic Stooges', *East Village Other*, iv/19 (9 April 1969), p. 15.

10 Ibid.

11 Karin Berg, 'Stooges', *East Village Other*, v/15 (17 March 1970), p. 9.

12 Ibid.

13 Ibid.

14 Nick Logan, 'The Stooges, Fun House', *New Musical Express* (19 December 1970), p. 9.

15 Ibid.

16 'Blind Date with Maggie Bell', *Melody Maker* (December 1970), and an equally dismissive review by a *Melody Maker* staffer, 'R. H.' (Roy Hollingworth?), are reproduced in Jeff Gold, *Total Chaos: The Story of The Stooges* (Nashville, TN, 2016), pp. 194 and 155 respectively.

17 Logan, 'The Stooges', p. 9.

18 Mick Farren, 'The Stooges', *IT*, 78 (24 April–7 May 1970).

19 Chris Hodenfield, 'Other Detroit Sounds', *Strange Days*, 1 (11–25 September 1970), p. 22.

20 Ibid.

21 Ibid.

22 Ibid.

23 Duncan Fallowell, 'Pop – American Sounds', *The Spectator* (12 December 1970), p. 779.

24 Ibid.

25 Ibid.

26 Ibid.

27 Ibid.

28 Ibid.

29 The apocryphal story of the MC5 defecating on stage was mentioned by Hodenfield in his piece on the band; Fallowell appeared happy to make myth and mischief out of the tale

(Chris Hodenfield, 'Rough Trade from Venus', *Strange Days*,
   1 (11–25 September 1970), pp. 28–9).
30 Ibid.
31 Ibid. Fallowell probably found this song title in Berg,
   'Stooges'.
32 Ibid.
33 Ibid.
34 Dave Marsh, 'The Incredible Story of Iggy and the Stooges',
   Zigzag, 17 (December 1970/January 1971), pp. 26–8.
35 Ibid.
36 Iggy's bodily functions were still making good copy late into
   1973, see Nick Kent and Roy Carr, 'Obscene and Heard:
   The Sordid World of Rock', *New Musical Express*
   (25 August 1973), p. 15.
37 Steve Mann, 'Alice Cooper Third Generation Rock', *Frendz*,
   4 (23 June 1971), pp. 20–21.
38 Ibid.
39 Jamie Mandelkau, 'Alice Cooper', *IT*, 106 (16–30 June
   1971), pp. 10–11.
40 Ibid.
41 Ibid.
42 Ibid.
43 Mick Farren, 'Killer', *IT*, 121 (13–27 January 1972), p. 19.
44 Steve Mann, 'Alice Cooper: Third Generation Rock',
   Frendz, 4 (23 June 1971), p. 20.
45 Mick Rock, 'David Bowie: A Spaced-Out Oddity', *Club
   International*, I/2 (August 1972), pp. 72–4.
46 Ibid.
47 Nick Kent, 'Alice Cooper', *Frendz*, 32 (July 1972).
48 Rock, 'David Bowie'.
49 Danny Holloway, 'David Bowie', *New Musical Express*
   (29 January 1972), p. 15.
50 Kevin Cann, *David Bowie, Any Day Now – The London
   Years, 1947–74* (London, 2010), p. 205.
51 Shortly after his meeting with Bowie, John Mendelsohn
   published 'Superstardom Is My Destiny', *Rolling Stone*,
   82 (May 1971), pp. 24–6. It was a rock critic's fantasy
   with lines that snake forward to Ziggy Stardust, especially
   Mendelsohn's admiration for Iggy. The Stooges had saved

his soul and fuelled the search to find his own 'psychedelic punk' to front his band Christopher Milk.

52 'Classifieds', *The Times* (30 March 1972), p. 32.

53 Rosalind Russell, 'Iggy and the Stooges', *Disc* (21 July 1972).

54 Nick Kent, 'Leaders of the Pack: The Class of '73 – Iggy Pop', *New Musical Express* (6 January 1973), p. 24.

55 Vaughn Masterson, 'Pouf Rock', *Knave*, v/2 (1973), pp. 46–8.

56 John Brown, 'Dada Weer All Krazee Now', *Cream*, 18 (November 1972), pp. 26–9.

57 Nick Kent, 'Punk Messiah of the Teenage Wasteland', *Cream*, 17 (October 1972), pp. 14–18.

58 Nick Kent, 'David Bowie, the Rise and Fall of Ziggy Stardust', *Oz*, 43 (July/August 1972), p. 48.

59 Nick Kent, 'In the Teenage Wasteland . . . Hawkwind', *New Musical Express* (12 August 1972), pp. 32–3.

60 Kent, 'Punk Messiah'.

61 Ibid.

62 Nick Kent, 'For Those Who Think Bowie a Trifle Lame . . . an Initiation into Iggy Pop', *New Musical Express* (29 July 1972), p. 28.

63 Ibid.

64 Nick Kent, 'Johnny Milkshake', *Frendz*, 29 (9 June 1972), p. 10.

65 Ibid.

66 Michael Oldfield, 'Caught in the Act', *Melody Maker* (22 July 1972), p. 36.

67 Ibid.

68 Ibid.

69 Ibid.

70 Ibid.

71 Charles Shaar Murray, 'David at the Dorchester: Bowie on Ziggy and Other Matters', *New Musical Express* (22 July 1972), pp. 18, 31.

72 Ray Fox-Cumming, 'Iggy and the Stooges: *Raw Power*', *Disc* (1973), www.rocksbackpages.com, accessed 19 November 2020.

73 Mick Rock, 'Sounds', *Club International*, II/9 (July 1973), p. 4.

74 Ibid.

75 Roy Carr, 'Albums: Bye Bye Johnny B. Goode, Welcome Iggy Pop', *New Musical Express* (February 1973), unpaginated cutting.

76 Ibid.

77 Simon Frith, 'Tubular Bells and Raw Power', *Let It Rock* (August 1973), p. 55.

78 Ibid.

79 Ibid.

80 Ibid.

81 Ibid. Jonathon Green also provided a comparative review in *IT*, here matching *Raw Power* with a Dean Martin album. He considered both efforts to be derivative (Jonathon Green, 'Punk Drunk Junk', *IT*, 157 (28 June–12 July 1973), p. 21).

82 Richard Williams, 'Teenage Insanity', *The Times* (2 July 1973), p. 9.

83 Ibid.

84 Ibid.

85 See Richard Cromelin, 'Iggy and the Stooges – Theatre of Cruelty', *Los Angeles Times* (23 June 1973), p. B5. 'A lot of people compare us,' said Alice about The Stooges; 'he's much more physical, just like Theatre of Cruelty sort of thing, that type of shit.' (Steve Mann, 'Alice Cooper: Third Generation Rock', *Frendz*, 4 (23 June 1971), p. 20.)

86 Mick Rock, 'Iggy Pop', *Music Scene* (February 1974), p. 12.

87 Michael Watts, 'Oh You Pretty Thing', *Melody Maker* (22 January 1972), p. 19.

88 Ibid., p. 42.

89 Richard Williams, 'Reed between the Lines', *Melody Maker* (22 January 1972).

90 Ibid., p. 25.

91 Ibid.

92 Richard Williams, 'Opinion: It's a Shame Nobody Listens', *Melody Maker* (25 October 1969), republished in Alfredo Garcia, *The Inevitable World of The Velvet Underground* (Madrid, 2012), p. 368.

93 Tim Souster, 'Through the Sound Barrier', *Observer Magazine* (5 October 1972), republished in Garcia, *The Inevitable World*, p. 366.

94 Tim Souster, 'Pop Music', *The Listener* (4 July 1968),
   republished in Garcia, *The Inevitable World*, p. 264.
95 For a fairly comprehensive set of references and clippings
   on the Velvets from the UK press see Garcia, *The Inevitable
   World*.
96 Geoffrey Cannon, 'The Who on Record', *The Guardian*
   (3 September 1971), p. 8.
97 Michael Watts, 'Loaded', *Melody Maker* (13 March 1971), np.
98 Andrew Lycett, 'Velvet Underground', *Melody Maker*
   (17 April 1971), p. 21.
99 Duncan Fallowell, 'Pop: On Velvet', *The Spectator*
   (3 April 1971), p. 467.
100 Ibid.
101 Ibid.
102 Ibid.
103 Ibid.
104 All of this material is collected in Garcia, *The Inevitable
   World*.
105 Williams, 'Reed between the Lines'.
106 Ibid.
107 Ibid.
108 Lester Bangs, 'He Walks It Like He Talks It (Usually)',
   Creem (July 1972), pp. 59–60.
109 Reed discusses the album in some detail in a long interview
   from early 1972 held in London (Robert Somma, 'Fallen
   Knights and Fallen Ladies', in *No One Waved Goodbye*
   (London, 1973)), which was also published in *Zigzag* (III/10
   (1973)): 'The thing I'm pleased about is that it's very straight
   ahead rock 'n' roll. I've been heading slowly but surely in
   that direction. Each album, if you follow it, gets more into
   straight rock. *Loaded* was a rock 'n' roll album that
   I thought was badly produced.'
110 Andrew Weiner, 'The Chuck Berry of the Seventies', *Cream*,
   II/4 (September 1972), pp. 18–21, 38.
111 Roy Hollingworth, 'Reed Section', *Melody Maker*
   (24 June 1972), pp. 28–9.
112 Ibid.
113 James Johnson, 'David Bowie', *New Musical Express*
   (17 June 1972), p. 22.

114 Tony Stewart, 'Lou Reed: A Voice from The Underground', *New Musical Express* (17 June 1972), p. 47.

115 Ibid.

116 'News', *New Musical Express* (24 June 1972), p. 3.

117 Hollingworth, 'Reed Section'.

118 Charles Shaar Murray, 'David at the Dorchester', *New Musical Express* (22 July 1972), pp. 18–19, 44.

119 Charles Shaar Murray, 'Back at the Dorchester', *New Musical Express* (29 July 1972), p. 12.

120 Charles Shaar Murray, 'Lou Reed/Kings X', *New Musical Express* (22 July 1972), p. 20.

121 Ibid.

122 See, for example, Charles Shaar Murray's review, *New Musical Express* (5 August 1972), p. 8.

123 Michael Watts, 'The Main Man', *Melody Maker* (22 July 1972), pp. 28–9.

124 Nick Kent, 'The Stones, Bowie, Roxy and Mott and What They Owe to the Inspiration of This One Man', *New Musical Express* (14 October 1972), p. 5.

125 Charles Shaar Murray, 'Lunch with Lou', *New Musical Express* (12 August 1972), p. 32.

126 Ian Hoare, 'Transformer', *Let It Rock*, 3 (December 1972), p. 58.

127 Ibid.

128 Weiner, 'Chuck Berry', p. 38.

129 Nick Kent, 'Lou Reed: The Sinatra of the 70s', *New Musical Express* (28 April 1973), p. 5.

130 Ray Fox-Cumming, 'Lou Reed: *Transformer* (RCA)', *Disc* (1972), www.rocksbackpages.com, accessed 19 November 2020.

131 Mick Rock, *Raw Power: Iggy and the Stooges* (London, 2005), pp. 14–15.

132 Jeff Gold, *Total Chaos: The Story of The Stooges* (Nashville, TN, 2016), p. 234.

133 Ibid.

134 Ibid., p. 153.

135 Iggy discusses the musical influences on *Raw Power*, ibid., pp. 248–9.

136 Rock, *Raw Power*, p. 175.

137 Mick Rock, 'Interview with Lou Reed – August 1972', in Lou Reed and Mick Rock, *Transformer* (Guildford, 2013), np.

138 Michael Watts, 'Wild Side Story', *Melody Maker* (9 June 1973), p. 11.

139 Ibid.

140 Ibid.

141 Ian Hunter, *Diary of a Rock 'n' Roll Star* (London, 1974), p. 22.

142 Nick Kent, 'A Walk on the Wild Side of Lou Reed', *New Musical Express* (1973), www.rocksbackpages.com, accessed 17 November 2020.

143 Nick Kent, 'Critic's Choice', *Let It Rock* (January 1974), p. 18.

144 Whatever the status history now affords Iggy Pop and his Mighty Stooges, in 1972–3 they were no more than a fleeting moment of interest in the pop rush of the day. A scrapbook of their cuttings from this period would only fill a few pages. Iggy didn't make the cover of a British music paper until *Sounds* (16 February 1974), which used a King's Cross image and featured a story on his LA exploits. The NME announced an 'Iggy Tour' on its front page just over a month later and in its news pages similarly used a King's Cross image to illustrate the announcement of gigs booked for the end of the month and into May, including two nights at Biba's Restaurant and eight further shows elsewhere in England. An *Old Grey Whistle Test* appearance was also expected ('News Desk', *New Musical Express* (6 April 1974), p. 3). Nick Kent remained true to the cause even when the pickings were thin and filed a lengthy piece for the NME (3 May 1975), which again covered The Stooges' backstory. He also gave some space to the recent demos Iggy and Williamson had recorded that would eventually become the *Kill City* album. As if covering for the emptiness at the heart of his story, or his own idolization of Pop, Kent's description of LA's queer predators managed, even in this age of often vicious homophobia in the British music press, to reach a new bilious low.

4 KILL ALL YOUR DARLINGS

1 Anthony Burgess, *A Clockwork Orange* (London, 2012), p. 8.
2 Robert Greenfield, 'The *Rolling Stone* Interview: Keith
  Richards', *Rolling Stone*, 89 (19 August 1971), pp. 24–7.
3 Ibid.
4 Andrew Loog Oldham, 2*Stoned* (London, 2003), pp. 173–4.
5 Ibid., pp. 153–9.
6 Michael Brent, 'Cults', *Men Only*, xxxvi/3 (August 1971),
  pp. 6–8.
7 Ibid.
8 Ibid.
9 Ibid.
10 Ibid.
11 Ibid.
12 Jaynie, 'T. Rex at Boston Saturday 15 January', *IT*, 122
  (27 January–10 February 1972), p. 18.
13 Ibid.
14 Simon Frith, 'Lest We Forget', *Cream*, 19 (December 1972),
  p. 32.
15 Tony Stewart, 'David Bowie and Roland Kirk – A Strange
  Duo', *New Musical Express* (29 January 1972), p. 14.
16 Danny Holloway, 'David Bowie *Hunky Dory*', *New Musical
  Express* (29 January 1972), p. 13.
17 Ibid.
18 Ibid.
19 Duncan Fallowell, 'Lady Stardust', *The Spectator*
  (29 July 1972), p. 181.
20 Ibid.
21 Ibid.
22 Frith, 'Lest We Forget', p. 32.
23 Nick Kent, 'David Bowie: *The Rise and Fall of Ziggy
  Stardust and the Spiders from Mars*', *Oz* (July 1972), np.
24 Nik Cohn, 'David Bowie – Superstar: He Camps, Vamps,
  Glistens and Sings', *Harpers & Queen* (September 1972),
  p. 94.
25 Ibid.
26 Ibid.
27 Ibid.

28 Ibid.

29 Ian MacDonald, 'Will David Bowie Commit Rockanroll Suicide to Become a Superstar?', *Cream*, 16 (September 1972), pp. 10–13, 41–2.

30 Ibid., pp. 10–13.

31 The advertisement is in *IT*, 121 (13–27 January 1971), p. 10.

32 Michael Watts, 'Oh You Pretty Thing', *Melody Maker* (22 January 1972), pp. 19 and 42.

33 Ibid., p. 42.

34 Ibid.

35 Robin Denselow, 'David Bowie at the Festival Hall', *The Guardian* (10 July 1972), p. 8.

36 Charles Shaar Murray, 'Where Star Trek Meets the Clockwork Orange', *New Musical Express* (9 December 1972), p. 10.

37 MacDonald, 'David Bowie', pp. 10–13.

38 Martin Walker, 'Lucky Glam Rock', *The Guardian* (2 September 1972), p. 8.

39 Ibid.

40 Ibid.

41 Ibid.

42 Ibid.

43 Pete Fowler, 'Skins Rule', in *Rock File*, ed. Charlie Gillett (London, 1972), pp. 10–24.

44 Peter Doggett, *The Man Who Sold the World: David Bowie and the 1970s* (London, 2011), p. 292.

45 Bowie made these comments in an interview with Paul DuNoyer quoted in Chris O'Leary, *Rebel Rebel: All the Songs of David Bowie from '64 to '76* (Winchester, 2015), p. 245.

46 Gordon Coxhill, 'Bowie Interviews Reserved for "Known Sympathisers"', *Music Scene* (December 1972), pp. 48–9.

47 Bob Edmands, 'The Last Bus Has Gone but the Millennium Has Arrived: Roxy Music in the Sticks', *Cream*, 24 (May 1973), p. 14.

48 Paul Trynka, *Starman: David Bowie – The Definitive Biography* (London, 2010), pp. 153 and 157.

49 Cohn, 'David Bowie'.

50 Pat Long, *The History of the NME* (London, 2012), p. 34.

51 Max Bell, 'Underground Overground', *Club International*, IV/9 (September 1975), pp. 6–7.

52 Trevor Hoyle, *Rule of Night* (Hebden Bridge, 2003), p. 85.

53 Ibid., p. 63.

54 Ron Ross, 'David Bowie: Phallus in Pigtails, or the Music of the Spheres Considered as Cosmic Boogie', *Words & Music* (1972), www.rocksbackpages.com, accessed 6 August 2021.

55 Julie Webb, 'What's Mott?', *New Musical Express* (16 September 1972), p. 8.

56 Allen Levy, 'Mott the Hoople: Memories of Years Past', *Changes*, III/3 (1 July 1971), pp. 4–5.

57 George Tremlett, *The David Bowie Story* (London, 1974), p. 129.

58 Nick Kent, 'Memoirs of a Street Punk: Ian Hunter', *New Musical Express* (19 January 1974), pp. 5–6.

59 Ian Hunter, *Diary of a Rock 'n' Roll Star* (London, 1974), p. 61.

60 Craig Copetas, 'Beat Godfather Meets Glitter Mainman: William Burroughs, Say Hello to David Bowie', *Rolling Stone*, 155 (24 February 1974), p. 25.

61 Ibid.

62 Dave Laing and Simon Frith, 'Bowie Zowie: Two Views of the Glitter Prince of Rock', *Let It Rock*, 9 (June 1973), pp. 34–5.

63 Ibid.

64 Simon Frith, 'Letter from Britain', *Creem* (October 1972), p. 79.

65 Ibid.

66 Charles Shaar Murray, 'Goodbye to Ziggy and a Big Hello to Aladdin Sane', *New Musical Express* (27 January 1972), pp. 5–6 and 54.

67 Charles Shaar Murray, 'Bowie-ing Out at The Chateau', *New Musical Express* (4 August 1973), pp. 12–13.

68 Ian MacDonald, 'David Bowie: Pin-Ups', *New Musical Express* (20 October 1973), p. 20.

69 Ibid.

70 Ibid. Writing at the end of 1973, just prior to the release of *Pinups*, McDonald held out great hope for the album, basing his enthusiasm on what Bowie had done with

'Let's Spend the Night Together'. But while he condemned his fellow critics, who had cursed that cover as some kind of assault on the canon of second-generation rock, which Bowie had long left behind, he ended up retreating back into the trenches with them. The track listing he gives for *Pinups* has Bowie's own 'London Boys' as the final track after The Kinks' cover. (Ian McDonald, 'The Prophet without Honour', *Music Scene* (December 1973), pp. 12–13.)

71 Charles Shaar Murray, 'David Bowie's *Pin Ups* (RCA)', *Oz*, 48 (1973), reproduced in Murray, *Shots from the Hip* (London, 1991), pp. 39–40.

72 Lester Bangs, 'David Bowie Flashes His Roots', *Creem* (January 1974), pp. 62–3.

73 For background on the suits design and sales see Paul Gorman, *Mr. Freedom: Tommy Roberts, British Design Hero* (London, 2012), pp. 114–15.

74 Charles Shaar Murray, 'If The Who Split . . .', *New Musical Express* (3 March 1973), p. 6.

75 Ibid.

76 Ibid.

77 Mick Farren and Edward Barker, *Watch Out Kids* (London, 1972), np.

78 D. F., 'Caught in the Act: The Who Liberal Hall, Yeovil', *Melody Maker* (23 July 1966), p. 16.

5 FOR YOUR PLEASURE . . . WE PRESENT OURSELVES

1 John Rockwell, *New York Times* (December 1972).

2 Robin Denselow, 'On a New Phenomenon in Rock Music', *The Guardian* (9 October 1972), p. 8.

3 Richard Williams, sleeve notes to super-deluxe edition of *Roxy Music* (Virgin/EMI, 2018), np.

4 Richard Williams, 'Roxy Music', *Melody Maker* (14 June 1972), p. 22.

5 Ibid. NME's introduction to the band also started with the cover image (Tony Tyler, 'The Answer to a Maiden's Prayer', *New Musical Express* (1 July 1972), p. 28).

6 Duncan Fallowell, 'Lady Stardust', *The Spectator* (29 July 1972), p. 181.

7 Nick Kent, 'Roxy', *New Musical Express*
(25 November 1972), p. 30.

8 Tony Tyler, 'Roxy Music', *New Musical Express*
(17 June 1972), p. 12.

9 Williams, 'Roxy Music'.

10 Denselow, 'On a New Phenomenon'.

11 Ibid.

12 Ian MacDonald, 'Foxy Roxy', *New Musical Express*
(12 August 1972), p. 12.

13 Ibid. Two weeks later the NME ran a piece where Ferry
discussed his influences, which included The Crystals, The
Shirelles, Ethel Merman, Dylan, Smokey Robinson, Lotte
Lenya, Charlie Parker, Billie Holiday, Frank Sinatra, The
Inkspots and The Beatles (Bryan Ferry, 'Whatever Turned
Me On', *New Musical Express* (26 August 1972), p. 6).

14 MacDonald, 'Foxy Roxy'.

15 Geoff Brown, 'Eno's Where It's At', *Melody Maker*
(10 November 1973), pp. 40–41.

16 Ian MacDonald, 'Roxy', *New Musical Express*
(23 September 1972), p. 5.

17 Ian MacDonald, 'Ferry Interesting Roxy', *New Musical
Express* (14 October 1972), p. 15.

18 Ibid.

19 News item, *Melody Maker* (22 July 1972), p. 5.

20 Nick Kent, 'The Prince of Sleaze Confesses All!', *New
Musical Express* (19 January 1974), pp. 18–19, 24.

21 Kent, 'Roxy'.

22 Nick Kent, 'A Flight of Fantasy', *New Musical Express*
(3 February 1973), p. 5.

23 Ibid.

24 Ibid.

25 Nick Kent, 'Roxy Music: It May Be Chic but Can You
Dance to It', *Frendz*, 34 (25 August 1972), pp. 7–10.

26 Ibid.

27 Ibid.

28 Ibid.

29 Ibid.

30 Tony Palmer, 'Pop: Easy Does It', *The Observer*
(15 April 1973), p. 37.

31 With the exception of Andrew Loog Oldham's interventions on the back of the first four Rolling Stones albums and Bob Dylan's ruminations on some of his early record sleeves, Puxley's text has subsequently been seen as a high water mark in liner notes for what has, otherwise, little interest for pop critics (I would add, to whatever list might be drawn up, Andy 'Wipeout' Wickham's note for *The Everly Brothers Sing*, which is both long and perversely autobiographical, with little to say about the music).

32 Tony Palmer, 'Shock Tactics from Roxy', *The Observer* (23 July 1972), p. 26.

33 Ibid.

34 Ibid.

35 Charles Shaar Murray, 'Roxy Airborne', *New Musical Express* (23 December 1972), p. 6.

36 Ibid.

37 Michael Bracewell, *Re-Make/Re-Model: Art, Pop, Fashion and the Making of Roxy Music, 1953–1972* (London, 2007), p. 385.

38 James Naremore, *More Than Night: Film Noir in Its Contexts* (Berkeley, CA, 1998).

39 'Ferry Merry Christmas', *Melody Maker* (22 December 1973), p. 1.

40 Michael Watts, 'Song and Dance Man', *Melody Maker* (29 December 1973), pp. 3 and 41, republished as 'Today's Heroes: Bryan Ferry', in *Rock Life: Melody Maker Special*, ed. Gavin Petrie (London, 1974), pp. 107–11.

41 Ibid.

42 Ibid.

43 Ibid.

44 Duncan Fallowell, 'Pop', *The Spectator* (7 April 1973), p. 432.

45 Stephen MacLean, 'They Came from the Closets! . . . and Some Even "Rocked" the Boat', *Gay News* (30 May 1973), pp. 10–11.

46 Pete Fowler, 'Fighting Off the Martians', *Let It Rock*, 34 (October 1975), pp. 22–3. For an earlier look at Roxy's audience still in its formative stage, see Bob Edmands, 'The Last Bus Has Gone but the Millennium Has arrived: Roxy Music in the Sticks', *Cream*, 24 (May 1973), pp. 14–16.

47 Fowler, 'Fighting Off the Martians'.

48 Kent, 'The Prince of Sleaze'.

49 Ibid.

50 'Rox in Your Head', *Penthouse*, VII/7 (1972), p. 23.

51 'Roxy Again', *Penthouse*, VIII/4 (1973), p. 22.

52 Neville Player, 'Profile', *Penthouse*, IX/7 (October 1974), pp. 44–6, 48, 136.

53 Bruno Holbrook, 'Coming in Handy', *New Statesman* (14 December 1973), pp. 992–3.

54 Ibid.

55 Ibid.

56 Paul Gorman, 'David Parkinson', GQ (June 2014), p. 70. For more on Parkinson, see also William English, *Perfect Binding* (Leicester, 2019).

57 Stephen Colegrave and Chris Sullivan, *Punk: A Life Apart* (London, 2001), p. 87.

58 Dick Masters, 'All Warholed Up at New York's Superball', *Club International*, I/4 (October 1972), pp. 58–61.

59 Extended scenes from *Club International* spreads and other magazines shot in 1972–3 are found in Jay Myrdal and Pete Smith, *JP Smut* (London, 2003).

60 Tym Manley, 'Sounds', *Club International*, III/6 (June 1974), pp. 4 and 6.

61 Ibid.

62 Ibid.

63 Ibid.

64 Ibid.

65 Chrissie Hynde, 'Everything You'd Rather Not Have Known about Brian Eno', *New Musical Express* (2 February 1974), pp. 24 and 29.

66 Ibid.

67 Reproduced in the deluxe edition of *Roxy Music*.

68 See www.paulgormanis.com.

69 Nick Kent, 'The Politics of Flash', *New Musical Express* (6 April 1974), pp. 20–21, 39.

70 See www.paulgormanis.com.

71 Simon Frith, 'The Roxy Picture Palace', *Let It Rock*, 20 (May 1974), pp. 22–3.

6 LOBBING MOLOTOV COCKTAILS INTO THE OPERA HOUSE

1 Roy Hollingworth, 'Music in a Dolls House', *Melody Maker* (24 November 1973), p. 13.

2 On the advent of the Dolls' London reunion, Malcolm McLaren wrote about his ardour: 'I thought they were so, so bad, they were brilliant. I was smitten – like my first real desire, first kiss, first everything . . . this was the first time I had fallen in love with a group.' ('Dirty Pretty Things', *Guardian Friday Review* (28 May 2004), pp. 4–6.)

3 Hollingworth, 'Music'.

4 Ibid.

5 Roy Hollingworth, 'You Wanna Play House with the Dolls?', *Melody Maker* (22 July 1972), p. 17.

6 Ibid.

7 Ibid.

8 Ibid.

9 Ibid.

10 Ibid.

11 Ibid.

12 Ibid.

13 Lou Reed and Mick Rock, *Transformer* (Guildford, 2013), np.

14 Dick Masters, 'All Warholed Up at New York's Superball', *Club International*, 1/4 (October 1972), pp. 58–61.

15 Around the same time as the costume ball, Hollingworth filed a report on the New York scene. Leaving aside the Dolls, who he had covered earlier in the year, he focused in on Suicide at the Mercer Arts Center: 'It is a heady stark trip. The starkest trip I've ever seen . . . It was fascinating. How two people could create such a thick wall of sound and atmosphere was an unbelievable achievement. It roared, and groaned, and the singer smacked himself on the head with the mike a couple of times, and then fell in a heap in a corner – and whimpered. Was this the end of music as we know it? Oooh it was creepy.' (*Melody Maker* (21 October 1972), p. 21.)

16 Ibid.

17 Ibid.

18 Ed McCormack, 'Subterranean Satyricon: New York City's Ultra-Living Dolls', *Rolling Stone* (26 October 1972), pp. 14 and 16.

19 Ibid., p. 14.

20 Ibid.

21 Ed McCormack not only wrote for *Rolling Stone* and *Andy Warhol's Interview* magazines but was managing editor on *Changes*, a New York-based journal. His bona fides as a reporter of third-generation rock was confirmed in his coverage of Alice Cooper at the Town Hall and Iggy and the Stooges at the Electric Circus in July 1971, which focused on the different forms of audience interaction both bands encounter: Iggy confronted his audience while Alice played to his. McCormack thinks the latter's single, 'Eighteen', at that time climbing the charts, rips off Iggy's vocal style. He's a fan (Ed McCormack, 'Shooting Gallery', *Changes*, III/3 (1 July 1971), p. 2).

22 Ian Hunter, *Diary of a Rock 'n' Roll Star* (London, 1974), p. 52.

23 Nick Kent, 'Memoirs of a Street Punk: Ian Hunter', *New Musical Express* (19 January 1974), pp. 5–6.

24 Grace Lichtenstein, 'Alice Cooper? David Bowie? Ugh! And Ugh Again!', *New York Times* (24 September 1972), p. HF1.

25 Ibid.

26 Ibid.

27 Roy Hollingworth, 'In New York', *Melody Maker* (14 October 1972), p. 6.

28 The following is the only music press news item I've found on the band's visit to the UK: 'The New York Dolls, currently creating considerable interest in their hometown, fly into London on October 15 for recording and concerts. They will appear at the Wembley Empire Pool – with the Faces – on October 29, and Manchester Hardrock on November 9.' ('Dolls Here', *Melody Maker* (14 October 1972), p. 4.) The NME's gig guide listed the Manchester support slot with Roxy Music, and paraphrased Roy Hollingworth: 'Together they are with the New York Dolls, who are apparently so good that Lou Reed won't

work with them.' ('Nationwide Gig Guide', *New Musical Express* (11 November 1972), p. 28.)

29 Nick Kent, 'Faces/Wembley', *New Musical Express* (4 November 1972), p. 28.

30 Mark Plummer, 'Let's Face the Music and Dance', *Melody Maker* (4 November 1972), p. 51.

31 Paul Gorman, *The Life and Times of Malcolm McLaren* (London, 2020), p. 263.

32 Glen Matlock, 'They're Where We All Come From', *Guardian Friday Review* (28 May 2004), p. 5.

33 I'm grateful to 'From the Archives' New York Dolls chronology for much of the information on the band's first trip to the UK: www.fromthearchives.com.

34 The Dolls are name-checked as part of the bill for the Wembley concert in David Wigg, 'Hot Rod Stewart', *Daily Express* (28 October 1972), p. 20, and then given another mention on the Monday following the gig: 'an outrageously glittering all-male rock band NEW YORK DOLLS making their British debut' (30 October 1972), p. 17.

35 'Pop Group Drowning Tragedy', *Kensington Post* (1 December 1972), p. 8.

36 Ibid.

37 Ibid.

38 Ibid.

39 'Ex-Bunny's Wigs Fooled Banks', *Daily Mirror* (20 February 1968), p. 4.

40 *Daily Mirror* (11 August 1970), p. 5.

41 Nina Antonia, *The New York Dolls: Too Much Too Soon* (London, 2005), pp. 62–6.

42 Ibid.

43 Ibid.

44 Michael Watts, 'The B Side of New York', *Melody Maker* (20 January 1973), pp. 16 and 38.

45 Barry Miles, 'They Simper at Times', *IT*, 148 (23 February–8 March 1973), p. 6.

46 Ibid.

47 Ibid.

48 Ibid.

49 The man who signed them to Mercury records called them
a 'travelling Fellini movie' in Kevin Avery, *Everything Is an
Afterthought: The Life and Writings of Paul Nelson* (Seattle,
WA, 2011), p. 451. Nick Kent kept Satyricon in circulation in
his January 1974 piece on the Dolls ('The New York Dolls',
in *Greatest Hits: The Very Best of NME* (London, 1975),
p. 61). In his memoirs Sylvain recalls the influence the film
had on his use of white pancake make-up (Sylvain Sylvain
with Dave Thompson, *There's No Bones in Ice Cream:
Sylvain Sylvain's Story of the New York Dolls* (London,
2018), p. 110).

50 Danny Holloway, 'Marc Bolan: A Weird Kid with 40 Suits
and No Friends', *New Musical Express* (12 February 1972),
p. 25.

51 Ibid.

52 Ed McCormack, 'New York Confidential', *Rolling Stone*
(15 March 1973), p. 12.

53 John Rockwell, 'Dolls "Revive" Rock in an Uptown Debut'
(3 February 1973), p. 19.

54 Ibid.

55 Arthur 'Killer' Kane, *I, Doll: Life and Death with the New
York Dolls* (Chicago, IL, 2009), p. 57.

56 Ibid., pp. 86–7.

57 Nick Kent, 'New York: The Dark Side of Town', *New
Musical Express* (5 May 1973).

58 Ibid.

59 Ibid.

60 The Dolls covered 'Back in the USA', which, according to
Sylvain, was as much a tribute to the MC5 as to Chuck Berry
(Sylvain, *There's No Bones*, p. 169). Not even two years
after its release in the UK Nick Kent reviewed the MC5's
album in the NME column Junkyard Angels – 'A Nostalgic
Look around London's Junkshops – The Scrapyards of
Rock'. How quickly things moved; from hip to history.
He labelled *Back in the USA* as 'THE American album. This
is THE album the kids can relate to.' (Nick Kent, 'Junkyard
Angels', *New Musical Express* (21 October 1972), p. 46.)

61 Nick Kent, 'Welcome to the Faabulous Seventies', *New
Musical Express* (25 August 1973), p. 38.

62 Richard Williams, 'New York Dolls', *Melody Maker*
   (18 August 1973), p. 31.
63 Ibid.
64 Denis Lemon, 'Decadent or Just Outrageous', *Gay News*, 31
   (6 September 1973), p. 14.
65 Ibid.
66 Ibid.
67 Ted Castle, 'David Johansen Interview', *Gay News*, 31
   (6 September 1973), p. 14.
68 For example, see news item 'New York Dolls Due',
   New Musical Express (27 October 1973), p. 3.
69 'New York Dolls to Play Biba's Rainbow Room',
   Record Mirror (17 November 1973), p. 6.
70 Deborah Thomas, 'Tuesday Scene', *Daily Mirror*
   (30 October 1973), p. 11.
71 'What's happening to rock 'n' roll when a band as obviously
   lacking in musical talent as the New York Dolls makes
   headlines up and down the country? Precious few people
   have seen them play in Britain (apart from their pre-
   Christmas debacle on the Whistle Test).' ('Glam Rock/Acid
   Rock/Fag Rock/Folk Rock/Soft Rock/Doom Rock and
   Now . . . Parody Rock from the New York Dolls',
   Beat Instrumental (February 1974), pp. 3 and 8.)
72 Letters Page, *Melody Maker* (26 November 1973).
73 Ibid.
74 Ibid.
75 Duncan Fallowell, 'Goodbye Tom, Hello Biba',
   The Spectator (26 January 1974), p. 113.
76 Jymn Parrett, 'Dolls in London', *Denim Delinquent*, 3
   (Spring 1974), p. 6. All eight issues of the fanzine have been
   reproduced in Jymn Parrett, *Denim Delinquent, 1971–76*
   (Chicago, IL, 2016).
77 Parrett, 'Dolls in London'.
78 Barbara Hulanicki and Martin Pel, *The Biba Years,
   1963–1975* (London, 2014), p. 177.
79 Michael Watts, 'The Band They Love to Hate', *Melody Maker*
   (8 December 1973).
80 Ibid.
81 Ibid.

82 Ibid.

83 The NME wasn't published for eight weeks between 24 November 1973 and 12 January 1974, so didn't cover the Biba shows.

84 Nick Kent, 'The New York Dolls', *Greatest Hits: The Very Best of NME* (London, 1975), pp. 61–4.

85 Ibid.

86 Nick Kent, 'Farewell Androgyny *n.* hermaphroditism (Gr. *Gyne*, woman)', *New Musical Express* (16 March 1974).

87 Ibid.

88 Ibid.

89 Ibid.

90 Ibid.

91 Ibid.

92 Nik Cohn, *Today There Are No Gentlemen: The Changes in Englishmen's Clothes since the War* (London, 1971), p. 29.

93 Ibid., p. 30.

94 There is a fairly liberal dose of poetic licence in McLaren's description of his King's Road encounter with the Dolls. He first met members of the band in August 1973 while in New York to promote Let It Rock. This would have been where Johansen had got the flyer that Ben Edmonds described in his report on the recording of the band's debut. That event, if it happened at all, and without producer Todd Rundgren's presence, would have occurred at a summer rehearsal for gigs to promote the album's release. The recording sessions had been completed two months before McLaren's trip to the States and the album was already in the stores by the time he arrived to take part in the National Boutique Show (Paul Gorman helped me sort out the McLaren/Dolls timeline).

95 Malcolm McLaren, 'Dirty Pretty Things', *Guardian Friday Review* (28 May 2004), p. 4.

96 'Queen of Max's back room' is how she is described in *Andy Warhol's Interview*, 28 (December 1972), pp. 10–14. See also, Cyrinda Foxe-Tyler with Danny Fields, *Dream On: Livin' on the Edge with Steven Tyler and Aerosmith* (New York, 2000), pp. 86–97.

97 'Stacia', *Club International*, III/4 (April 1974), p. 4.

98 Kent, 'The New York Dolls', p. 63.

99 'Sensor', *Club International*, III/3 (March 1974), p. 7.

100 Bob Dunne, 'New York Dolls: Rock's Roots?', *Beetle*, v/5 (December 1973), np.

101 John Rockwell, 'Dolls "Revive" Rock in Uptown Debut', *New York Times* (February 1973), p. 19.

102 S. Davey, 'Sophisticated Boom-Boom: Confessions of a New York Doll', *Beetle*, v/12 (November 1974), np.

103 Ibid.

104 Ibid.

105 Martin Kirkup, 'Dolls: Shangri-Las of the 70s', *Sounds* (24 November 1973), p. 10.

106 Charlotte Greig, *Will You Still Love Me Tomorrow: Girl Groups from the 50s on . . .* (London, 1989), p. 55.

107 Greil Marcus, 'How the Other Half Lives: The Best of Girl Group Rock', *Let It Rock*, 20 (May 1974), pp. 24–6; Mitchell S. Cohen, 'Shall We Dance? The Shangri-Las', *Let It Rock*, 24 (December 1974), pp. 21 and 56.

108 Marcus, 'How the Other Half Lives'.

109 Ibid.

110 Ibid.

111 Ed McCormack, 'The Gold Lamé Dream of Bette Midler', *Rolling Stone* (15 February 1973).

112 Marcus, 'How the Other Half Lives'.

113 Ron Ross, 'New York Dolls: *Too Much, Too Soon*', *Phonograph Record* (1974), www.rocksbackpages.com, accessed 6 August 2021; Dave Marsh, 'The New York Dolls: *Too Much Too Soon*', *Rolling Stone* (20 June 1974), p. 79; Nick Kent, 'The New York Dolls: *Too Much Too Soon*', *New Musical Express* (27 April 1974), www.rocksbackpages.com, accessed 6 August 2021.

114 Phil McNeill, 'New York Dolls – *Too Much Too Soon*', *Gay News*, 52 (26 June 1974), p. 16.

115 Kirkup, 'Dolls: Shangri-Las of the 70s', p. 10.

116 See Peter Stanfield, *A Band with Built-In Hate: The Who from Pop Art to Punk* (London, 2021).

117 Avery, *Everything Is an Afterthought*, p. 246.

118 Ibid.

119 Nik Cohn, 'Rebecca and the Teen Dreams', *Cream*, 17
    (October 1972), pp. 8–12, 43.
120 Ibid.
121 Ibid.
122 Ibid.

CONCLUSION

1 Filmed in November 1969 the 45-minute documentary
   The Rock and Roll Singer was broadcast by the BBC in 1970
   as part of the 'Late Night Line Up' series.
2 Mick Farren, *Gene Vincent: There's One in Every Town*
   (London, 2004).
3 Waxie Maxie, 'Super Sexy. That's the Ballsy Rock 'n' Roll
   Allstars', *Curious Pillow Book* (1972), np.
4 Ibid.
5 Ibid.
6 Eve Punk Adrien, 'Trash', *Rock and Folk*, 84 (January 1974),
   p. 27.
7 Paul Alessandrini, 'Poupees', ibid., pp. 63–9.
8 Paul Gorman, *The Look: Adventures in Rock and Pop
   Fashion* (London, 2006), pp. 163–4.
9 With Richard Gere from the Broadway run in the cast,
   Grease opened in Coventry in June 1973 and then moved
   to London in July. Reviewed by Dennis Detheridge, *Melody
   Maker* (9 June 1973), p. 53.
10 Charles Shaar Murray, 'The Who: Exorcising the Ghost of
   Mod', *Creem* (January 1974), pp. 36–41.
11 Sleeve note on the picture sleeve of Ronnie Spector and the
   E Street Band's 1977 single 'Say Goodbye to Hollywood'.
12 Dave Marsh, *Born to Run: The Bruce Springsteen Story*
   (London, 1981), p. 6.
13 Ibid.
14 Ibid.
15 Ibid., p. 7.
16 In his review of Springsteen's *E. Street Shuffle*, Nick Kent
   read the same elements Marsh had lauded in wholly negative
   terms: 'I FIND HIM SO OFFENSIVE. There's just something
   about a guy who entices you into believing all this grandiose

gup he's spitting out about greasers and gypsies getting into knife fights down on the Kokomo, screwing Spanish waitresses and so forth that makes one think that he's really done nothing more than sit around listening to *Highway 61 Revisited* all day, and doing some heavy duty down at the movie house that shows *West Side Story* after midnight during the weekends.' (*New Musical Express* (2 February 1974), p. 31.)

17 Mick Johnson, 'Pop Prostituted', *Melody Maker* (29 December 1973), p. 48.
18 Simon Reynolds, *Shock and Awe: Glam Rock and Its Legacy from the Seventies to the Twenty-First Century* (London, 2016), p. 408.

SELECT BIBLIOGRAPHY

Antonia, Nina, *The New York Dolls: Too Much Too Soon*
(London, 2005)
Auslander, Philip, *Performing Glam Rock: Gender and
Theatricality in Popular Music* (Ann Arbor, MI, 2006)
Avery, Kevin, *Everything Is an Afterthought: The Life and
Writings of Paul Nelson* (Seattle, WA, 2011)
Balfour, Rex, *The Bryan Ferry Story* (London, 1976)
Birch, James, and Barry Miles, *The British Underground
Press of the Sixties* (London, 2017)
Bracewell, Michael, *Re-Make/Re-Model: Art, Pop,
Fashion and the Making of Roxy Music, 1953–1972*
(London, 2007)
Burgess, Anthony, *A Clockwork Orange*, restored edn
(London, 2012)
Cann, Kevin, *David Bowie, Any Day Now – The London Years,
1947–74* (London, 2010)
Castle, Alison, *The Making of a Masterpiece: Stanley Kubrick's
'A Clockwork Orange'* (Cologne, 2019)
Cohn, Nik, *Today There Are No Gentlemen: The Changes in
Englishmen's Clothes since the War* (London, 1971)
——, and Guy Peellaert, *Rock Dreams: Under the Broadwalk*
(London, 1973)
Colegrave, Stephen, and Chris Sullivan, *Punk: A Life Apart*
(London, 2001)
Deakin, Rich, *Keep It Together! Cosmic Boogie with The
Deviants and the Pink Fairies* (London, 2007)

Doggett, Peter, *The Man Who Sold the World: David Bowie and the 1970s* (London, 2011)

English, William, *Perfect Binding* (Leicester, 2019)

Farren, Mick, *Watch Out Kids* (London, 1972)

——, *The Texts of Festival* (London, 1973)

——, *Give the Anarchist a Cigarette* (London, 2001)

——, *Gene Vincent: There's One in Every Town* (London, 2004)

Fountain, Nigel, *Underground: The London Alternative Press, 1966–74* (London, 1988)

Garcia, Alfredo, *The Inevitable World of The Velvet Underground* (Madrid, 2012)

Gold, Jeff, *Total Chaos: The Story of The Stooges* (Nashville, TN, 2016)

Gorman, Paul, *The Look: Adventures in Rock and Pop Fashion* (London, 2006)

——, *Mr. Freedom: Tommy Roberts – British Design Hero* (London, 2012)

——, *The Life and Times of Malcolm McLaren: The Biography* (London, 2020)

Green, Jonathon, *Days in the Life: Voices from the English Underground, 1961–1971* (London, 1988)

Greig, Charlotte, *Will You Still Love Me Tomorrow: Girl Groups from the 50s on . . .* (London, 1989)

Hoskyns, Barney, *Glam! Bowie, Bolan and the Glitter Rock Revolution* (London, 1998)

Hoyle, Trevor, *Rule of Night* (Hebden Bridge, 2003)

Hulanicki, Barbara, and Martin Pel, *The Biba Years, 1963–1975* (London, 2014)

Hunter, Ian, *Diary of a Rock 'n' Roll Star* (London, 1974)

Huxley, David, *Nasty Tales: Sex, Drugs, Rock 'n' Roll and Violence in the British Underground* (London, 2001)

Kane, Arthur 'Killer', *I, Doll: Life and Death with the New York Dolls* (Chicago, IL, 2009)

Kent, Nick, *The Dark Stuff: Selected Writings on Rock Music* (London, 1994)

——, *Apathy for the Devil: A 1970s Memoir* (London, 2010)

Kramer, Peter, *A Clockwork Orange* (Basingstoke, 2011)

Long, Pat, *The History of the NME* (London, 2012)

McLenehan, Cliff, *Marc Bolan, 1947–1977: A Chronology* (London, 2002)

Marsh, Dave, *Born to Run: The Bruce Springsteen Story* (London, 1981)

Melly, George, *Revolt into Style: The Pop Arts in the 50s and 60s* (Oxford, 1989)

Murray, Charles Shaar, *Shots from the Hip* (Harmondsworth, 1991)

Myrdal, Jay, and Pete Smith, *JP Smut* (London, 2003)

Naremore, James, *More Than Night: Film Noir in Its Contexts* (Berkeley, CA, 1998)

O'Leary, Chris, *Rebel Rebel: All the Songs of David Bowie from '64 to '76* (Winchester, 2015)

Parrett, Jymn, *Denim Delinquent, 1971–76* (Chicago, IL, 2016)

Paytress, Mark, *Ziggy Stardust* (New York, 1998)

——, *Bolan: The Rise and Fall of a 20th Century Superstar* (London, 2002)

Pih, Darren, ed., *Glam: The Performance of Style* (Liverpool, 2013)

Reed, Lou, and Mick Rock, *Transformer* (Guildford, 2013)

Reynolds, Simon, *Shock and Awe: Glam Rock and Its Legacy from the Seventies to the Twenty-First Century* (London, 2016)

Rock, Mick, *Raw Power: Iggy and the Stooges* (London, 2005)

Savage, Jon, *England's Dreaming: Sex Pistols and Punk Rock* (London, 1991)

Sylvain, Sylvain, with Dave Thompson, *There's No Bones in Ice Cream: Sylvain Sylvain's Story of the New York Dolls* (London, 2018)

Tremlett, George, *The David Bowie Story* (London, 1974)

Trevena, Nigel, *Lou Reed and the Velvets* (Falmouth, 1973)

Trynka, Paul, *Iggy Pop: Open Up and Bleed* (London, 2007)

——, *Starman: David Bowie – The Definitive Biography* (London, 2010)

Visconti, Tony, *The Autobiography: Bowie, Bolan and the Brooklyn Boy* (London, 2007)

Welsh, Chris, and Simon Napier-Bell, *Marc Bolan: Born to Boogie* (London, 1982)

ACKNOWLEDGEMENTS

The first exchange I had about this project was with my good friend Lawrence Jackson on a long drive from Kent to Dorset and back. I thank him for listening and for sharing his experience of the dread he felt when first hearing Ian Hunter in 'All the Young Dudes' beckoning to the kid in the audience – 'yeah, you in the glasses'. I share his fear of looking such a man in the eye. The book is dedicated to my pals Graham Henderson and Eddie King, who have been with me on this adventure for the past thirty and forty years respectively: their thoughts on what rock 'n' roll is, and might be, have made the difference and have left their mark. My fine friend and fellow scholar Will Straw was the first to read a draft. He gave me confidence in the project when I most needed it and a better sense of where I might go before I could consider the job done. My editor, Dave Watkins, has again shown faith in me and helped steer this ship. I am most grateful.

My thanks also go to Andrew Krivine, who generously offered to supply a serious number of gorgeous full-colour posters from his collection. Too few are used here but some can be seen in *Too Fast to Live: Punk and Post-Punk Graphics* and in his next project, *Reversing into the Future: New Wave Graphics*. A similar debt of gratitude is owed to Paul Gorman for answering a good number of the questions I threw at him. His research has encouraged me to explore areas I might not have found for myself, or at least not so readily. His blog is an essential port of call: www.paulgormanis. com. It was a privilege to talk about Mick Farren and the Underground with Jonathon Green, who met with me just as the copy-edited manuscript was about to be returned. His *Days in the Life: Voices from the English Underground* is the seminal text on the topic. Lastly, an especial thank you to my brother Andy for photoshopping the book's images.

This volume was written on the southeast coast of Plague Island during the lockdowns of 2020, a horrible year for many and a difficult one for most everybody. Long, early morning walks with my partner, Julie, helped keep things together; she has my love. Hey! Sidney: A-wop-Bop-a-loo-Bop, A-wop-Bam-Boom!

PHOTO ACKNOWLEDGEMENTS

The author and publishers wish to express their thanks to the below sources of illustrative material and/or permission to reproduce it. Every effort has been made to contact copyright holders; should there be any we have been unable to reach or to whom inaccurate acknowledgements have been made, please contact the publishers, and full adjustments will be made to subsequent printings.

All images from the author's collection, except for those courtesy of Julian Brown/Mirrorpix/Getty Images: p. 256; Tom Copi/Michael Ochs Archives/Getty Images: p. 117; P. Felix/Daily Express/Hulton Archive/Getty Images: p. 241; Andrew Krivine: pp. 97 (top), 217; Michael Ochs Archives/Getty Images: p. 180; David Warner Ellis/ Redferns/Getty Images: pp. 206–7.

INDEX

Page numbers in *italics* indicate illustrations